Xmas 2022

ERA OF GREAT BENEFIT:

The Age of Human Empowerment

TO

Ali Bali Bee

By
The Balanced View Team

First Edition 2013

Balanced View Media: Mill Valley, California USA 2013

The Age of Human Empowerment and Era of Great Benefit by the Balanced View Team is licensed under a Creative Commons Attribution-Noncommercial-No Derivative Works 3.0 United States License

Based on a work at www.balancedview.org

ISBN 978-0-9886659-4-1

Contents

Editor's Introduction   *v*
Preface   *vii*
Foreword   *xvi*

1. An Introduction to the Age of Human Empowerment
   and Era of Great Benefit   1
2. Relying on Open Intelligence for Short Moments
   Many Times   16
3. The Wish-Fulfilling Gem   28
4. Open Intelligence Becomes Obvious at All Times   45
5. Expanding the Power   57
6. The Emerging Society of the Age of Human
   Empowerment and Era of Great Benefit   72
7. Spontaneous Benefit and Altruism   91
8. Education in the Nature of Mind and Identity   104
9. Discovering Our Gifts, Strengths and Talents   117
10. What Won't Wear Off   128
11. The Domain of Pure Pleasure   143
12. Social Activism in Intimate Relationships and Parenting   155
13. The Beneficial Speech of Social Change   173
14. The Social Profit of Empowered Discernment   187
15. A Skilled Trainer   199
16. An Authentic Training   210
17. A Lifelong Community   223
18. Real Connection, Real Intimacy   232
19. Benefit in Everyday Living and Dying   244
20. The Ultimate Resource   253
21. Organizations and Leadership Rooted in Open Intelligence   262
22. Empowered Relationships Are the Basis of Social Change   275

Balanced View Resources   *286*

Editor's Introduction

The basis for this book comes from talks given by Candice O'Denver, the founder of Balanced View, over a three-year period. Beginning with some particularly powerful talks in 2009, clearly there was a new direction that was appearing—one which pointed to the increasing emphasis on the education in the nature of mind as well as to an emerging Age of Human Empowerment and Era of Great Benefit. It became very evident right from the start that these potent talks needed to be put into book form so that a broader audience might be able to benefit.

The process of formulating any of the Balanced View books begins with the talks and the writings from Candice herself, who has wholeheartedly dedicated her life to bringing this incredible message to the world. We on the editing team would like to take this occasion to offer our immense gratitude to Candice for all that she has contributed till now and for all the extraordinary innovations she will surely bring about in the coming years.

Various service groups were created to make the book possible, and the process began with the recording and editing of the talks, which were then posted on the Balanced View site for free download in video and audio form. A team then transcribed approximately 150 spoken talks into text form, and once that was completed, a group of editors corrected and collated the texts. Next, the compilers went through the whole body of material to select the most powerful texts for inclusion in the book. After the appropriate texts had been selected, compiled and set into a series of chapters, another team of editors, including Candice herself, went through the book repeatedly line-by-line to shape it into form.

Hence, the book which you have before you is the result of many thousands of hours of devoted service by numerous volunteers from around the world whose passionate wish is that others will be able to benefit from these trainings as they have.

We, the Balanced View Team, are very happy and grateful to be able to present to you this wonderful new book.

May, 2013

PREFACE

This book presents the Age of Human Empowerment and Era of Great Benefit. This is one of a collection of texts written by the Balanced View Team especially to bring global human society a foremost standardized education in the nature of the human mind. Moreover, it is not as though there are several texts like it. It is the only text of its kind. This book is an encyclopedia of Balanced View's core trainings and explains their exact results of benefit to all.

The unique breadth of knowledge coupled with the topmost realization of the nature of mind offered by the team of teachers/trainers and participants preparing this book make it a profound contribution to the world. The excellence infused with the rarity of this writing brings to the world a social change of benefit to all—one of premier evolutionary importance. As one of the crowning jewels of the Balanced View movement's empowerment of people on all continents, it offers a new way of life for the human species—one filled with satisfaction, flourishing, increased intelligence and the benefit of all.

A world of benefit, prosperity and generosity has arrived in which this text will be cherished in particular. In the decades to come, Balanced View's decoding and unraveling of education in the nature of mind will be recognized as one of human culture's most significant contributions during this era. This book presents a pioneering feature set of the extraordinarily beneficial qualities and activities of the human mind, speech and body as well as direct access to them.

Support is given within the text for its special language, vocabulary and literary techniques, such as repetition and similes, in order to make the book completely understandable, empowering and harmonious for the reader. It furthers a complete education in the inexhaustible nature of mind, discovered to be an open, universal intelligence at the foundation of mind which serves all.

THE CONTEXT

This book has no references or bibliography. It represents a completely fresh attempt by a worldwide team to develop a standardized solution to education in the nature of mind to be applied individually and collectively. It is a work of in-depth scholarship, research, development, implementation, and revision based on feedback—all ongoing.

It began forty years ago with the advent of a computational comparative analysis on education in the nature of mind drawn from the first online bibliographic research services. The comparative analysis continues to provide new data on education in the nature of mind in all of the world's cultures and subcultures as more data become available.

A natural result of the comparative analysis is a flexible, comprehensive map of education in the nature of mind. The development of the Balanced View educational methodology is based on this comprehensive map. Balanced View has taken root all over the world as the standardized solution in education in the nature of mind—unique to this time, place and circumstance of rapid transition and global social change for the benefit of all.

A STANDARDIZED SOLUTION FOR EDUCATION IN THE NATURE OF MIND

This book presents an amazing breadth of knowledge which does not stop there, because it is presented in a way that will satisfy everyone for a very long time—bringing to light a seed of all-beneficial conduct germinating within humans everywhere.

The scholarship in this book is a most important means to an end, for it is used to introduce the opening of intelligence's beneficial potencies, and it is used as such by a qualified trainer to support participants in Balanced View in the introduction and recognition of the powers of benefit naturally present in everyone. It is meant to be the educational means of beneficial potency of mind, speech, body, qualities and activities accessible to all of human society. Not only does proper education in the nature of mind bring forth our naturally beneficial nature, it also nurtures to fruition our most unique strengths, gifts and talents that otherwise would be unknown or barely known.

The uncoding or unraveling of the beneficial potencies of mind is inexhaustible; thus, its supply is available in unlimited quantities. It is the most important of all educational subjects and has been taken far too lightly. That Balanced View is the first standardized solution in all of human history is appalling—akin to not teaching or allowing someone to walk or talk. So basic to human health, life satisfaction and flourishing and the very basis of an ever-expansive intellectual, intrapersonal and interpersonal capacity, education in mind is the exact means for world peace as well as enrichment of everyday relations. Additionally, as the caregiver of our environment, the mind is the utmost priority.

To leave the mind to its own devices is unethical and doomed. With the international presence of attention and legislation, we must regulate education in the nature of mind with a standardized solution such as Balanced View. Likewise, at one time there were no solutions to racism, gender bias, domestic violence, child abuse and so forth, which were and still are to some degree accepted within society. How pivotal a beneficial mind is to all!

Many countries now prohibit all of the social outrages mentioned above, yet the mind's hatred of one for another cannot be regulated through laws. It must come from the individual's recognition that hatred is poisonous—personally and collectively. Then, active means must be taken through education to train up the energy called "hatred" into its native beneficial potency. Most people on the face of the earth do not even know that hatred is a very limiting definition of the mind's beneficial power called "wrath." Wrath is the recognition of wrong coupled with the skillful means and insight to change the circumstances for the benefit of all.

The speech, body, qualities and activities are all at the mind's beck and call. However the mind defines a situation, the speech, body, qualities and activities will follow its lead. The speech, body, qualities, and activities are never separate from the mind's power. This bears repeating again and again until it is spontaneously known to be fact. Much of this book is based on repetition as a literary device to completely confirm an all too obvious fact about the mind that either has been completely overlooked or had another agenda added to it, such as money, power, prestige, politics, religion, spirituality and so on. Education in the nature of mind stands on its own; it is its own category, class and field of study. This is essential to the mind's freedom—the most basic human right.

The mind must be given the freedom of its powers of great benefit that are so obvious upon proper training. It is quite simple to recognize the type of mind-education needed by a child early in life. Really, no person should have a child unless they have the essential basis of successful training in the nature of mind. Obviously, no child should be given an ill-suited education in the nature of mind, and the education must match the child's ability.

Balanced View is for those who take to it most easily, and the results of the training are the most powerful means of attracting others to Balanced View. We now have worldwide coverage in terms of opening education in the nature of mind to all who are most suited.

A future will come when no one alive remembers the extreme mind that is used now. Our minds have evolved little beyond the fight-or-flight syndrome of earlier humans. Any creature with the social and intellectual capacities of a human also has spontaneous altruism—the automatic response to be of benefit—engineered into their development. All basic human drives, such as bonding, defense, acquisition and comprehension are best informed by education in the nature of mind.

THE ENDOWMENT OF THIS WORK AND ITS AUTHORS

A progression of increasing profundity can be seen within the texts of Balanced View, which is the only standardized solution for education in the nature of mind. As unusual as this claim may be, it is inevitably met by the question, "Does there exist a standardized solution for education in the nature of mind, one that is straightforward and easily identifiable?" At some point in thinking about this question, there would arise other inquiries, such as, "When and where did I receive education in a standardized solution for education in the nature of mind?"

When we find that we have received none, or one was received that was so culturally specific as to be of use to very, very few, we are likely to feel aghast that such a foundational aspect of education has been overlooked, left entirely vague or worse yet, left in the hands of religions which are creationist and have the point of view—without any scientific evidence at all—that human beings are fundamentally flawed. Following on from that, almost all of the institutions and organizations of human society likewise address humans as flawed, disempowered and able to change only through life-altering events, such as adopting religious beliefs which have no result aligned with what a human actually is, let alone one of true education, empowerment and mobilization of the individual's mind as an ever-expansive natural resource of open intelligence.

Balanced View continues to be innovated by a mostly anonymous team. Anonymity among the primary staff is the best insurance policy for authenticity in many regards. To name a few of the advantages, anonymity erases the dislikable ignorance, desire, pride/arrogance, hatred/anger, envy/jealousy that most often arise in organizations. These traits arise only because there is no education in the nature of mind as the foundation of employee health, work satisfaction and flourishing.

When compared to the ordinary intelligence used nowadays, each Balanced View book is a pinnacle text on a particular aspect of the subject of open intelligence—the natural and single intelligence of the universe—and its benefit to all. Additionally, the excellence of the authors and their capabilities and attainments in the nature of mind induce the instinctive recognition of open intelligence in the reader or listener, thus verifying the excellence of the book itself. "Induce" means the work and its authors are very much unlike most works and authors in their highly skilled use of successful transmission of open intelligence through symbolic and non-symbolic skillful means, which ensure permanency in the retention of open intelligence and its inexhaustible aspects of purity (the realization that nothing is of a kind different then open intelligence), spontaneous presence, openness, indivisibility, benefit, prosperity, generosity and open-ended knowledge creation.

Mostly, the greatness of Balanced View is in the amazing breadth of knowledge that has come about from a team of people motivated solely by the benefit of all. The greatness of their achievements also rests in the areas of scholarship, research, writing, training, use of computation, telecommunications and transportation technology as means of communication and teaching, as well as worldwide community organizing and organizational capacity. Only a team spontaneously motivated by the benefit of all with the best of leadership—open intelligence—could achieve this most noteworthy of accomplishments.

To an extraordinary degree the team is endowed with utmost excellence in terms of the details of innovative theory and practice it provides, as well as with its background in an unerring history of education in the nature of mind. We are able to present pristine open intelligence—naturally imbued with the spontaneous motivation to benefit all—in a way that arouses ever-deepening realization of its sheer inexhaustibility within the reader or listener. An unending source of strength is discovered which provides beneficial knowledge to the mind, speech, body, qualities and activities. Beneficial knowledge is always specific and directly serves the circumstance, acquiring information from the vast expanse of its auspicious inexhaustibility and processing it in a way that serves the benefit of all. This knowledge is not learned and is naturally occurring in always-on open intelligence. Perhaps most awe-inspiring of all is that open intelligence has the pervasive feature of immediate benefit, unendingly.

Curiosity is inspired by the book due to the lack of exposure humans have had in the past to a standard solution for education in the nature of mind that is aligned with reality itself. The incredible results of education in the actual nature of mind now promise a future of benefit, prosperity and generosity.

This new period of civilization we have entered is known as the Age of Human Empowerment and Era of Great Benefit, and the date of its inception, 1965, coincides with Balanced View's decision to research, develop and implement a result-oriented standardized solution to education in the nature of mind for all—one that will surely unify a global human culture into a beneficial, prosperous, generous, peaceful society.

There is enormous confusion these days about the meaning and capacity of mind in all of its aspects. The utter chaos of offerings on topics such as the brain and mind, awareness, consciousness, neuroscience, positive psychology, mindfulness and so forth has led to much misunderstanding, harm and often passivity. Lack of education coupled with money, power and prestige enshroud these sadly mistaken attempts, wherein the super-factual powers of mind such as spontaneous skillful means, discernment and the purposeful insight that benefits all are overlooked in favor of self-centered aims. As the use of the term "awareness" is particularly erroneous in its presentation, Balanced View has provided a standard solution for education in awareness at www.timelessawareness.org. However, awareness as it is taught by most is not the nature of mind at all and is only a contrived point of view devoid of spontaneous compassion and altruism.

A simile here will serve better than any other formation of words in terms of open intelligence really fulfilling the current requirements of a robust, global human culture's need for education in the nature of mind. Due to lack of education in the nature of mind, the sensorial capacities of most humans engage a vague comprehension of a world of subjects and objects with no true discernment based on certainty of definition. A glance is given, and that is it. Similarly, moonlight is sometimes noticed, yet few discern moonlight as luminosity created by the union of sunlight and moon.

Thus, the open-intelligence view, based on an exact understanding of the nature of mind—particularly the crucial juncture of open intelligence and data—is so specific that it is just beyond the scope of all but a very few due to lack of education. Open intelligence's crucial juncture with data is spontaneously present, giving off a luminous aura due to the great purity of open intelligence coupled with data, which are its inseparable light signals. From this ultimate vantage, it is instinctively recognized that the world, subjects and objects discerned in moonlight and elsewhere are a great spread of equalness and evenness—an unending expanse and aura of great luminosity, comprehensive intelligence and benefit. Great purity is the very essential light of light—a light of such brightness that it outshines all data. Similarly, sunlight outshines the darkness of the moon, leaving a luminous glow and the aura of that glow which is moonlight.

All of this writing remains only a jumble of words unless beautified and simplified by a special kind of communication required for comprehension. This special kind of communication is called "pure transmission through symbolic and non-symbolic means." What this indicates is that instinctive comprehension and recognition take place beyond ordinary rules of logic and reason.

Likewise, moonlight is an immense light due to the crucial juncture of the moon and the sun involving a complex combinatory pattern. Only when moonlight is thoroughly comprehended via open intelligence can it be instinctively understood both as a metaphor for open intelligence's combinatory pattern of the Four Mainstays as well an immense power source beyond the abilities of most to process and simultaneously extract its profound realization of beneficial power. How exactly is the resultant moonlight a metaphor for the Four Mainstays? This book answers that question.

When there is lack of education in the nature of mind, the immense benefit of open intelligence moment-to-moment and overall is completely inaccessible. In a word, it is lost, solely due to this lack of education.

Balanced View presents a formal and full education in the nature of mind. The long sought after results to be found in realizing the nature of mind are ensured once and for all. No effort is needed in the book's reading or listening, as the transmission of open intelligence is always on and spontaneously quickened in the exposure to it. What a wondrous marvel it is!

FOREWORD

A FEW IMPORTANT INSIGHTS

As unusual as it may seem to some who are changed forever by this remarkable book (and in a way they never dreamt possible), this has occurred only because their human knowledge has been thoroughly cleansed and its spontaneous brilliance has shown through.

It is obvious that we are the greatest civilization amongst the highly accomplished human societies who have lived on Earth, and now we have proven that we hold within our vast, open intelligence the knowledge of the universe(s) in a usable way. This is a time of rapid transition and social change. Though some are just coming along for the ride, it is important to rejoice in their companionship as we would that of a dear friend, for everyone without exception is swept up already by the Age of Human Empowerment and the Era of Great Benefit.

The seamless reality of all of existence is showing its radiant countenance, and this can no longer be denied. We are not divided. Not a single thing has ever had an existence of division. However, this strange belief in divided existence is at the root of any instance of pain or misery that flashes across the mind, cell phone, TV and computer screen. Actually, we only have been hiding out from reality and hiding in a strange mix of lack of education, desire, hate, pride and jealousy. Most of us recoil at the former statement, thinking, "This does not apply to me." Yet, we live with all of this pain stuffed inside us, often without knowing it. A term to apply to this condition is "internalized oppression."

The great sadness of the term is to be found in its profound meaning, which is that people believe, act on or enforce the dominant system of beliefs about themselves and members of their group. Until we clarify our own internalized oppression and that of the collective of human society, we cannot possibly make accurate decisions. The urgent importance of exposing internalized oppression has been bypassed until now by all attempts at education in the nature of mind. Due to this strange mix of factors, the very leadership of these efforts at education has been in denial about their own points of view, thus coloring their projects with meager results.

Humanity's own tremendous capacity for knowledge took the wrong turn in describing the world as a reality of the independent existence or interdependent creation of subjects and objects living in a world. Two terms for this belief are "materialism" and "reification." This is merely popular information and not true knowledge at all, for reality tells us the truth *as it is*, unaffected by popularity contests, money, power, prestige and a rabid gender bias which does not permit the rich gifts of both women and men. To explain, whenever there is such extreme bias between groups, both groups are severely oppressed.

What reality tells us loud and clear is that not a single thing can be found to independently exist or can come to be through interdependent creation. Even if we try to make two different things, in actuality there will never be two. Throughout this book, when you see the words "reification," "reify," or "reified," you will know that each one points to the belief that people, places and things each have an independent nature.

Our friend the linear particle accelerator has assisted us in learning once and for all that the belief in the independent nature of subjects, objects and worlds is false. Billions upon billions of dollars have been spent to build an accelerator that will find the absolutely smallest existent particle; however, the failure in this is actually an enormous success. And what has been found? Reality! In this book, we face reality together in open-ended knowledge creation for the benefit of all.

TEAMING

The team that created the masterpiece that is this book is exceptional in both capabilities and attainments. For the reader or listener, their overall excellence is a premier basis for being truly open to the factual nature of mind as it is presented herein. The amazing breadth of knowledge infused into the writing from team members all over the world has never before saturated the topic of education in the nature of mind. This is long overdue.

It is very daring, yet true, to state that this team and its results represent the greatest knowledge of all, which can come only from openness and deep listening for the exact word-facts which have led to the first global standardization of education in the nature of mind with proven results for all participants. Many do not realize that merely giving talks on the subject of the nature of mind is light-years apart from lifelong education in the inexhaustible nature of mind.

The fine-tuning of each person's strengths, gifts and talents in all aspects of mind, speech, body, qualities and activities is happily provided by Balanced View twenty-four hours per day around the world, and this will continue as long as there is a request for it. The life satisfaction, flourishing and enrichment of insight brought by this type of education to our planet and the others we explore are a truly remarkable achievement.

This book represents consummate scholarship of a new order—that of the global mind. The reader in the not too distant future will have access to well-documented biographies which will give more details of the team's life. The team's extensive background in the subject gave great skillful means and insight to the elaboration and actual application of highly-refined editorial, information-theoretic and computational methodologies utilizing the Internet and telecommunications. Thus, we have thoroughly laid down the necessarily flexible conceptual foundations for this new area of result-oriented education in the nature of mind.

The significance of the Balanced View Team's accomplishments challenge the beliefs of some readers who do not understand how a team operating outside of all known institutional or organizational frameworks can stealthily infiltrate the minds of people on all continents and most of the world's cities.

First of all, our qualities and activities as a team come from education in the nature of mind—open intelligence—which has empowered the un-doable to be done. Open intelligence is the singularity talked about in science. Secondly, we have people on our team, among our many accomplished members, who were first introduced to computing and programming in the 1940s— three sisters and two brothers whose father designed the first worldwide computer network for food distribution.

The system was based on reducing each product to a bar code, among many other extraordinary aspects of computational architecture, which created a revolution in distribution of food around the world, greatly reducing starvation and other maladies stemming from lack of fresh food. The sisters and brothers on our team heard their father's engaging talks (given just for them!), and each one of them grew into their own success in different revolutionary applications of information-theoretic and computational methodologies.

Lastly, our team has an outstanding background in community organizing at the local, regional, national and global level. Again, the elders on the team started out in community organizing in the Civil Rights movement of the 1960s, the global movement of students against the war in Vietnam, the international women's political caucus, gathering women together from all over the world to further and to support their political initiatives, which then grew into actual laws against domestic violence and all types of assaults on children. This grassroots experience has been invaluable in initiating meet-ups and ongoing meetings, all of this adding up to the burgeoning Age of Human Empowerment and Era of Great Benefit.

Chapter One

AN INTRODUCTION TO THE AGE OF HUMAN EMPOWERMENT AND ERA OF GREAT BENEFIT

Human society is undergoing a massive change—a paradigm shift in which we, the people of the world, are bringing forth the power of open intelligence to completely transform ourselves and society. This is the Age of Human Empowerment and the Era of Great Benefit.

Rather than seeing ourselves as separate subjects and objects, more and more we are seeing ourselves as expressions of the intelligence of nature itself, the very intelligence that is the basis of all things. One could also call this natural intelligence "open intelligence," a force and presence that includes everything that is, just as space includes all that appears within it.

Society is shifting once and for all, and the shift is extraordinary, profound and unparalleled. This shift is so incredible because it is not only a matter of people changing as individuals, but it involves the changing of every single institution, belief system and assumption of a society that we have relied upon for millennia. Therefore, our way of being human is becoming totally subsumed by open intelligence and its powers of great benefit. This is the evolutionary imperative of our times. We are living in a period of rapid transition—one of education in the nature of mind and the empowerment and mobilization of open intelligence.

Increasingly, people are living in a space of vast and radiant open intelligence simply through the use of electronic and telecommunications. We are empowering the benefit of open intelligence and allowing it to inform the actions of mind, speech, body, qualities and activities. Our very own open intelligence is connecting with the space of reality, and a new beneficial knowledge opens up—the most comprehensive intelligence and knowledge that exists. More and more we will relate to open intelligence as our primary body and its potency

1

of benefit as the informant of all we think, feel, sense or otherwise experience.

Mostly when we think of things, we think of them as exhaustible—a finite resource—but the benefit of open intelligence is an inexhaustible resource. No matter how long anyone or anything might exist, there will always be more open intelligence and more empowerment of great benefit.

Beneficial potency and flourishing are at the core of each and every person, and the ability to contribute one's gifts, strengths and talents for the benefit of all is taking over society from within. Worldwide, people are living daily life in the greatly beneficial place of open intelligence. This isn't an era which brings about a number of superficial changes then exhausts itself and ends. No, this is an inexhaustible Age of Human Empowerment, marked by a society committed to the recognition of and reliance on open intelligence to empower our innate potency. Those who are recognizing this and are gaining assurance in their true identity as open intelligence are the pioneers of this new era.

This age is a treasury in which a beneficial, prosperous and generous society emerges unendingly. There isn't really a way to put this into a historical perspective; it is simply the shining forth of the primordial intelligence that has always been.

This book introduces the Age of Human Empowerment and Era of Great Benefit and presents a model of how to fully accomplish open intelligence and its powers of complete life satisfaction and flourishing, clarity, mental and emotional stability, profound insight, increased intelligence, spontaneous altruism, superb skillfulness and consistent power to fulfill creative intent of benefit to all. Concise key points are given for the education in the nature of mind as well as for increasing the extraordinary beneficial powers of open intelligence in everyday life. The text is filled with the inexhaustible resource of the reality of open intelligence that pervades every single aspect of being human.

The entire text is based on barely edited talks by the founder of Balanced View shared in a daily series from 2009 to 2012.

PERVASIVE INTELLIGENCE

By relying on and gaining assurance in open intelligence, the power of the mind, speech, body, qualities and activities are clarified, normalized and demystified. People are empowered to re-know all knowledge according to the greatly profound view of open intelligence's permission field, which allows everything to be *as it is*. We do not need to mystify our nature any longer. We can now state clearly and without reservation that open intelligence is the basic and complete identity of everyone. Our true nature is very straightforward, and it is time to familiarize ourselves with it.

Open intelligence clarifies all accumulated mistaken knowledge with its tremendous lucidity, openness, spontaneous presence and indivisibility. Increasingly, we instinctively recognize that not a single thing has a nature independent of open intelligence. The clarity of open intelligence sees through all things with alertness and precision; it knows what is entirely useful and what is to be set aside.

This intelligence of the multiverse is naturally present in human beings in a usable way. All the knowledge that has been discovered and that is to be discovered in the future is located within that same intelligence. In relying on open intelligence for short moments, the intelligence of the multiverse is simply *noticed until it is obvious at all times*. One sees that there is a very clear intelligence pervading everything; our own intelligence that allows us to know ourselves and to know others *is* this pervasive intelligence.

Introduce yourself to open intelligence by stopping thinking just for a moment. What remains? Alertness, clarity and openness remain. When the next thought comes, it shines forth from the same open intelligence that is present when not thinking. Not thinking and thinking both shine forth as open intelligence. Open intelligence and its data are indivisible like the sky and the color blue.

"Data" is a term that is used to describe everything that is thought, done, felt, sensed and experienced—that is to say, all phenomena, every single thing that is known by open

3

intelligence. Data are the dynamic energy of open intelligence. In other words, data are the liveliness or light signals of open intelligence. Given the fact that open intelligence encompasses all, how could data—thoughts, emotions, sensations, experiences—possibly have an independent nature separate from open intelligence? Data and open intelligence are inseparable, just as lightning is inseparable from vast space.

When the terms "reification" or "to reify data" are used, this means giving an independent nature to data and seeing them as having an existence separate from open intelligence. So, "reification" involves making a thing into something it is not

A common idea is that open intelligence is somehow separate from data. However, only from the vantage of incomplete education of the mind is there separateness. From the vantage of open intelligence, there is no separateness at all. Thoughts, emotions, sensations and other experiences—all data—appear within open intelligence just as a rainbow appears within space.

Like space and a rainbow are inseparable, data are inseparable from open intelligence. Recognition of, assurance in and reliance on the truth of the inseparability of data and open intelligence is the foundation for the Age of Human Empowerment and Era of Great Benefit. Instinctive comprehension and recognition of the indivisibility of data and open intelligence is the crucial juncture of its powers of great benefit.

There is a natural intelligence within us that is completely carefree, potent and powerful. Each short moment of this incredible intelligence gives us an openness to explore potency and power in a way that is not possible when we are confined to data-driven intelligence alone. This is an order of intelligence that is much more powerful than the one that comes from sorting data into positive, negative and neutral categories. This more comprehensive order of intelligence always knows what to do and how to act, and it does so in a very beneficial way.

Great meaning is embodied in the term "*open* intelligence." Open intelligence refers to a vast, all-inclusive, intelligent space that humans can realize through a simple education in the nature of mind. There is nothing that is independent of or apart from this all-embracing open intelligence. It is the basis of reality— the basis of the entire universe and everything we see and do not see. The same open intelligence that creates the human mind, speech, body, qualities and activities also creates the great oceans, mountains, planets, time, space, dimension and the whole cosmos.

INTRODUCTION TO SHORT MOMENTS

"Short moments of open intelligence repeated many times" is the key to alignment with reality. Open intelligence is alertness, clarity and cognizance that is open like a cloudless sky, and one short moment of open intelligence is the instinctive recognition of inexhaustible open intelligence, the treasure trove of benefit, prosperity and generosity.

We should never underestimate the incredible potency of a single short moment of open intelligence; it is very, very powerful. By relying on open intelligence moment-by-moment—rather than on the data stream of thoughts, emotions, sensations and other experiences—society becomes increasingly more stable and beneficial.

This textual introduction to short moments of open intelligence many times may at first seem radically different, while at the same time very common and ordinary, and the text itself may seem repetitive and unusual in other ways. A new view of the world springs into everyday reality through the literary skillful means of the written word coupled with the pure transmission of open intelligence.

Once there is the introduction to open intelligence, we allow ourselves to follow the simple instruction: to rely on short moments, repeated many times until recognition of open intelligence becomes natural and spontaneous. Uncontrived short moments will allow open intelligence to be steadfast. So, once again, this is key: uncontrived short moments, repeated many times, becoming spontaneous and continuous. The uncontrived quality of these short moments is the unwavering introduction to truly real open intelligence.

When open intelligence becomes continuous, its potency grows inexhaustibly, fueling our strengths, gifts and talents with a completely new intelligence. As open intelligence becomes increasingly constant, we find that it has an immense power we never dreamt possible. There is an incredible capacity to invent, innovate, solve problems and act skillfully, collaboratively and harmoniously in all situations. When it is recognized that this innate intelligence resolves our personal problems, the conviction begins to emerge that it has the power to solve the problems of the world as well. We are awed by how obvious open intelligence is and amazed that for so long we had not recognized it, even though it has always been present.

See for yourself what this is all about in your own life experience. You decide if what is being stated here is true or not. It is a simple choice; do you choose to go with all the data streaming through you in the form of thoughts, emotions, sensations and other experiences, or do you choose to return again and again to short moments of open intelligence until automatic? That is the choice.

You can read what is being stated here, but to really experience it you need to have a vivid and instinctive recognition of it in your own life. This instinctive recognition is the intelligence you rely on. It is an instinctive recognition with depth and breadth. It extends in all directions and is filled with the power of beneficial qualities and activities. By the power of short moments, many times you will see more and more of this instinctive recognition in your own life.

Again and again return to open intelligence, revisiting it again and again, for short moments many times. In doing so, you experience open intelligence's increasing lucidity, openness, spontaneous presence and indivisibility without even trying to gain it.

The awesome adventure of connecting with open intelligence occurs in short moments, repeated many times until this thriving intelligence is recognized spontaneously and uninterruptedly. This practice is our homage to and acknowledgement of the great natural intelligence that gives us the life we live.

Empowered by the practice of short moments we can all join together in open-intelligence society for the benefit of all.

The alignment with reality that comes from relying on open intelligence for short moments many times leads to a way of life that is joyful and beneficial, which is filled with the potency of our intrinsically powerful human nature. This alignment with reality reveals the fundamental truths of human nature *as it is*— fundamental truths that change us and the world forever.

THE AGE OF HUMAN EMPOWERMENT AND ERA OF GREAT BENEFIT IS RIGHT HERE, RIGHT NOW!

This alignment with reality is the dawning of the Age of Human Empowerment and Era of Great Benefit that is occurring right now. This era is truly emerging—an era in which humankind is coming together in realization of its own open intelligence as a force of unity, service, potency and peace. With greater certainty in open intelligence, the conviction in its innate power dawns brighter and brighter and there is the increasing realization of the unavoidable basis that is our indestructible resource and support.

People all over the world are relying on open intelligence rather than on outdated knowledge about human nature that has trained their own stream of thoughts, emotions, sensations and experiences. The excessive negativity about the way society is now moving is one of these data streams. Because we have entered the Age of Human Empowerment and Era of Great Benefit, many things are new and unfamiliar, and most people cannot accurately assess the very positive nature of what is occurring. Many marked changes in society are coming about— incredible changes that people said could never happen— because humanity is opening up to the reality of things as they are. We have had lots of ideas about the way things are, but now we are discovering amazing characteristics and qualities about which we were totally unaware.

We are not cut off or separate in any way from open intelligence; we are ourselves representatives of open intelligence and of its entirely beneficial expanse. Yes, surely, we are nothing but open intelligence, and that fact is true for everyone—not just for special someones—but for everyone.

Human beings no longer need to be thought of simply as biological entities at the whim of their data. We exist as intelligent entities with a totally open intelligence, and we are truly inseparable from it. This is very, very important to know and experience. We no longer need to be constantly accumulating positive experiences and structuring ourselves into a closed system of "the perfect person with the perfect data."

We have to be willing, moment–to–moment, to set aside all of our preconceptions about what the world is and what the world does, about what individuals are and what individuals do. This is the responsibility we take on when we become familiar with open intelligence. This taking responsibility is not only tremendously beneficial to each of us and to society in general, but it is the legacy that will be passed on to future generations. This is a legacy we should really care about, because it is one that will give people mental and emotional stability no matter what is happening for them and give them an opportunity to provide beneficially for each other.

Everything pours forth from the great benefit that is you yourself. Through pure aspiration, motivation, commitment, refinement and manifest realization of tremendous benefit in society, the pioneers of open intelligence make evident the condition of original benefit. Most of us have not been living from that place of original benefit because we have not seen it before, but now more people *are* living from there. We are seeing minds that are as vast as sky; we are seeing endless displays of benefit and good will, as well as circumstances that are prosperous and generous in all regards.

HUMAN SOCIETY COMING TRULY ALIVE

This is a particularly exciting moment where human society comes truly alive. Truly alive! Who generated all this? *Humanity* generated it through evolution. We did it through our commitment to comprehending ourselves. It is not like this shift came from a dimension we do not know anything about. No, it came from more and more people relying on and gaining confidence in their own open intelligence as an integral, evolutionary advancement of body, speech, mind, qualities and activities.

We, the people of the world, have launched the Age of Human Empowerment and Era of Great Benefit. The beneficial, prosperous, generous disposition of so many lives is evidence of this change in society. By the power of open intelligence this shift is more and more obvious—replacing lack, scarcity and greed, and shifting entirely to benefit, prosperity and generosity. Life is seen to be a vast expanse of prosperity and spontaneous benefit in which, fundamentally, there is no problem, and which is filled with open-ended knowledge creation and open-ended solution creation. What a marvel this is!

There isn't a destination to get to; open intelligence flourishes as the very nature of who we are. Spontaneous accomplishments come about beyond our wildest dreams. We are completely relaxed and changed forever. We can have a life fueled by the power of open intelligence and have a balanced perspective—personally and collectively—about all of life. We can see the past clearly, we can see what is going on right now clearly, and we can see the future clearly. With that kind of balanced and open perspective, we can take action in a very direct way that will serve all. We are not merely responding to life from a stance of indulgence, avoidance or replacement of data.

All these words are very satisfying and soothing and are something we all would like to hear, but what is even better is to see the benefits displayed in people around the world. Many, many people have shown up for a complete relationship with open intelligence, and the results are very compelling. These personal examples of open intelligence displayed in a human life are very convincing.

We are evolving very rapidly to a way of life that may have been unimaginable before, but a life that will be profoundly better for all beings. It will be a life that is profoundly abundant, with all the resources that human beings need—resources which in the past had been unavailable for most people.

Most convincingly and amazingly, the Balanced View movement has been brought about by grassroots community organizing, and many very positive changes have been brought about through the same means. To name a few: the right for women to vote and to have reproductive rights, the right to education from early childhood through the highest levels of education for all people regardless of gender or race, equal pay for equal work for women and for all people, the Civil Rights movement, the Domestic Violence movement and special educational programs for the gifted and the disabled.

In the past, the gifted and the disabled may have endured a lifetime of bullying. These populations deserve the very best we have in terms of educational support and funding. The opportunity must be provided to pursue the exact advanced education needed to produce the innovation that will bring about the transformation of human society.

THE TOOLS OF OPEN INTELLIGENCE

In the Age of Human Empowerment and Era of Great Benefit, the greatest of all human rights and freedoms are presented in a language that humans can understand and relate to in their own lives. Usually when we think about "human rights" and "freedom," we think of civil rights and other human rights. It is very unusual to think that we have a right—a birthright as it were—to govern the power of our own mind; however, that above all is the most inalienable of human rights.

We have the necessary tools and frameworks for maintaining open intelligence. It absolutely is the case that every person has innate open intelligence, and through using the right tools each person can avail themselves of that open intelligence, and they can avail themselves of complete mental and emotional stability. All the tools are now in place: a simple practice, a worldwide community, clear trainings and committed trainers.

There are now open-intelligence tools to be turned on in all of society—free, open-source tools that are available to everyone. Each person can take comfort in them to their heart's content. There is no limit. There is always-on support—as much as one would want—and this is very powerful. Providing complete mental and emotional stability for everyone takes a few caring people coming together and making the tools available. The tools are definitely being provided to people, yet the personal examples provided by those who fully rely on open intelligence are the most powerful tool, more powerful than any words that could be spoken.

We live in a time of incredible good fortune because these trainings on the open intelligence of mind are widely available in a plainspoken and clear language. There is no more auspicious time that has ever been in human society than this current time, but we are also at a critical juncture. We have a unique occasion right here where we can go beyond the outdated ideas we have about ourselves. What we have before us is an incredible opportunity to shape ourselves and all of our societal institutions in a beneficial way.

One of the greatest tools of the present day is the incredible information and telecommunications technology we have. Global society is now connected due to the power of communications technology and the Internet. For the first time we can organize ourselves on a global level and provide a training that applies to everyone equally. This is a huge change, because in previous times there was not the same ease of communication between people, nor was there a common training available to many, many people around the world.

This technological revolution we are experiencing is a real endorsement of what we are as human beings. We are innovators, explorers and discoverers; we are always looking for something new and something better. In the present day, we have finally reached the point where people are connecting with one another worldwide through this extraordinary technology, and many people are using that technology to speak meaningfully about happiness, peace, prosperity and benefit as a standard for all.

The next great frontier of human endeavor will be this discovery of the full and complete capacity provided by open intelligence. The great pioneers of open intelligence will come to the fore in the next ten years and will be known by everyone. Due to their work the greater advances that will be made in science and other technologies in the coming decades will occur via this new frontier of open intelligence.

The means to discover this new frontier will become the most valued knowledge on the planet. Whether it is in relation to business or to everyday life, this knowledge will become something that everyone wants. When people find out what the capacities of open intelligence are, that will be what they want, and they will be willing to go to any lengths to know more about it and experience it themselves.

This is a crucial time in history, and it is important to know that we are on the brink of a new frontier and that there are people who are expert guides into this new territory. We desperately need people who are altruistic, beneficial and generous to be at the forefront of all fields, and we need people who know that the purpose of life is to benefit themselves and others. These are the people who should be in the forefront of human life and who should be trusted as our leaders, and more and more they will be. They are going to bring about incredible technological innovations, and they will radically influence human culture and the evolution of humankind for the simple reason that they will be fully utilizing open intelligence as the basis of their action. This is the era in which many people will come forward who care more about their desire to benefit all than their desire to build a personal life based on self-concern.

THE FOUR MAINSTAYS

The core technology or algorithm of the Age of Human Empowerment and Era of Great Benefit is the Four Mainstays. Once the introduction to open intelligence takes place, it is a matter of making use of the basic educational program for all human beings. The Four Mainstays are: 1) The simple practice of short moments of open intelligence, repeated many times until open intelligence becomes obvious. 2) The trainers who support each individual in optimizing the instructions for powerful everyday use. 3) The trainings and the training media: written and spoken instructions which radically increase the momentum and power of open intelligence. 4) The worldwide community.

The Four Mainstays elicit the power of human society to enter into a period of great benefit, prosperity and generosity, and they provide the enhancement environment for every individual equally and for all of human society with no one left out. The Mainstays empower everyone individually to enjoy the benefits of open intelligence as well as to benefit the world. They help provide the fundamental education in the nature of mind and the lifelong enhancement structure for every single human being on earth. This is the basis from which to go out and do wonderful things in the world!

Each expression of the Four Mainstays enhances open intelligence, and its enhancement through exquisite skillful means is beautiful to observe. Enhancement and enrichment are provided to all of society through gaining assurance in open intelligence, resulting in the perfect life satisfaction and benefit inherent in the Age of Human Empowerment and Era of Great Benefit.

Having a full-on relationship with a trainer is extremely important. A trainer is another person just like you who has made the one hundred percent commitment to open intelligence and who is willing to go to any lengths to assist and support. Why is that relationship important? Because they have been where you are now, and they know how the same data you have were resolved in their own lives. There are many pitfalls that will be avoided through that profound relationship.

The Four Mainstays are a powerful combinatory pattern of instruction. They are an instruction set—an algorithm—that leads unerringly to a specific result. This algorithm or instruction set will not only be used by people living today, but also by people in the future, because when we become an open-intelligence society, we pass that set of instructions on to the next generation. That is the legacy we leave for the future.

Anyone who commits to the simple set of instructions of the Four Mainstays and follows the instructions for a period of time can ensure themselves inexhaustible mental and emotional stability. The natural stability comes from recognizing in every moment the pristine nature of our own inner environment—no matter how disturbing that inner environment may at times seem to be. Complete mental and emotional stability is not out of our grasp; it is very much within our grasp—swift and sure.

OPEN-INTELLIGENCE SOCIETY

By relying on short moments as one of the Four Mainstays altogether, we come to see that very powerful beneficial qualities and activities are already present as the basic identity we all share. As individuals we take a look at where we have been, where we are now and where we are going in the future, then collectively we take a look at where we have been as a society, where we are now and where we are going in the future, and then we act decisively and wisely from the vantage of open intelligence. What is true for the individual is true on a global level as well.

An Age of Human Empowerment and Era of Great Benefit takes place in a society based on each person relying on open intelligence for one short moment at a time. Each person puts a building block in place for the society of great benefit, and each person can take responsibility for her or his beneficial nature in a very simple and straightforward way. We take responsibility for ourselves one moment at a time. There is no authority figure that will jump in and save us. As a species, we each have to step up and take responsibility. This is authentic governance.

In open intelligence there is freedom of two types. There is individual emancipation and then there is emancipation for the sake of all. Emancipation for the sake of all is the source-power of great benefit in society and in each individual's mind, speech, body, qualities and activities.

14

In this society of open intelligence that we have insisted upon and that we are taking a stand for, we are stating that we will not live with a standard of mental and emotional *in*stability any longer. We have innate mental and emotional stability engineered into us, and we will not live with mental and emotional instability for another moment. We have the power within us for mental and emotional stability, and we will empower that by using the Four Mainstays, which can be likened to using the best software to run the most excellent program available.

Open intelligence is all-encompassing and instantaneously pervades everything—a formidable force which orchestrates all of human society. By tapping into that powerful force we are actually part of it in a way that is very enduring for us, in a way that really gives us a sense of solidity and indestructibility. Right here, right now, no matter what we are thinking, no matter what our emotion is or what that twitch in our body is, it is all saturated by open intelligence. The fact that we are realizing that we actually are representatives of open intelligence—the pervasive intelligence of nature itself—is a tremendous turning point for human society. Indeed, within us we hold the intelligence of the universe in a usable way. Open-ended, beneficial knowledge creation is the result of the creation of an Age of Human Empowerment and Era of Great Benefit.

If we as a society want to thrive, then that thriving will occur from open intelligence. Open intelligence has been present all along; however, we are now at the evolutionary turning point in human existence where it is being recognized, and also at the point where it *must* be recognized.

The Age of Human Empowerment and Era of Great Benefit is an invitation to humankind—a call to action—to come together in realization of our own open intelligence as the force of unity, service, potency and peace. In realization of the unavoidable bind of benefit that is our indestructible resource and support, we are just beginning to comprehend what the fruits of this great benefit might be.

Chapter Two

RELYING ON OPEN INTELLIGENCE FOR SHORT MOMENTS MANY TIMES

The Four Mainstays—the practice of short moments many times until continuous, the trainer, the training media, and the worldwide community—is a system of instruction and a combinatory support structure which empowers everyone individually to enjoy the benefits of open intelligence and its great benefit to the world. The Four Mainstays are the basis from which to go out and do wonderful things in the Age of Human Empowerment and Era of Great Benefit.

Once the introduction to open intelligence takes place, it is then a matter of practicing short moments in everyday life, utilizing the trainer, trainings and the training media and having a relationship with a community of people who are committed to the inexhaustible benefit of the Four Mainstays.

The first of the Four Mainstays is the reliance on open intelligence for short moments many times. If you are new to the practice of short moments, know that this practice is what you can count on. You can *really* count on this. Anyone can practice short moments—anyone. Even in moments of doubt, the doubt too is the shining forth of the open-intelligence view.

Maybe the first day that you hear about short moments, it might be remembered only once or twice, yet persist nonetheless. Maybe other people are more obsessive about it. "Got to recognize it, got to recognize it," and they focus on it all the time. Whatever the particular tendency is, all of that will eventually smooth out. We are each unique in our circumstantial data, but the key in any case is a one hundred percent commitment to this simple practice.

Until we began to recognize open intelligence, data were prioritized, and so we only knew about the data. But by acknowledging open intelligence in this simple, direct way of

16

short moments, it becomes very obvious and very potent. In that initial short moment, all of the potent benefit of body, speech, mind, qualities and activities is activated. The doors of beneficial, prosperous and generous qualities and activities swing wide open.

Open intelligence may not be all that obvious to us in the initial short moment, but in retrospect we will see very directly the great benefit that it is to us and to everyone. At first we may have different responses to the recognition of open intelligence. We may think that it is working for us or we may think it is not working for us or it might be seen as something in between; however, the potency of the open-intelligence view is super-complete from the start and very profound in every circumstance.

THE INSTINCTIVE RECOGNITION OF OPEN INTELLIGENCE

As we begin our exploration of what exactly relying on open intelligence for short moments many times is, we should first experience a short moment of open intelligence directly. To do so, we simply stop thinking just for a moment. In this way, by stopping thinking we can observe right here and now in a decisive way just for an instant that basic alertness is present. Where is it? Is it in the brain? Is it in the heart or in the mind? What is present in that moment is a naked and alert basic cognizance, and that basic cognizance is exactly *as it is*. By tuning into that rather than tuning into the stream of data, open intelligence becomes more and more obvious, until it is continuous at all times. In that naked view is a splendid and even perception of everything that appears in the here-and-now.

When thinking is stopped, an inseparable mind-treasure is automatically prioritized—an alertness, clarity and basic cognizance. This mind-treasure can be trained up in short moments repeated many times until it is continuous. It is prioritized as the center of observation and information, and all of what we perceive is then viewed from the vantage of open intelligence—in, of, as and through open intelligence.

Descriptions arise which are due to the bare cognizance of open intelligence. A thought comes into open intelligence and resolves in open intelligence; then the next thought comes and resolves; then the next thought comes and resolves—but all of it occurs in open intelligence. There may be a gap in the thoughts or no gap, but the gap between the thoughts is itself open intelligence. The open intelligence that is present in the gap is also present when there are thoughts with no gap. The appearance-duration-resolution of thought is just a description of open intelligence. Indeed, *everything* is a display of open intelligence. By seeing the simple process in our own thinking in this very direct way, we will understand how the whole world of descriptions comes about.

The instinctive recognition of open intelligence does not require thought or reason. We can comprehend it intellectually, but that is not the same as instinctive understanding. We only have a true comprehension of the open-intelligence view when it is instinctively recognized. There is nothing to do, no effort to make, nothing to achieve—very simple, very clear, very open, very right-here.

A short moment of open intelligence is the log-in and password into a culture of gratitude and respect, a culture of openhearted, powerful participation. One moment after another, the power to know and to do for the benefit of all is right here. When we *really* feel this instinctive truth in our hearts, then we know we are in the right spot. Through the power of our own practice of short moments, we are participating in an era of benefit, prosperity and generosity.

THE POWER OF THE SHORT MOMENTS PRACTICE

The best advice for everyone, everywhere, every single day would be, simply stated, to commit one hundred percent to the practice of short moments of open intelligence and to all the Four Mainstays. The incredible power of the short moments practice cannot be overestimated. By just continuing on with the practice whenever you remember to do so, it will avail great, great benefit. By this simple practice alone, open intelligence will become continuous. There is no need to look for any benchmarks as to what should be happening or any levels to achieve or things that should occur. Just know that if you fully commit to this practice, open intelligence will become obvious and continuous. The trainer, training media and worldwide community are available twenty-four hours a day to support obvious realization of open intelligence at all times.

Open intelligence is already present; it is simply a matter of recognizing more and more that it *is* already continuously present. Do not try to prolong moments of open intelligence. Open intelligence already is, so it does not need to be prolonged. Simply become accustomed to its obviousness; that is all. These short moments naturally grow longer and longer, and open intelligence comes into the foreground rather than being in the background, outshining everything in splendid equalness and evenness. Its power shines in every aspect of life. Whether you are you are president of a country or a parent bringing up children or you are selling fruit by the roadside, the potency of open intelligence shines forth in that situation or activity.

At first all the data may seem to be enemies, yet as open intelligence becomes more obvious, the data become friendlier and friendlier—until they are completely outshone. Initially, we might be a little hesitant because the data have seemed to cause us so much trouble, but we eventually come to see that the data are self-releasing. We do not have to keep a watch on them, and we do not have to categorize things any longer. By the power of open intelligence we have profound insight into the meaning of all definitions and all interactions. This is where life gets very, very real.

In the midst of a significant personal struggle, we might suddenly see that the data surrounding that struggle entirely self-release. In actual fact data never were a problem, are not a problem now and will never be a problem in the future. They appear and disappear like a line drawn in water.

We may hear the words, "Open intelligence is vast like infinite space," but the recognition of that actually becomes real to us in our daily life. It isn't just a bunch of words anymore; it is very real in our own experience that open intelligence is a vast expanse like pure space and that open intelligence and data are indivisible, like the sky and the color blue. It becomes obvious that open intelligence is not limited within the skin suit of a body.

Each short moment of open intelligence sharply accelerates the benefit of all. The auspiciousness of such beneficial activity is the crowning of society. The Age of Human Empowerment and Era of Great Benefit—the singularity of greatly beneficial open intelligence—is the greatest of successes. In this context, our civilization reaches an unending zenith.

THE BASIS FOR ALL OUR ACTIONS

Taking short moments together with people who are committed to open intelligence is a very powerful practice. If we are constantly around people who are talking about all their data and how meaningful they are, then data will seem to be very urgent and important. To choose open intelligence over data and to be with other people who are doing the same is a simple and important choice.

At the same time, everyone is self-responsible and self-governing. There is no one else who can do this practice for you. Other people can give you tremendous support; however, when it comes right down to it, it is a matter of *your own* recognition of open intelligence. It is such a tremendous boon to make the choice to rely on open intelligence for short moments many times. You have made an excellent choice that will enrich you and others lifelong—a choice which is so much a part of the emergence of the Age of Human Empowerment and Era of Great Benefit in yourself and in the world.

You benefit yourself enormously by relying on short moments. This is one thing you can do for yourself in your everyday life for the rest of your life. If you continue to rely on the practice, open intelligence becomes automatic and continuous, and in doing so your mind becomes clear, rather than being filled with excessive negativity. However, *you* must take the action. When you do so, you show yourself that the person you have been told you are through the bias of society's excessive negativity is not truly who you are. Use the negativity as a support for the practice. For instance, you could watch your most disliked news programming while allowing open intelligence to outshine it. By doing this, you may find insight into the most comprehensive discernment, rather than staying with kneejerk reactions to disliked statements.

Solid and clear within every individual is the bright mind of open intelligence, and that bright mind of open intelligence is the basis for all your actions, all your thoughts, all your sensations and all your emotions. Regardless of circumstances, you can count on this. Even if there is a great natural disaster like a meteor hitting the Earth, open intelligence remains the basis of everything.

It is important to rely on a practice that will give you a very significant and substantial result in your life. You want to see a real change, and you want to open up to the great powers and abilities within yourself. Relying on open intelligence for short moments many times has a consistent result that can be counted upon; it brings about the spontaneous power to be of benefit to all.

The potency of open intelligence is always fully present, so the sense of arriving at a destination—"I've got it now"— becomes obsolete. Yet, there is always a sense of augmentation, of increase, of expansion and obviousness of open intelligence, regardless of the situation. Inexhaustible open intelligence is the key point.

Short moments isn't a thing to do forever. It is a way of seeing what is actually going on, and after a while open intelligence is just obvious all the time, regardless of what is going on. Many, many things can be going on for people everywhere right now, yet for those relying on short moments, open intelligence remains always-on.

These short moments become continuous. Open intelligence recognized in short moments is self-kept. Open intelligence does not go anywhere. The open intelligence that is recognized, whatever amount that is, is self-kept and cannot be lost or diminished. Any thoughts that open intelligence is lost or diminished are themselves fueled by open intelligence.

ORIGINAL BENEFIT

The world in which we live is a dimension and lineage of original benefit. The names that have been concocted to describe the world are just one way of describing it. If we read books to try to account for ourselves and the world, we only have secondhand knowledge that we have learned from others, but we have no firsthand experience. However, when we experientially take a look in, as, of and through open intelligence at who and what we are and what the world is, then we arrive at a clear understanding. We arrive at crystal clear intelligence.

By the power of short moments, we discover how to account for ourselves, others and the world. We determine this in a very direct way and not by relying on secondhand knowledge. In our own experience we arrive at a direct account of ourselves and the world that we can count on. This is a very powerful stance. Anything else in books or any kind of secondhand knowledge is of little use unless we have this firsthand knowledge. With this firsthand knowledge, all other knowledge makes sense.

These short moments open up a treasury of natural resources within human life, and it really is quite astounding to witness so many people settling into short moments and discovering these natural resources. By each person's short moment of open intelligence, there is an expansion of society's intelligence and the power to exhibit beneficial qualities and activities.

A short moment is a demonstration of incredible benefit, where we actually notice that our life has shifted from self-focus to the benefit of all. We have not cultivated it or contrived it; it is spontaneous in short moments. When we take a short moment of open intelligence, we are ensuring the Age of Human Empowerment and Era of Great Benefit. The building blocks are this alone—short moments. This is a very profound contribution, and it only takes a short moment!

By the power of many individuals committing to short moments, this era is instantiated in society. We have the right to live *in* this pervasive benefit and *as* this pervasive benefit. This is our actual birthright. The great benefit, prosperity and generosity that are our birthright are evident from the beginning of that first moment of complete mental and emotional stability. When the pure benefit that is at the basis of everything is potentiated and utilized as the basis of human life, we have access to the best of our innate strengths, gifts and talents, and we find a human society rich with inexhaustible prosperity and generosity.

THE RESET BUTTON

Taking short moments is like pressing the reset button, bringing us back to open intelligence again and again. After a lifetime of hearing, reading and writing so many different things about ourselves and who we are, now it is the reset button again and again—reset, reset, reset to open intelligence. "Oh yes, that's right; OH YES, that's right!" The resonance grows strong, reverberating throughout everything without doubt or confusion. We hit the reset button again and again. Each time that reset button is hit by any individual, not only is the reset button hit for that person, but for all of human society.

From the time we were born we have grown accustomed to relying on data, but now we utilize short moments many times to grow accustomed to our natural state. Luminous open intelligence shines with benefit, and initially the most important thing is just to recognize this. Open intelligence should be picked out again and again until its recognition becomes spontaneous. We just identify the open-intelligence view; we do not have to do anything to keep it in place.

We want to uninstall the software we have been running that led us to indulge all the data. This new software is completely free, and in fact, it is already installed! That is how user-friendly it is, and if we forget that it is already installed, we just press the reset button! Short moments of open intelligence is always spontaneously upgrading, so we do not have to do anything to it.

It is the core operating system for the recognition of open intelligence. This unavoidable open intelligence that binds us all together simultaneously protects, defends and nurtures. It is an unavoidable charity that nurtures us in every moment. It guards us, fundamentally speaking. It resets us to natural vigor, benefit and brilliance.

Give this a try and you will see in your own life what is described here. Those nagging worries you have always had do not have to nag and worry you any longer. By relying on open intelligence for short moments many times you will find you have complete freedom in all the nagging and worrying. The freedom isn't somewhere other than in the nagging and worrying! There is complete freedom in immediate perception and complete perceptual openness in all experience. The practice of short moments spontaneously presses the reset button of open intelligence again and again—until all of human society becomes a society of open intelligence.

OMAT AND ODAT

Each one of us has to live our human life, and how can we best do that? We do it one moment at a time, one day at a time—OMAT and ODAT—"One Moment at a Time" and "One Day at a Time." In a similar way, we get into the swing of relying on short moments one moment at a time. We lighten up and relax by relying on open intelligence for short moments— one moment at a time, one day at a time. In each moment we completely confirm open intelligence rather than the data. If we want to know things about the world or we have decisions to make or we have things to do in our life, like we all do, the best information is going to come through the recognition of open intelligence. It is not going to come from rummaging around in all the data.

By relying on the open-intelligence view, in a very natural way we gain trust in it over time. We gain trust through familiarization, just like we gain trust in any situation. We familiarize ourselves with it to the degree that it becomes completely obvious at all times. It becomes always completely and obviously present—so evident that it does not even need to be talked about. We just go along our happy way.

We human beings have developed a lot of incredible things; however, in terms of what we take ourselves to be, we have basically been living in a very primitive way. But that is now changing. Emerging from within society is a whole new way of being, one moment at a time!

The spontaneous self-release of the here-and-now is guaranteed. It is a one hundred percent guarantee—one moment at a time—OMAT, OMAT, OMAT, OMAT. There is no way to grab OMAT or nail it down. OMAT cannot be made into a thing; it is here and gone, never to be duplicated again.

We see the benefit of OMAT and ODAT in our own lives from the outset, and through that practice we also begin to benefit others as well. Little by little—OMAT and ODAT—we come to see that we have access to intelligence and to qualities and activities that we never imagined possible. When we release our hold on the stream of data involved in conventional thinking—conventional ideologies about everything, including science and technology and all the constellations of data associated with those things—we open up an expanse of intelligence that contributes directly and profoundly to the benefit of all in every single area of human knowledge.

RECOGNITION, COMMITMENT, ASSURANCE

There are three declarations that completely confirm the practice of short moments of open intelligence, make clear its key points, and elicit clarity, power and benefit. The three declarations are: "recognition," "commitment" and "assurance."

We have to *recognize* what open intelligence is in order to be able to commit to it. No matter how dim or bright that recognition may seem initially, open intelligence is always present. By recognizing it, we know what it is, and this serves as the introduction to open intelligence. If the open-intelligence view is not recognized, the preservation of that view does not occur. So, initially to recognize open intelligence is essential.

The next declaration is the *commitment* to the practice of taking short moments of open intelligence many times. One hundred percent commitment means, "I will rely on open intelligence no matter what happens." It is the most important commitment we can make in our lives, because all other commitments depend on that one. The commitment is a one hundred percent commitment; it should not be partial. Just as we cannot mix oil and water, we would not be best served by trying to mix a partial commitment to open intelligence into our lives. That would just lead to confusion.

The third declaration is to attain complete *assurance*. Assurance in open intelligence does not come from mental analysis. It is in the one hundred percent commitment to short moments that we find the assurance. If we have not made the one hundred percent commitment, it is not possible to find the assurance. If we try to mix in other means along with short moments, then we never know the full potency of the unadulterated skillful means of short moments. Short moments is the most skillful means of all skillful means for human beings of this era.

A bird has wings, but unless it uses the wings to fly, it never really has complete assurance of their capacity. It is the same with open intelligence. We may already know that we have an open-intelligence nature, but unless we actually familiarize ourselves with it, acknowledge it and then put it to use, we do not know its full power.

The transition from relying on reified intelligence to relying on open intelligence can happen quickly or slowly, and while for most people it happens relatively slowly, there might be quantum leaps here and there. But whichever it is, we become more and more familiar with and adjusted to open intelligence. As we do so, our plans and activities do not have so much stress and tension in them, and eventually the stress and tension disappear completely.

Gaining assurance in open intelligence is similar to gaining a new friend. It usually takes a while to grow in trust with that friend, and in the same way it may take a while to grow in trust and assurance with open intelligence. We grow in trust with the spontaneity of open intelligence and its laser-like decision-making capabilities and the ability to apply the correct solution in the moment.

We can see how far we have come, and because of that we can trust ourselves, and we can trust that this process will continue to unfold moment to moment. Open intelligence prepares us for any eventuality. We grow more and more secure, even to the point of knowing, "Well, death could come at any moment, and no matter what that might entail for me, I am ready."

We become simple and direct. Complete stability is available here and now—yes, here and now! Things play out however they do, and in whichever way they play out we are totally stable and secure. In this way we have made the best investment in our future that we could possibly make.

Wherever we go, there we are, and that is where the full force and power of short moments of open intelligence is. We do not need to go anywhere else to get it or to demonstrate it in some future time or remember some past time when it was demonstrated and now it isn't. There is a fierce power that is right here, right now. It is in the current moment, whatever that current moment is presenting for us. All the games are over. No matter what the presentation is here and now, it is a presentation of the full force of the body, speech, mind, qualities and activities of open intelligence, and this is recognized completely through short moments many times.

Chapter Three

THE WISH-FULFILLING GEM

The view of lucid open intelligence called the balanced view is capable of quickly correcting all wrong knowledge and placing you in the reality of correct knowledge, love and beneficial activity—like the sun quickly evaporates mist leaving space clear and shining. In the practice of short moments of open intelligence, the very powerful natural intelligence at the basis of everything—known and unknown—comes to the forefront as a greatly beneficial leader and guide.

Because you are reading this, you naturally have the strength, capacity and intelligence to be benefitted by open intelligence, which means you already do instinctively comprehend and recognize the profound meaning of open intelligence and its powers of great benefit. The instinctive comprehension and recognition of open intelligence will continually be more obvious to you, as will its powers of knowledge, love and capability.

To repeat again what has been mentioned previously, to experience a short moment of open intelligence, first of all stop thinking. Now that you have stopped thinking, what remains where the thought was? Alertness, clarity and power remain. Alertness means sharpness and readiness; clarity means accuracy and brightness; power means the ability to do or accomplish something. Take a moment to enjoy resting in the potency of open intelligence by stopping thought completely just for an instant. What a marvel this is!

We find our entirely beneficial natural state to be alertness, clarity and power. What is more, this very power is available to us all the time and is the fuel of all thoughts, emotions, sensations and other experiences. Whether the experience is positive, negative or neutral, open intelligence pervades all.

The dynamic quality of open intelligence choicelessly, ceaselessly, spontaneously and pervasively enacts the benefit of all. It is necessary to empower the sun of realization of open intelligence in all moments, letting its primal reality be *as it is*. Reality is none other than open intelligence. Short moments of open intelligence repeated many times leads to obvious open intelligence at all times, without any effort to keep it in place. Short moments is nurturing and celebrates open intelligence. Our entire attitude changes to one of gratitude and respect.

KEY POINTS AND PITH INSTRUCTIONS

Everyone has the strength, intelligence and capacity to empower the authentic reality pervasive of everything. Leave open intelligence in its natural state. The results are immediate and permanent. To repeat, the results are immediate and permanent. There is nothing else in life that can promise both immediate and permanent satisfying results at all times. The beneficial power of open intelligence to provide life satisfaction and flourishing is always on; it is inexhaustible.

And to make it even better, Balanced View offers support through all the Four Mainstays, not just through the one Mainstay of short moments of open intelligence. The other Mainstays are the worldwide community, multimedia trainings and wonderful trainers. Live chat is offered twenty-four hours per day to those who request it.

Basically, what I would say from my own experience is that you must allow yourself to empower the potency of open intelligence and its great powers of speech, body, qualities and activities. This comes spontaneously and naturally through the powers of open intelligence.

A magnificent peacock merely looks like a large dark bird until it spontaneously displays the magnificence of its exquisitely decorative wings. Likewise, until we show our true colors of open intelligence, we do not know of our powerful capacity of love, knowledge and accomplishment.

When I was in my thirties, I stayed for two summers on the edge of a peacock grove at a remote house in coastal northern California. The first time I saw the mighty birds come to the window, I was in a Japanese soaking tub, totally quiet and relaxed. Suddenly, I looked up through a long redwood window and there was a flock of about thirty peacocks, some displaying their feathers and others not. I gasped in awe at the unexpected gift of nature. Similarly, each moment is an unexpected gift of open intelligence.

By completely confirming your own open intelligence, each moment gives you the key point of this most important instruction: open intelligence is always on, outshining each moment from within. Each moment is spontaneously self-releasing. There is no way to keep it in place or to measure or adequately describe it other than to say, "Relax, and open intelligence will be *as it is*." Just as the noonday sun outshines the dark of night, open intelligence outshines the here-and-now. Its great outshining brightness is inexhaustibly obvious. Its powerful intelligence is the most comprehensive intelligence, and it discerns everything precisely and beneficially for all. To go about life in any other way is like putting a target before you and then shooting an arrow in another direction. How useless that would be!

The key points of open intelligence must be employed. You must realize that everything you have learned prior to the empowered view taught here is completely wrong if it has not totally severed the root of incorrect knowledge. Thought, speech and action are mostly coarse and primitive due to incorrect learning. Whether we know it or not, we allow ourselves to be dragged here and there by urges and data that severely limit our life satisfaction, flourishing and beneficial activities.

THE DIRECT CUT

A direct slice must cut the root of this disabling knowledge, just like a very sharp blade makes a clean cut, leaving a finger or head on the chopping block. Ah yes, my friends, embolden your open intelligence with the metaphors and other similes used here. Their tone will never leave you as they strike the mark, outshining with sheer perfection the mind's muttering. Confusion's stories immersed in describing everything and everyone are outshone by simple, uncontrived recognition of open intelligence until obvious at all times. Likewise, a line drawn in water leaves no trace when left *as it is*.

Regardless of its appearance, open intelligence takes the form of potently pure, lucid, unstopped benefit. Its own entity, transparent and naked, is like a flawless crystal ball. Open intelligence as the ground of shining forth gives rise to the stoppage-less liveliness of beneficial activity. Everything and everyone within open intelligence shine forth like images appearing and receding in a crystal ball. A shimmering crystal ball emits the image of anything nearby. Similarly, open intelligence is the beginning, middle and end of its intangible images.

No matter what way it shines forth, open intelligence is not lost in the appearance or its description. So, exactly *that*— shining forth as the liveliness that does not move away from naked open intelligence—is the potency of beneficial activities. Inseparable open intelligence and its liveliness are in reality indivisible. If when an appearance of open intelligence shines forth as data and is left *as it is*—spontaneously present open intelligence—the data are seen to be the power of great benefit. Likewise, when a muddy pond is left unstirred, it settles naturally into clear and clean water.

Hey! My friends, please realize the meaning of allowing data to proceed to shining-forth-release as the expanse of pure open intelligence. No covering up needs happen any longer due to the mere appearance of the play of data. It would be like a poor person going begging who doesn't realize that he lives on the Isle of Gold. Thus, to resolve the root of open intelligence, go about it like this, you fortunate ones, knowing that all that is known and unknown constitutes the Isle of Gold itself.

Give up your right to be a victim of imposing an independent nature on appearances. Like luster cannot be separated from gold, data appearances cannot be separated from open

31

intelligence. Data are the light-signal luminosity of open intelligence—a great luminosity unlike any other light. Realize this in lucid direct perception, free of the elaborations of mental analysis, and all that shines forth is manifest as transparent open intelligence.

ENTERING THE AGE OF HUMAN EMPOWERMENT AND ERA OF GREAT BENEFIT

Human society has truly entered the Age of Human Empowerment and Era of Great Benefit. This is not a mere fantasy; it is happening right now all over the world. This is an era in which there will always be increasing pure benefit, generosity and prosperity for all. These qualities are inexhaustible and are therefore self-augmenting. All of the ways that we live today are changing enormously.

This is the era in which we are living *right now*. There have been people who have been relying on open intelligence ever since human society began; however, this practice has never been pervasive throughout the global society in which it was occurring and was only present in a few random cultures here and there. But now throughout global human culture we see a powerful commitment to short moments of open intelligence until obvious at all times forming an open-intelligence society.

The people of planet Earth are creating a world that is based on the solution-orientation of open intelligence rather than on the confusion of data-naming. It is as simple and powerful as that, and it all begins with each one of us. Yes, to repeat, *it all begins with each one of us*. Each short moment acknowledged by each person in the world creates a great storehouse of open intelligence that becomes more and more powerful and spreads throughout the world. We need to see that we do indeed have incredible power and potency within us. We are not helpless, disempowered and powerless; indeed, we carry in us the potency of the incredible and awe-inspiring natural power that created the entire display of natural wonders that make up this universe.

When we empower open intelligence these are the results: the mind will become stable and strong, and emotional and mental stability and physical health will become the standard. This is going to come about very quickly. All of the knowledge that we need for this to occur is already present within us as open-intelligence's great and most comprehensive knowledge, and it is only by going to this source that we will be able to provide for human beings, for all beings, and for planet Earth. In order to understand who we are and what our place in the cosmos is, we really must rely on open intelligence.

When we recognize the discomfort, tension and disharmony caused by emphasizing data, this really motivates us to gain confidence in open intelligence, and we begin to rely on the open-intelligence view. By the power of this we see that the open-intelligence view shines forth, unveiling a profound capacity that is not available when only relying on the descriptions of data. As open intelligence shines forth within human society, everyone is affected, and bit by bit the entirety of human culture upgrades to always-on open intelligence and its powers of great benefit. Make no mistake about it; this is always already the case.

Through simply making open intelligence your basis rather than mental analysis, you join the growing force that realizes that the greatest capacity of intelligence is insubstantial and pure intelligence, which is also called "the nature of mind." Again, make no mistake about it; this is the greatest power. Look at your own mind to see if it is like that or not.

In short moments you look at the nature of mind until it is obvious at all times—alert, clear and beneficial. This alone brings the greatest of what can be found in life: perfect intelligence as well as beneficial disposition, conduct and results.

ABSOLUTE ASSURANCE

Practice short moments, one moment at a time, whenever you remember to do so. Keep it simple, one short moment at a time, one day at a time. Absolute assurance is gained by simply relying on open intelligence for short moments many times until it goes continuous. By the power of this assurance, your approach to life begins to alter immediately and you start to experience increasing soothing and potent energy.

By this simple, radical and revolutionary practice, open intelligence *will* become continuous. You will see increasing open intelligence and increasing beneficial qualities and activities in your life and throughout your entire lifespan. For many people progress in gaining assurance in open intelligence is made gradually; however, the typical length of time in gaining assurance will shorten as more and more people worldwide rely on open intelligence. It will become easier and easier for people to recognize open intelligence, and each new expression and permutation of open intelligence will outshine the preceding ones. With more and more people practicing open intelligence, the instinctive recognition of open intelligence and the full flowering of the outshining of all data will become easier and easier for everyone.

Each short moment of open intelligence practiced by each person in the world is a contribution to the Age of Human Empowerment and Era of Great Benefit. So, know that each short moment of open intelligence is the greatest gift you can ever make to society.

The rules that once governed us no longer will. For example, the greed for money, power and prestige will naturally and spontaneously be replaced by benefit, prosperity and generosity as our primary result. Without any need to think about anything, our needs will be taken care of: beautiful places to live, lovely clothing to wear, wonderful friends, the best food to eat, health care, education and all the other tools we need to assist in our beneficial aims. Everything is provided.

Upon the flourishing of open-intelligence society, all are recognized to be the mind, speech, body, qualities and activities of the dimension of benefit, prosperity and generosity. Even though we have lived as though we were always suffering from lack—wanting something more, hoping that certain things will occur and fearing that they will not—this cannot alter the reality of our natural state of original benefit.

THE ALL-ABUNDANT GIFT

There are people who have had access to all kinds of privilege and wealth, and even with this extraordinary privilege, even *greater* privilege and wealth is to be found through the power of open intelligence. Open intelligence really is the wish-fulfilling gem—the all-abundant gift—because it provides everything anyone could wish for. "The wish-fulfilling gem" is a wonderful metaphor and describes all of life. All of the facets of life are a wish-fulfilling gem of endless and inexhaustible benefit for all. The very energy of your mind, your speech, your body, your gestures and actions, your different qualities and activities—all of these are aspects of the wish-fulfilling gem of open intelligence.

Human beings have been living a certain way for a long time, bogged down by reified intelligence and the metaphors of internalized oppression which depict limitation and inadequacy. We need some new metaphors, so why not "the multiverse of blazing jewels" and why not "the wish-fulfilling gem"?

Open intelligence isn't a means *to* a wish-fulfilling gem; open intelligence *is* the wish-fulfilling gem. When open intelligence is prioritized and it is the primary aim of one's life, then its beneficial boon comes into play. This is what we actually hold in our hands and hearts, and this is what our whole body is made of. Every single cell and subatomic particle is a wish-fulfilling gem, and the means for tapping into that are very easy and available.

The increase in beneficial, prosperous and generous outcomes is a sign of emancipation from reification, and we already see this taking place today all over the world. People are gathering together in open-intelligence society in such a way that everything flows along in beneficial harmony, and everyone is taking care of everyone else with plenty of resources for all.

How glorious it is to look out and be able to see people as their beneficial qualities and to see everyone's essential being as a wish-fulfilling gem capable of providing untold good fortune! It is just awe-inspiring to watch the miracles of benefit unfold in this way. There is an expanse that reaches out endlessly, and we cannot even really say what is there, yet we know open intelligence is our reality—what we actually are. Open intelligence is entirely beneficial and will lead us from being a fractured, fragmented human culture to one of great singularity and benefit—where everything is interoperable and interactive in an entirely positive way.

In conventional society there is a great deal of emphasis placed on diversity of nationality, culture and ethnic background, yet we are coming into a period where people will be less and less likely to refer to themselves based on their country or cultural background. That identification is loosening up; people are becoming much less identified with the nation that they are from and more identified with a global human society.

By the power of open intelligence we come together in the unbelievable richness of unity of open intelligence. It does not mean that we lose diversity; it means that we enhance diversity from the power of open intelligence. However, it is not the diversity of personal identity that is enhanced; it is diversity of beneficial qualities and activities that is enhanced. We go from a self-focused kind of diversity to an amazingly diverse display of beneficial qualities and activities from many, many different people.

We need the intelligence provided by short moments to solve the problems that have been created. Initially we solve our own individual problems, and we thus become assured that, within us, beneficial power and energy is present and spreads out everywhere. In a society where this is occurring, people really do take care of each other. It is a society of total sharing, caring and dignity.

Relying on open intelligence means that in our own experience we see that we do not have to go into some kind of extreme point of view—such as austerity at one end of the spectrum or wasteful overspending at the other. By the power of open intelligence in every moment, we learn that we do not need to go to extremes in *any* way. It is not a matter of renunciation of anything; it is a matter of human dignity and human reality. The negativity and suffering are outshone by the power of open intelligence.

Many, many people all around the world can say with absolute conviction about their lives, "Each year just gets better and better!" No matter what great things they may have projected for themselves, it has always been better than anything they could have imagined. This is the reality of what open intelligence brings. This is such a profound insight into human nature, and the insight brings vitality, total vigor and the alertness of knowing who we really are.

PIONEERS

We are really the first generation of people in human history to have opened up to ourselves as inseparable from and interoperable with the indivisible open intelligence of the universe, and who have done so in a way that has connected people around the world. We are the first mass wave of humanity to pass into this comprehensive order of intelligence that we have always had as human beings.

In reality, our mind, speech, body, qualities and activities *are* the vast expanse of open intelligence. The open intelligence of the universe is embedded in us as intelligent entities, and we can expand the openness of that intelligence in inexhaustible ways. There is no limit to it; it isn't as if we are made only of physical and mental stuff, or that we are locked within a skin line and we are always inside there and are never anywhere else. Rather, our intelligence reaches out infinitely.

People are naturally attracted to having a happy life filled with satisfaction and flourishing, but they have not always known where to turn to receive it. Right now in human society some people are very receptive to open intelligence and they take to it right away. First, some people adopt open intelligence, and through seeing the evidence of the result in the early adopters, other people say, "Wow, that's for me," and then things flow from there. This is the way it has been throughout human history. Open intelligence innovators are pioneers who start the first wave of human adaptation.

We could look at this circumstance as being similar to settlers going off to the New World hundreds of years ago. The initial pioneers took a chance and went out to see what it was like in this new place they had heard about. They sent back reports, and many said, "It is a rich land filled with promise, and you can come and prosper as we have." Those who had a positive experience attracted many others to come, and now there are hundreds of millions of people living in what was then called the New World.

It is similar with discovering open intelligence: initially there are pioneers who are willing to adopt an entirely new way of looking at the world, a way that brings life satisfaction and flourishing, but soon their reports of joyful success draw many others. The original pioneers shine forth, carrying the message of instinctive recognition of open intelligence with beneficial capacity, and when people see bright, shining faces and beneficial activities, they see a reflection of themselves and how they want to be.

Because these original pioneers have firmly decided on their open-intelligence nature, their conviction and conduct encompassing the benefit of all directly influences others. New participants in open intelligence understand that they are simple human beings just like the others who have gone before them, and they know that what was possible for others is possible for them as well. This gift of recognition is so very precious.

The demonstration of benefit is so convincing that doubts have nowhere to take hold. Doubts may arise when one is new to relying on open intelligence, but very quickly they are seen through—knowing that even the doubts are open intelligence at their basis! All the preoccupation with doubt, skepticism, negativity and unsolvable problems shifts into a seamless solution orientation that is always-on, and many, many people are attracted by that demonstration of open intelligence.

At the same time, it is not a matter of comparing oneself to someone else. There is only unending flourishing and benefit for everyone. While there are iconic figures to honor and emulate, this honoring and respect are of enormous value in recognizing our own similar beneficial qualities and activities. We are the heroes we have been looking for. Each person is the hero, and each short moment is the real building block of the demonstration of benefit.

This generation of human society is a generation of new ideas and new models. The first generation of open-intelligence pioneers is spreading throughout human society, and this group will grow larger and larger until it is present in all of human society. From birth people will be trained in open intelligence, and the prioritization of open intelligence will be taught to children everywhere, even before they learn their ABCs.

IMMEDIATE AND PERMANENT BENEFIT

Open intelligence is an evolutionary imperative. Our reified intelligence has taken us as far as it can take us, and now we are empowering a greater order of intelligence. We as a human society are moving out from where we have been. We have expanded into a comprehensive order that sees the reified intelligence we have been living from as only one of the orders of intelligence that is available. We are also seeing that we are all really connected in a way that we perhaps never had known before.

Relish and enjoy the unfolding of these incredible beneficial qualities and activities in your own life. Feel and completely appreciate the total heartfelt gratitude for the spontaneous explosion of your own mind, speech, body, qualities and activities as they ramp up and burst open with benefit. What a wonderful way to live—each of us enjoying that in ourselves and enjoying it in each other. This is just so special, so wonderful and so very empowering.

It is important to never underestimate the incredible value of the contribution of a short moment of open intelligence. A short moment of open intelligence opens up a huge frontier of knowing and doing that is unparalleled. The reified intelligence that we have used up to this point is being transmuted into beneficial open intelligence.

The mere accumulation of knowledge need not be the ultimate goal of knowledge-creation and knowledge-seeking. What we really want to get to is the very basis and nature of knowledge. We want to look at knowledge from the perspective of "what is the nature of knowledge" rather than just "knowledge for the sake of knowledge."

Open intelligence is the basis of all knowledge—not just the basis of reified knowledge—but of all knowledge. Open intelligence is not a thing, an object or a function located in a particular part of the mind that spreads throughout the network of the mind. It is all-pervasive; it cannot really be located. However, if the power of open intelligence isn't used, it will be ignored, but simply by using it, it is trained up into powerful and beneficial knowledge and action.

By empowering open intelligence, we see what we are able to beneficially know and do. Benefit becomes what is expected, rather than merely what is hoped for. Right now as a general condition of society, we spend a lot of time *hoping* that things will get better; however, in open-intelligence society we *are certain* things will get better and better. We have so much confidence in open intelligence that there is a deep assurance in continuous benefit. We no longer have to drain our energy in hoping for benefit and fearing that it will not come about. We have entered into the intelligence at our basis that allows for benefit in all circumstances.

Science and technology have come to the point where the attempt is being made to replicate the functioning of human intelligence in computational resources; yet, we really need to know the capacity of our own intelligence before we start attempting these sorts of things. The only really stable view from which to do that is through the open-intelligence view;

otherwise, the attempt to replicate the functioning of human intelligence will be infused with all kinds of misleading data streams. It is important for teams that are working on such things to be very clear about what the true capacities of human beings really are and to not rely on misguided and outmoded ideas.

Human beings have been seen as inherently flawed, and all of our categories of self-identification are permeated with the conviction of being originally flawed. We see ourselves as flawed and we see each other the same way—living in a state of lack and insufficiency in which we cannot overcome this original flaw. The idea of human imperfection has saturated all of our institutions—hospitals, prisons, education, politics and so on. They are all saturated with the view that human beings are imperfect creatures who basically are profoundly flawed and need to be fixed. These ideas are based on concepts that no longer work and have never really worked.

Internalized oppression is the result of lack of education about open intelligence's powers of great benefit. This internalized oppression would not exist without the real external oppression that forms the social climate in which we exist, a climate in which open intelligence's powers of great benefit are ignored in favor of viewing humans as innately flawed. Once oppression has been internalized, we are unknowingly submissive to data streams. We harbor inside ourselves a wide variety of data streams—pain and memories, fear and confusion, negative self-images and low expectations—turning them into weapons with which to harm ourselves every moment of our lives. The keen education and knowledge of innate open intelligence's power of benefit overcomes and outshines internalized oppression completely.

Open intelligence's power of benefit is the remedy for internalized oppression of all kinds. Human society has internalized the oppressive forces of highly codified ideologies and pedagogies that infiltrate every level of society, including the human brain, which is now largely running the equivalent of a software program that tells people that they are disempowered and can only live by what they have been taught to think or not think and do or not do.

As human beings we have some very basic drives, and one of those is the drive to belong. We want to belong and we want to love and be loved, and these are very basic to every human being. However, the way we train ourselves is completely at opposites with our basic drive to belong and to love and be loved. We train ourselves in a way so that we do not love ourselves, and if we do not love ourselves, we do not love others. The constant faultfinding within ourselves is projected out onto others, and then we never feel that we belong, nor do we feel truly lovable. This is quite an ironic state of affairs, when we consider that we are entirely capable of being totally strong, clear, loved and lovable.

What a relief to stop living life as though each day were the Judgment Day! We use the power of our own body and mind to come to a conclusion about this in a very personal way. Within ourselves we have to see that we have an incredible power that we did not know we had when we were assuming that we were flawed. Our nature is that of immediate and permanent benefit—this is reality itself.

THE EMANATION OF GREAT BLISS-BENEFIT

Countless labels and descriptions cannot change our fundamental nature: we are the emanation of great bliss-benefit. *This* is our fundamental nature. So, every single thing about us, whatever it is, is an emanation of great bliss-benefit. In our very own experience we come to recognize this by acknowledging it rather than ignoring it. It is as simple as that. Rather than affirming again and again our independent nature as flawed beings, we rely on our basic state of great bliss.

By relying on open intelligence for short moments, it becomes very clear that everything abides as great bliss, and there isn't a single thing that does not rest in great bliss. The instinctive recognition of that in our own experience comes through the power of simple open intelligence.

In open intelligence itself we find a great sense of humor and a joy and exhilaration. We do not take ourselves as seriously as we once did. We find the whole project of human life to be filled with incredible possibility. We find that we are totally empowered, and we seize the power for complete mental and emotional stability, and we claim that mental and emotional stability as our own. We do not follow the dictates any longer of society that tell us what our thoughts, emotions, sensations and experiences mean. Instead, we find out for ourselves what these really mean in the light of the pure benefit of spontaneous existence.

The discovery of rich, untapped resources within human intelligence provisions a tremendous upgrade to beneficial qualities and activities—individually and collectively.

Those of us who are using digital devices often want to upgrade our software or hardware. In a similar way, by resting in the powers of great benefit we get into the seamless feed of the pure-benefit upgrade. We find within ourselves that we have an intelligence upgrade in beneficial open intelligence that is always going on, and we do not even have to ask for this upgrade.

This is easy to recognize in our life because we feel such a sense of increasing stability and satisfaction, and we look at others who are undergoing this profound augmentation of intelligence and life satisfaction and we say, "Wow! This is so much fun! It is right here in all of us. We don't have to go anywhere else to get it. It is always on." So, we gather together in this context, and it is a very relaxed and joyful way of life.

PURE BENEFIT

The open intelligence that provides the profound meaning to the powers of benefit comes forth inexhaustibly.

As the entity of completely pure benefit, there is spontaneous existence encompassing all, where complete purity means that beneficial potency is completely pure of the entirety of reification. There is no *object* of view—not open intelligence or data—and benefit does not depart from a nature of dazzling primordial purity, spontaneity and devotion to all, in which forever there is not known the separate existence of particularity.

Similarly, the nature of this completely pure benefit is that it is *as it is* in its spontaneous existence without parts or moments.

Completely pure benefit is the nature of this spontaneously arising benefit at the crucial juncture of open intelligence and data. Human beings are the crucial juncture of open intelligence and data; thus, we rest potently and only as the power of great benefit.

Chapter Four

OPEN INTELLIGENCE BECOMES OBVIOUS AT ALL TIMES

Through instinctive recognition and comprehension of open intelligence's beneficial potency, data spontaneously release and open intelligence becomes inexhaustibly obvious. Complete empowerment of open intelligence occurs through the Four Mainstays lifestyle of Balanced View. The combinatory pattern of the Four Mainstays ensures full and complete empowerment.

Similarly, sunshine pours forth from the sun, empowering photosynthesis to make plants grow. Our empowerment of mind, speech, body, qualities and activities occurs fully and factually through the Mainstays, a perfect match and fit with reality itself.

This can only come about through gaining true perspective on the actual definition of everything and everyone *as it is*. "As it is" means as it actually and in full reality *is*. First of all, not a single thing—no matter what the datum is called by name—has a nature independent of open intelligence, which is the totality of everything and everyone together—known and unknown. To define anyone or anything without including this fundamental definition is a great error and mistake. The full definition of everything and everyone must be included and understood, not just the definition we see in a dictionary or other reference book.

Dreams, for example, shine forth as open intelligence just like all data. In actuality, the shining forth of waking life is non-different and indivisible with sleeping life. All shines forth and is subsumed into open intelligence. Similarly, reflections shine forth and recede in a crystal ball. What a wondrous marvel it is! Living freely and openly as the great intelligence shining forth and simultaneously outshining its own data, which are the light signals of open intelligence.

45

Know that dreams, whatever they contain, are supporting further opening of the great inexhaustibility of unchanging open intelligence. We gain incredible assurance in open intelligence and trust it completely through its recognition in dreams and sleep. We come into total trust of ourselves and everything we say, do, think or act. Identification quietly slips open from self-centered concern to the bright powers of open-intelligence benefit. No longer is there the feeling of being trapped inside the skin line. Instead, there is tremendous ease and potency that fuels each moment.

Like the sun outshining all planets and stars in brilliant daylight, the power of open intelligence outshines thoughts, emotions, sensations and other experiences. The planets and stars are present, but they are no longer noticed, as they have been outshone by the bright light of the sun. This is a very powerful metaphor.

So, it is like that with the resolution of data in open intelligence. The more powerful open-intelligence commitment is in your life, the less data are noticed, until finally there are just a few data that might be the subject of attention now and then. Finally, though, even those data are outshone beyond notice, and instead there is profound and pervasive open intelligence as well as a comprehensive overview into the nature of existence. Similarly, at daybreak only a very few planets and stars can be seen; however, assuredly these remaining appearances are outshone by the light of high noon. Likewise, open intelligence outshines all data—every single one into its very great inclusivity and indivisibility.

This outshining of data can sometimes come in the midst of the sort of data stream which we are certain cannot be an expression of open intelligence—like wild and out of control jealousy for instance—where there are extremely afflictive thoughts and emotions. But all of a sudden it is recognized that open intelligence is simultaneously and spontaneously present, outshining all the onrushing emotions of jealousy. Rather than the data streams being a huge oppressive flood that carries away our energy, they are not even noticed. That is what "outshining" is. It does not mean that data go away; it means that we live life with their presence in a much different way.

Some very negative and agitating data streams can come up, but the more negative the data, the greater the shining forth of beneficial activity. This is timeless benefit; the greater the afflictive states, the greater the benefit and the greater the welfare of all beings. We even get to the point where we can say, "Those afflictive states, well, bring them on!" With freedom in immediate perception and complete perceptual openness in all experience, we know who the commander is. The sovereign monarch of all data is the open-intelligence view, and the data have no independent power or influence of their own through name or definition.

The outshining of data comes about by being able to preserve open intelligence and have it be predominant even during huge blasts of data. It becomes clear that open intelligence is powerful at all times. Open intelligence does not have any bias about this or that datum; it is open, clear, potent and abundantly present without preference. When we practice short moments of open intelligence repeated many times, it becomes continuous, and by the practice of short moments one is introduced to the possibility in one's life of outshining all data. We allow the data to flow on by while we maintain open intelligence—the open intelligence that shines forth from within the data stream itself.

Instead of sitting around tortured with thoughts, emotions and sensations and looking for experiences to make us feel better, our data are outshone by blazing open intelligence. As data are outshone, sometimes there are still a few data which linger, but as we gain more and more assurance in open intelligence, we are not even bothered by those anymore.

EXPANSIVE OPEN INTELLIGENCE

We spontaneously train up beneficial power through always-on open intelligence. There is no reason to be in a rush or to hurry open intelligence, because it is already present. The thing we might notice is that it gets brighter and brighter. Open intelligence can take any form whatsoever; one person may consider a data stream positive, another would consider the same thing very negative and someone else would not think about it at all. Whatever the costume of these data may be, they are all the adornment of open intelligence. Open intelligence is in fact our own nature, a vast expanse, like pure luminous space beyond anything imaginable.

When we are introduced to open intelligence, the direction we have been looking in—positive, negative or neutral data—is subsumed and held in expansive open intelligence that has no point from which to view. That is what a balanced view is: no point from which to view. Sometimes adopting one datum, other times adopting another as tools of expression and communication, but not as fundamental statements about reality.

The data no longer have power and influence. For example, if in the past someone ruined your day by looking at you the wrong way, then that was just a choice you made. They could then do something else, and if your day is ruined by that as well, once again, it is totally up to you. On the other hand, you can choose to stand strong in your own open intelligence, and no one would be able to take that away from you.

When we choose to recognize open intelligence we have real choices in life. We have the way it was before the introduction to open intelligence and the way it is after. At that point we have been exposed to both possibilities, and we can make a simple choice: either continuing to be carried away by data or relying on open intelligence.

We see that by really, *really* letting all of our data be exactly as they are, we open up a vast expanse of incredible power and benefit. Instead of living in a world of scarcity, lack and tension-filled relationships, increasingly we live in a world of abundance, generosity, prosperity and easeful relationships. One sees the "before and after" for oneself and for everyone else— the "before" of addiction to data and the "after" of complete relief from data.

When we turn all the energy and attention that we had previously focused on data towards open intelligence, naturally within ourselves we find that without any effort at all we are filled with beneficial qualities and activities. We find that data do not have any power or influence over us at all.

A POWERFUL TRANSFORMATION

You can physically see the difference in yourself, and other people can see it in you as well. "Wow! What happened to you? You look so different!" As you continue to rely on open intelligence, it will take over your entire body, speech and mind in a very obvious way. Your skin will actually start to glow and your eyes shine, and this is because you are relying on your natural state. This is a very powerful transformation for human beings, and it is so simple, so direct and so easy. There is a marked distinction between what was before and what is now, and this marked distinction grows brighter and brighter—never failing to grow brighter and brighter and never going backwards.

At the break of dawn daylight is barely noticed amidst the dark; but then by high noon light obviously has infused everything, outshining darkness completely. All these data shine within the view of open intelligence, and the view shines from within all its own data. Each experience is that union of the view and points of view. Instead of the decades-long focus on data, we allow ourselves the complete simplicity of letting everything be *as it is*. It is a matter of seeing all things as "the view and points of view" or "open intelligence and data." To see it that way keeps things totally simple. Otherwise, the stories surrounding the data will be too engaging.

Whatever the story may be, it is made up only of data. If you stay in the data, it is like a maze that you cannot get out of. However, by relying on open intelligence—poof!—it is all gone. There is complete openness, and that is just the way it is. This is the simple choice that we have. We can choose the turmoil of data-naming or the great outshining.

Having data and merely noticing them versus having data and *being all wrapped up in them* are two entirely different things. Having data and not noticing them is what outshining of data is. You look out and you see the same things as before, you hear the same things and smell the same things; however, it does not have the same kind of impact. The only impact is one of the complete primordial purity, luminous openness and the spontaneous presence of very rich and beneficial indivisibility. The data are handy as tools for a lifestyle of beneficial potency; however, they are no longer the objects of attention. Rather, open intelligence becomes obvious at all times.

Without hesitation, be devoted to open intelligence, and each moment of open intelligence will turn everything you do into all-beneficial qualities and activities all of the time. This is the demonstration of great accomplishment in the Age of Human Empowerment and Era of Great Benefit, in which the precious treasury of the way of great benefit abounds.

By the power of open intelligence in *this* moment, you will be able to relax completely with the troublesome worry you have had all your life. If the worry continues to come up, rely on the Four Mainstays and soon you will see that your old worries and troubles have been completely clarified. Open intelligence is now obvious instead of the worry and trouble. You see in a very direct way that your own troublesome worries are gone beyond in the power of open intelligence's lucid clarity.

Open intelligence brings total strength and resilience to human intelligence right here. All these words, spoken and written, come and go in open intelligence and are due to the power of open intelligence alone. This is the spark by which you know you are. What could be more simple and direct? Right here, right now, that is the "you" that is being spoken to and that is speaking. No struggle, no effort to make, everything is wide-open like the seamless sky.

Uncontrived open intelligence is absolutely key—just allowing that great outshining to take place, to notice that this is already the case, that all afflictions whatsoever have been outshone from the outset. Primordial open intelligence has not had affliction and has never been named or labeled. This is what is recognized in short moments of open intelligence: that any name or label is open intelligence itself.

In the great outshining of all data, there is greater and greater clarity about one's true identity. Rather than focusing on the data-descriptions about who you take yourself to be, you know yourself to be simply what's looking! The open-intelligence view—what's looking—is like space filled with light. That is your identity: a vast expanse filled with lucid pure benefit. If you want to know what you are, then "space filled with lucid pure benefit" and "space filled with light appearing as data signals" are a lot closer to what you truly are than what you see in the mirror.

Even if you think you are somebody with a fixed identity, then it is very good to know that a fixed identity is totally impossible! You are not even the same as you were a second ago. The only thing that continues on year after year as you look in the mirror is total open intelligence and its power of great benefit. To truly and completely know this is the total outshining of all data streams having to do with self-identification.

The first time you look in the mirror when you are a small child, what's looking? When you are seventy years old looking in the mirror, what's looking? It is always exactly the same—open intelligence, which is never-changing and vivid luminosity, available throughout life to live as and draw on as the greatest natural resource. If you look in the mirror right now, you could ask, "Is what's looking any different than what was looking twenty years ago? Has what's looking aged? Has it changed in any way?" And we see that what's looking has never changed at all. Even if we look at ourselves and say, "Whoa, gained some weight here," or "Got some gray hairs now," what's looking never changes. Open intelligence does not get old, it does not get gray hairs and it does not realize reified states of birth, life and death, waking, dreaming and sleeping.

What's looking is flawless and radiant and has power over all of its self-shining data. What's looking is always-on, and if you know that what's looking never changes, then you can pass through all of life with steadfast ease and potency. You will

51

know what to do in all situations and you will live a life of benefit to all.

When we examine the looker based on our own direct experience, we find only open intelligence there; we do not find an actual individual looker. What we find is that what's looking is the same in everyone. It is *exactly* the same in everyone, so what we all have is total connectivity in this field of what's looking.

Open intelligence is the pure knowing or pure intelligence beyond all intelligences that could ever be conceived. It is the pure knowing, the pure intelligence at the basis of everything. It knows with its own special knowing and it does with its own special doing. When we have access to that, we are endowed with very special qualities and activities that are not accessible in reified intelligence. Intelligence based on data-naming is subsumed into the great power of open intelligence.

Sights and sounds of all beings are seen and heard by what never changes. Isn't that amazing? We can see right here in our own direct experience that what's looking is the same in everyone. What's looking is indivisible; it is impossible to divide it up into an individual looker. It only seems to be an individual looker when it is filtered through the perspective of reified intelligence. We are really living at all times as the presence of what's looking.

No matter what kind of experience we go through, what's looking is at the heart of all experience. It is the intelligence inside all experience—the intelligence that fills up all experience and subsumes all experience. The basis of everything is unchangeable; no matter what words are spoken, no matter what is happening, everything is unchangeable in its essence.

BENEFICIAL KNOWLEDGE

All over the world more and more people are living daily life in the greatly beneficial place of open intelligence, and they are empowered to comprehend all knowledge according to the greatly profound view of open intelligence. We go back to basics and we ask, "Who are we and what are we made of? What do we have within us that we might not know about? How can we draw on our maximum potential?" In our essence we are open-ended benefit creators, and as open-ended benefit creators what our eyes see is a world full of solutions. What we need to discover those solutions is a training that will allow us to see that we *truly are* open-ended benefit creators.

We have not been trained by society to see that we are open-ended benefit creators! Instead, we have had so many other conceptual frameworks and ideas influencing our behavior. Because of how we have been trained throughout our lives, we have come to think of ourselves as finite. We think, "Oh yes, I'm this little "me" inside this skin line of a body, and I'm not anywhere else." However, this isn't the case; our intelligence is vast and completely networked with everything and is not limited to a body or mind.

For a very long time we have looked at our body, speech, mind, qualities and activities only in terms of being a physical body, but now we are beginning to see what has been completely ignored: the overarching aspect of open intelligence that pervades every aspect, every quality and every characteristic of our being. Our body is the body of open intelligence, our voice is the empowering resonance of the primordial sound of open intelligence, and our mind, qualities and activities are radiant with the blazing potency and clarity of open intelligence. When we adopt this knowledge and instruction—which is simply the prioritization of our own basic cognizance instead of the data—we realize the open intelligence and great benefit, prosperity and generosity that are our birthright and which are the evidence of the Age of Human Empowerment and Era of Great Benefit.

Who we are has been mystified by all kinds of categories of knowledge, but now we can get right back to basics—to how we *really* work. We need to comprehend all knowledge from the open-intelligence view and see what all knowledge looks like from that vantage. All the knowledge contained within the vast expanse of open intelligence is within us. Wherever we go, the open-intelligence view will always be there with us.

Open intelligence is clear seeing and clear knowing and also the ability to stand up and shout out the truth, and this is what the open-intelligence view allows. To re-know all knowledge according to the greatly profound view of open intelligence means that new beneficial knowledge opens up—all kinds of knowledge we never had before—and we are able to courageously live from that knowledge and not from conventional norms.

Just as the scientific world came to agreement as to how subatomic particles—protons, electrons and neutrons—would be named, similarly we can come to agreement about how to talk about "open intelligence" and "positive, negative and neutral data." It is a simple way of standardizing language so that everyone is instinctively talking about, comprehending and realizing the same thing. It is a way of sharing our knowledge in an open and potent way so that we can really understand each other.

Completely relieved from the superstition of conventional methods, we prosper. In each moment of instinctive recognition of open intelligence, all of human society takes a quantum leap. The commitment to open intelligence is so ingrained and so imbedded, and that is what "instinctive" means: ingrained, imbedded and always already present without needing to do anything.

ORIGINAL POTENCY: A FUNDAMENTAL SHIFT

As all of this is occurring, society itself is shifting and this shift cannot be reversed. The shift is profound, unprecedented and so incredible because it fundamentally changes us as individuals as well as every single one of our institutions and organizations. Hence, it is a shift in our very way of being. What we have before us is an incredible change that will issue forth because of a drive to comprehend that is now being expressed in so many people.

Each of us has tremendous power and tremendous potency. We were indeed born with original potency, and not with original sin and bad karma. One of the characteristics of human society today is the feeling that so many people have of being small, of being helpless, of being powerless, of not being able to do things the right way or of not being able to fit in, when in fact original potency is what we were born with. The idea of being originally flawed and unworthy has been affirmed over and over again, yet this unworthiness is simply a datum within open intelligence. Plain and simple, our original nature is pure, lucid and beneficially potent.

Data are subject to the law of impermanence, so no matter how many positive or negative data we have, all of them appear and simultaneously disappear as open intelligence, and these data concerning our unworthiness are no different. We human beings are so much more powerful than the guilt and unworthiness that we have taken on. It is simply that we have made a basic yet pervasive error about the nature of our existence, but we are in the process of correcting that mistake. And it is not just a few people correcting the perceptual error; it is happening on a mass scale through global organizing of Balanced View communities at the local level.

Some of these data streams, such as humans being basically flawed, are very deeply ingrained within human culture. However, they are a fiction and do not speak to who we really are. They mystify who we are until we have no idea of our fundamental nature or identity. We sometimes find it difficult to have even one happy day, let alone to experience complete life satisfaction and flourishing in every aspect of our life, when in fact complete life satisfaction and flourishing are our birthright. To go beyond the data streams requires that all humans come together as the great force of open intelligence itself. This is what gives us the power as a human culture to outshine all these ideas that diminish and weaken us.

The power of nations, governments, corporations, religions, medicine and psychiatry to define us is lessening. In the past we may have ceded our power to their control, but no longer. Now we see that it no longer needs to be this way at all. We find within ourselves what is exhilarating in every moment, no matter how much we have felt powerless in the past. We depend on the durable power of open intelligence to bring forth our own mental and emotional stability. Durable power is perpetual power that goes on augmenting itself, so whenever it is realized as one's own, there is greater and greater increase of this perpetual, unchanging power.

Even though great things have been achieved in the past, there isn't anything that has achieved durable beneficial power in humans on a mass scale. Due to fragmentation, lack of durability and extreme biases, the outdated institutions of human society are falling by the wayside. We need to find our most durable and beneficial power as a species and evolve from there. Ever-present open intelligence is always on and is our most durable power. It does not move this way or that way. Inexhaustible, it does not have any perimeters and is without edges or corners. We have not expressed this power before as a society, but we are beginning to see what wonders it can bring to human life. We can count on it throughout life, and that is the meaning of "durable power."

What we are is very precious, and it isn't due to some kind of divine grace. We are naturally graced—we are always living as a state of grace—and that state of grace is our natural great completion. So, here we are in our state of grace, our great completion, and that is really what it means to be powerful and graced.

By everyone empowering themselves with short moments of open intelligence, we the people of the world are unifying as the force that brings about actual world peace. Through Balanced View's vast movement of open-intelligence empowerment around the world, the Age of Human Empowerment and Era of Great Benefit shines forth inexhaustibly.

Chapter Five

EXPANDING THE POWER

The supposed independent nature of all our data is something we are trained up to believe as we move through life; however, each one of us is always completely able to choose our relationship with what we have been trained to believe. No one ever need be a victim of their acquired data, not ever. No one is held or bound by any perception that has occurred. It is up to us to allow our open intelligence to be our predominant identity and to potently inform mind, speech, body, qualities and activities. This crucial empowerment, education and mobilization is occurring with each individual, and thus collectively.

The ways and means of open intelligence are those of the intelligence that is the most comprehensive and far-reaching, the most discerning and all-beneficial. Here we are, perhaps having lived our life until now with very little truly real knowledge—the knowledge that is only present in the obviousness of open intelligence.

The Twelve Empowerments and Four Mainstays of Balanced View provide us with an empowering and comforting lifestyle-enhancement community and enable us to take empowerment, education and mobilization all the way with through the purest transmission-potency of open intelligence. Just as some satellites are more powerful in their transmission capacity, so too Balanced View's skillful means and insight provide the most powerful transmission capacity for open intelligence.

THE PAST

There is nobody and nothing to blame for the data we have accumulated—not our mother, father, our past, our societal circumstances or anything. There is just *us*, strong in the open intelligence that is our complete identity. From that position, there are not any victims, because every single person is responsible for their own recognition of open intelligence. By relying on open intelligence, we give up the right to be a victim of all our data concerning people, places, things, our personal ego, our emotional life and whatever the other stories about our past might be. Amidst all of these stories, what is always right here? Open intelligence. It is not possible to actually verify a past and hold it to be real in this moment—absolutely impossible. It cannot be done. This is due to the reality of open intelligence right now as the only reality that was, is or ever will be.

The term "expanding the power" emphasizes the fact that open intelligence is indeed inexhaustibly powerful and that this power can be recognized and claimed even from the most afflictive data. To actually have the capacity, as we all do, to expand the power in all of our data is extraordinary.

Many times there is a mistaken idea that open intelligence is some sort of exalted state from which the afflictive states are excluded; however, it is really important to recognize that open intelligence includes everything. There is no way really to encompass the reach and range of that power through thought and reason; it can only be experienced instinctively in open intelligence, wherein data are recognized as they are—the shining forth of open intelligence itself.

By expanding the definition of data in open intelligence, the beneficial power of all data is recognized. By staying shut down in the closed intelligence of reified data we do not recognize the immensely beneficial power of mind, speech, body, qualities and activities which is always-on in open intelligence.

Sometimes we blame ourselves because we have difficult and negative data, and then we are damaged further by self-blame. We may eventually become deeply disturbed by our focus on data, yet it is important to understand that data are countless, ceaseless and unpredictable and that they arise spontaneously as the display of open intelligence. Whatever our own circumstantial data may be, it is always possible for us to rely on open intelligence and to no longer be controlled by data.

When all the indulging, avoiding and replacing of data comes to a complete stop, we cease trying to fix the flow of ordinary experience. We get totally real for the first time, letting everything be *as it is*. One day we may have thoughts that we are the best thing on earth, the next minute we may think that we are awful, and then we have all kinds of other feelings in between. We expand the power—the natural resources within ourselves—mining the gold from within every single datum. We do not get lost in the labels or in made-up notions about what a human being is, but we find that core in ourselves that will take us through thick and thin. We find what we can really rely on, no matter what occurs.

By the power of open intelligence we become willing, maybe for the first time, to see ourselves totally clearly. We become totally open to ourselves and others in the context of the way we actually are—not in the context of our make-believe ideas about what we are or what we might be. We become open to our real selves, moment-to-moment, exactly as we are—up and down, in one emotion or another, with one thought or another, having one sensation or another, with this, that and the other thing. We expand the power in all of it. The appearances appear, they flow on by and they disappear, and all the while we are expanding the full power inherent in them through relying on open intelligence. In short moments repeated many times, open intelligence becomes obvious at all times.

OPEN INTELLIGENCE INSEPARABLE FROM AFFLICTIVE STATES

Many different kinds of things appear in life—arrogance, pride, depression, desire, anger, hatred, jealousy, fear, rejection—but we can expand the power of great bliss-intelligence in them. When these powerful surges come over us, we rely on open intelligence, and in this way we see that open intelligence is inseparable from that energy that is flooding our being. That energy is the super-alive potency of sheer benefit, and that is what those feeling-states are. Whatever name we have chosen to give to them, they are only the blazing potency of sheer benefit.

Now, for some people these afflictive states can be very challenging; however, no matter what the afflictive state is, by relying on open intelligence the power of that affliction will lessen until it is outshone completely. That thing that used to obsess us so much is no longer the focus of our attention.

Initially it may seem too overwhelming to rely on open intelligence amidst strong negative states, but we can be sure that we can rely on any of the Mainstays. We do whatever is required and we are willing to go to any lengths to rely on open intelligence and to seek support. Then gradually there will be the experience of openness within the negative states. The negative states will not seem so "other" to us; they will not seem like a force that can take us over.

We find that there is nothing in our experience to be afraid of; there is only open intelligence itself. What seemed at first like an overwhelming foe becomes a little friendlier, and then over time it becomes quite familiar. The affliction gradually becomes a great companion on a grand adventure, then it self-releases like a snake effortlessly unknotting its body, and finally it is known to be nothing but the dynamic energy of beneficial power. That's it: the datum is no longer noticed as a thing with some kind of substantial authority of its own.

"Everything is indivisible"—this is the royal view. Because it is recognized that everything is indivisible, there is no longer the need to try to change the afflictive states. That is where the power is; this great, great power of benefit is *in* the afflictive states themselves. Wow!

When you enter the Four Mainstays combinatory pattern of instruction, you are together with all the other people around the world who are engaged in the same practice of short moments. That means that there is a very large group of people who know what reality is, and when these people get together they know that each person is responsible for their data. No one else is responsible, so the whole trip of blaming people, places and things for afflictive states comes to a complete stop.

We are never out of control. "Being-out-of-control" is a datum that makes us think we are a victim of our thoughts, emotions and experiences, yet by fully relying on open intelligence we give up the right to be a victim. In open intelligence, out-of-control does not exist as some separate realm where we exist apart from open intelligence. Open intelligence is in command and is sovereign in all phenomena. Out-of-control is actually filled with the power-packed beneficial qualities and activities of open intelligence itself.

We can be at rest with all our out-of-control afflictive states in this way; we can rely on the Four Mainstays to expand the profit and power of these afflictive states. If we just fool around with our afflictive states in isolation and continue to take them to be real, they can potentially bring us great harm. But if we rely on the combinatory pattern of the Four Mainstays, then we can expand the power and the potency in them without harming ourselves or anyone else.

If there is any kind of support we need, it is always available from Balanced View. If we get into some kind of situation where we find ourselves confused and lost, who are we going to rely on—someone who is confused and lost or someone who is clear and potent with a balanced view? If we do not know where to go for advice, then we cannot get good advice. The Four Mainstays are the insurance policy—the guarantee—for inexhaustible open intelligence.

BENEFIT FOR ALL

Through this simple practice of expanding the power of afflictive states, a vast expanse of total potency and benefit is opened to us. We are the ever–living, loving presence of open intelligence itself. We are the potent force of pure benefit, and we affirm this through relying on open intelligence amidst afflictive states. When we see how much benefit there is in open intelligence, we can also see how much benefit it will bring, not just to us, but to everyone. In doing so, we are no longer focusing just on ourselves. Our attention spreads out to include everyone, and this is what true benefit is.

It does not matter how many financial accounts a person has accumulated or if they have none at all, how old they are or how young they are, what kind of an education they have or don't have, it is clear that in regard to making sense of afflictive states, everyone is in exactly the same boat, and there isn't anyone in a different boat. Open intelligence is the natural equal opportunity program, the fundamental great equalization of all data.

In the great openness of open intelligence there is the ability to not only know our own thoughts, but to know the thoughts of everyone. Whatever data-driven state may be present for us, there are countless other beings experiencing exactly the same state at exactly the same moment. In this spontaneously arising understanding is a whole new reach and range of experience. No longer is there obsessive self-focus. There is wide-open intelligence containing all data—not just our own, but all data, and not only those just now, but in the past and in the future as well.

We each take responsibility for who we are, and we know exactly where the other person is coming from. If I encounter all my own data through the direct, vivid intelligence of open intelligence, then I know exactly what makes you tick. There isn't any mystery at all about what makes you or me tick. Not only do I feel totally comfortable with myself, but I feel totally comfortable with you. I know what you are about, and no matter what you might be doing, I will understand why you are doing it.

Whatever we are doing or however we are living, negative data are going to appear. Even if we got into some kind of continuous flow of positive data, at some point the negative data would reappear. This is one of the contradictions in trying to achieve only positive states; at some point the negative data will come back again. If we are actually able to maintain positive states for a while, what we are doing is temporarily neutralizing our negative states through contrived replacement of negative states with positive states.

These replacements are called antidotes. But what happens with antidotes and neutralization? The negative states are not outshone and the power is not acknowledged in them; they are only being neutralized. When we get very sick or are facing death or are experiencing great loss or another very afflictive situation, the negative data will most likely return, because they have not been resolved, but only neutralized.

By the power of the instinctive recognition of open intelligence, all data are normalized and resolved in open intelligence; rather than being neutralized through reshaping the data, they are expanded by the open-intelligence view. Data are a source of beneficial energy, sovereignty and command in all situations. In other words, the power of the mind is seized through the greater power of open intelligence. In this way, no matter what shines forth in the mind, it will be no problem, because all shining forth is known to be the shining forth of open intelligence itself, including the shining forth of the mind.

Confusion comes from the belief that life satisfaction could never be found in the negative state. Open intelligence shines from within all data—positive, negative and neutral. There isn't any datum that is excluded. By relying on open intelligence we will come to see that the afflictive state is completely pervaded and outshone by open intelligence. Everything about the description, no matter what it is, shines with open intelligence.

Give this precious knowledge to yourself; it is the greatest gift of a human life. There isn't really anything to call this gift; we could say that it is total okay-ness in which everything is flourishing. The marvel of expanding the power is that each life experience becomes an experience of satisfaction at the deepest level, no matter what the name of the experience might be.

THE PRACTICAL RESULTS

The depths of every single afflictive state—the ghosts and shadows, the dark thoughts, the terrifying anxiety—can be experienced without fear. Maybe one minute we are thinking of murdering someone, the next minute we are thinking, "How could I possibly think that? I am just so awful." But whatever these thoughts are, they are the spontaneous and dynamic display of open intelligence. They are all labels of the same thing, so why should we toil and trouble over them?

By relying on open intelligence we know how to handle situations, and we find that harmful behaviors we once had slip away without our having to work on them or do anything about them. All we do is rely on open intelligence. As open intelligence becomes more and more obvious, negative conduct fades away. Sometimes negative habits that were worked on for years completely resolve and disappear without a trace. They are not merely neutralized; they are transmuted into beneficial energy and activity.

This kind of decisive, direct experience of open intelligence in the moment is one where every single cell of our body is drenched with aliveness. It is not a spaced-out or disempowered state; there is totally raw, vital open intelligence that gets things done in a real way. There is no need to sit around and talk for hours about everything; we are too busy getting it done! We could all sit around and criticize this, that and the other thing, but getting in there and actually changing things is much different.

So, in a very simple and uncomplicated way, when that beneficial energy and activity begins to appear more and more in our lives, the old sourpuss face that we used to have will start to brighten up! The skin that was so gray and lifeless before is now all of a sudden completely healthy and radiant. We look at our eyes in the mirror and they look like shining suns. These are natural and everyday changes that come about from a practice that is really bringing a result.

There is a collapse of the framework of neediness, scarcity, lack and inadequacy—that we are not good enough or that we do not have the right tools to give ourselves true peace. All of these go by the wayside. We can see clearly how to gain assurance in open intelligence and introduce it to others. This is happening right now; it is not a future projection. This is already in occurrence, turning up in every single life that is committed to fully relying on open intelligence.

NO LONGER BELIEVING THE STORIES

When it is said, "expand the power," another way of looking at that is as simply allowing the ever-present energy of the instinctive recognition that is all-encompassing and all-inclusive—the unavoidable bind that knits everything together in indivisibility—to be *as it is*. That is the great power that we are resting as at all times. The capacity to expand the power in afflictive states is fundamental to the Age of Human Empowerment and Era of Great Benefit.

We do not need to do anything to make that power happen, because it is already present and already totally and completely available to everyone, and it is burgeoning forth ceaselessly. Nothing needs to be done to try to create something that is already here. It is simply a matter of the acknowledgement and instinctive recognition.

When we believe that these energy-rushes that we call anger, fear, depression or hatred can control us, that is just a story-line we are running. It is a fiction; it is something we have made up and believed. We are thereby abandoning the power we actually have to see what that energy really is. That energy is our power to be of benefit to ourselves and to the world, but this is recognized only if we let the anger and depression flow on by as we rely on open intelligence. If we let the afflictive states flow on by, they do not have any power to do anything. If they are left as they are, then what emerges from them is the natural power and potency to be of benefit—ensuring our own well-being and the well-being of others.

The sovereign seat of this mighty power of naturally perfect benefit—where is it? It is in each one of us. Rest in this power of great benefit, totally at ease, and know it to be so in your own direct experience.

Open intelligence gives us this power. We get out of the habit of looking to a future that we hope is going to be a certain way; we give up trying to forget about or change things from the past, and we get into the liveliness and vitality of what is here right now. Each one of us in this moment is fully alive, turned on, juiced up and ready to go. This is what life is all about; it is about getting real with what we actually are in the here-and-now. Whatever may be going on with us, nothing is more real than this very moment.

Whether we are high, low or in between, we expand the power of open intelligence, which is always vitally present. The power isn't found anywhere else. This power does not require a lot of different variables in order to put it into swing. It is in whatever we are thinking—whether we are anxious, afraid, happy, ecstatic, feeling empowered or disempowered. To know this keeps things very simple and very real.

At the outset there will be certain data to which we are completely blind, and if there are certain ways in which we can be blindsided, then our friends in the community can support us. The connection with an empowered trainer and community allows clear seeing to open up in a safe, comfortable environment where we can encounter all our data streams and expand the power in them.

Assurance in open intelligence comes with direct, decisive experience of open intelligence and its benefits. Many people have found that by relying on open intelligence a certain data stream is completely resolved, and that when that data stream is resolved, many other data streams are also resolved at the same time.

Let's say that we have had a hard time because of painful memories from the past of a break-up or abandonment, and this pain might still intrude in our lives. When we rely on the open intelligence of that datum rather than the reified description of it, then we not only resolve that datum, but we may realize that at the same time we have resolved many other kinds of data— such as fear of ostracism, fear of failure, or hesitation to be in close relationships. Even though our intent may have been to merely resolve this one datum, relying on the open intelligence within the painful-memory datum had a far-ranging effect in terms of resolving many data. For those people who have experienced this, it is completely amazing.

EXPANDING THE POWER IN REJECTION

Human beings are pack animals, and we want very much to get along in our group. We have a drive to belong; yet, we have situations in society, in institutions, in communities and between people which are based on the subtle threat of exclusion. We have all been in situations where we are threatened with rejection or exclusion. Sometimes even our own family is like that; there is a subtle or overt threat that if we do not act a certain way, we will be excluded.

To be rejected is a frightening thought for so many of us—bundled as it is with the things we have been trained to think about rejection, our past pain from being rejected, coupled with all the ways in which we feel we are rejected each day. From this limited vantage, every day can be a set-up for more rejection, so we are walking on eggshells to avoid rejection, and this fear of rejection is present in many of our relationships.

If I am worried about whether you are going to reject me or not, or I have made certain appraisals about you based on acceptance or rejection, then that very much alters our relationship. The encounters we have are filled with all kinds of make-believe ideas about you and me and how we need to account for each other. But, on the other hand, when I see you and I am relying on open intelligence, there is nothing there but the radiance of pure being and a truly intimate connection that we are meant to have with everyone. By relying on open intelligence instead of indulging fears of rejection, we expand the power in rejection, and the beneficial endowment that is at the basis of the data stream of rejection pours forth.

We are then looking at life as it really is by letting everything be *as it is*. This is how we become mature human beings. We face reality instead of continuing to engage in all sorts of avoidance mechanisms. We find a solid sense of ourselves, where we know what to do and how to act in each situation in life.

In the past we may have let our emotions have all kinds of effects on us, but now we rely on open intelligence to see what this cause-and-effect mechanism is really like. We ask ourselves, "If that person doesn't like me, does that mean that I have to suffer from rejection in my relationship with them?" Instead of believing that we have been rejected and then going with all the stories surrounding that rejection, we can take a new look at the situation through open intelligence.

Instead of trying to avoid rejection or replace it with a more pleasant emotion, we can expand the power of rejection. When we see the other person who has rejected us in the past, we can be totally present with the person without any worry about what they will be thinking about us. In that we have found the resolution for rejection, and we have found at the same time the super-energy inherent in open intelligence.

We ask ourselves, "Can rejection really destroy my innate indestructibility?" and we look at things from that extraordinarily profound level. By the power of instinctive open intelligence we grow to trust that open intelligence is very real. We see that there is a total indestructibility at our basis and that it is extremely potent and forceful and that nothing can knock it off-balance. From that we see that all these names and descriptions for data—while they might appear to have a power and influence—only have as much power and influence as we give them.

If our activities are guided by open intelligence and the assurance that comes from the power of letting things be as they are—rather than being guided by what other people think about us—this gives a much broader reach and range than when our qualities and activities are limited by fear of other people's negative opinions. If we believe all the rejection stories, we are limiting our own power, whereas in open intelligence we grow strong in, of, as and through the indivisible, indestructible and vast nature of our pervasively beneficial intelligence.

A GENUINE RELATIONSHIP WITH LIFE

Open intelligence enables you, me and everyone to be able to face everything squarely, without any pretend notions or fantasies about the way things are. If you get comfortable with your own self, then you can be comfortable in any situation. It is not possible to have a genuine relationship with life or with another person without having a genuine relationship with yourself.

To be entirely ready to rely on open intelligence rather than on data requires humility. Humility is not a state of weakness, but of strength. This is the naturally occurring humility of open intelligence in which all data are perfect. It does not mean inferiority, resignation or submission. When we are humble, we are willing to accept support, knowing that with it we can progress easily in gaining assurance in open intelligence. In the naturally occurring and bold humility of open intelligence, we increase our capacity to rely on open intelligence rather than on data. We accept ourselves as we are, including all our data. In this way, all situations can be utilized to intensify and gain assurance in open intelligence.

We must not give up on our commitment to relying on open intelligence. These brief moments of open intelligence, as momentary as they may be initially, have a tremendous impact of expansion and depth. The benefits may not be so obvious at first, but the key is to stay interested in open intelligence. We have to have the kind of resolve where we can say, "I will never give up!"

This simple approach of short moments guarantees authentic, unending open intelligence—an open intelligence with capacity and potency to accomplish incredible things and the power to benefit all beings. When we find the bedrock of open intelligence within ourselves, we could say that we find the ultimate satisfaction. There isn't anything to compete for or anyone to compete with. It all gets down to our own open intelligence, and then we find an endless source of solace, comfort and power, and we find it right within ourselves.

The lineage of human society is a lineage of pure benefit, and that lineage is now coming to full fruition in the Age of Human Empowerment and Era of Great Benefit. It is not a matter of getting into some kind of mental state called "open intelligence" or "happiness." The true lineage of human society is our innate quality and characteristic to be of benefit to ourselves and each other, and that is present for us right now.

NO DESTINATION TO REACH

The totally powerful intelligence that everyone needs is in our own experience. If we feel angry, that is where open intelligence is. If we feel so depressed that we do not think we can make it another minute, that is also where open intelligence is to be found. It is not in changing the depressed state into something else.

In a way, everyone is depressed—oppressed, repressed, suppressed—because when we have internalized all these oppressive ideas about ourselves, then naturally we are going to feel that way. But if we rely on open intelligence and take the pill of short moments many times, the short moments of open intelligence become expansive. We can just face ourselves exactly as we are, not needing to rely on anything else but open intelligence, knowing that it is going to take us all the way.

Each of us has different things going on in our life—from our past, from what is going on right now or what we anticipate will be in our future, but open intelligence subsumes all these ideas about time, about who we think we are and about all the baggage we have carried to this moment concerning how we came to be as we are. All the projections we have about a future, whether they are good or bad—that is where open intelligence is. It is in every single thought, emotion, sensation or experience. There isn't anywhere else to look.

There is no destination to reach, no place to go to. We do not have to search high and low, climb mountains, get qualifications or read all the books. There could not possibly be a destination, because open intelligence is inexhaustibly present. In the beginning there might be the thought, "Oh I am going to get somewhere, then I will know it, and I will have reached my goal." However, the destination never comes, so finally we just relax and say, "Wow, I never knew I had anything about me that was inexhaustible. I never knew that I could count on a lifetime of having thousands of very powerful realizations." Yet, the realizations just keep coming one right after another; there isn't *a* realization but *many* realizations. The realization that is important to the moment, whatever it is, that is what it is—inexhaustible realization.

Chapter Six

THE EMERGING SOCIETY OF THE AGE OF HUMAN EMPOWERMENT AND ERA OF GREAT BENEFIT

We human beings may feel in some ways special and unique, but we live in and as a vast expanse of open intelligence with many realms and universes, and this human realm is just one of them—a very tiny speck amongst countless realms. We have no idea how many realms and universes there are in the multiverse, so when we use a term such as "human society," we must understand it in the ultimate context in which it belongs.

All of these realms and universes, including the human realm, are pervaded by pure benefit, and pure benefit is taking over the human realm in this burgeoning of the Age of Human Empowerment and Era of Great Benefit. There isn't anything that can be done to stop it; it is already underway. We have far more capability and capacity than we ever thought possible to be of benefit to ourselves and to each other, and that will only become more and more evident, outshining all outdated habits of intelligence.

Yes, dear friends, the profound entity that is the crucial juncture of open intelligence and data is similar to the sun's matrix, in that its nature is luminosity; any reified and inaccurate definition of it burns off at inception. In open intelligence, free of elaborations, where could there be confusion of its identity; where could there be an independent datum? In pure benefit, free of closed definitions of data, where could there be anything other than the very great mind, voice, body, qualities and activities of open intelligence's inexhaustible beneficial potency?

Reification—pure beneficial potency—has nothing independent mixed with it anywhere. The extremes of reified data are thus comprehended and outshone. Spontaneously pure are the ever-expansive mind, speech, body, qualities and activities.

Relaxed and potent indivisibility is the crucial factor. With nothing to pick out or choose as independent, all is settled in pristinely pure liveliness, the most comprehensive, all-pervading openness of an intelligence pumped with optimal beneficial capacity. The great fortune of spontaneous existence and responsivity is that it is appropriate to time, place and circumstance.

Growing and increasing rapidly, without changing at all, pure-benefit magic subverts all attempts at holding it at bay. Effortlessly disabling all reified intelligences based on indulgence, avoidance or replacement of data, the consummate intelligence—open intelligence—is the great force outshining all ways and means of the severely crippling, reified human intelligence now in its death throes of excessive negativity. Severe and violent pain and struggle slip away in the easygoing empowerment, education and mobilization of the great exaltation of human nature. The sweeping momentum and concentration of stable social change throughout the world ensures the unity, liberty, benefit, prosperity and generosity of all.

PURE KNOWING

In this human realm that we inhabit, we have the three dimensional coordinates of length, width and depth that are visible to us, and we are trained to see only these three and to see all data as independently existing within that framework. We are trained to believe that data are encompassed by these dimensional coordinates, but this three-dimensional space that we perceive is only one aspect of countless dimensions that exist for our beneficial qualities and activities.

The most comprehensive order of all of these dimensions is that of pure knowing—pure open intelligence. It is the most comprehensive because it is the only aspect that pervades all these countless other dimensions; it is their essence and nature. A dimension like ours might have three dimensional coordinates and seven basic colors, and another one might have eighteen dimensional coordinates and no colors, and there could be untold variations of dimensional coordinates and descriptive factors associated with innumerable other dimensions. Just as we human beings live in a 3-D realm and we recognize this as a familiar place, each one of the dimensions in the multiverse is a place that would be recognizable to the beings that exist there— and glowingly present in all these data of the multiverse and existing as the basis of all knowing is open intelligence.

All data existing in all dimensions have no nature apart from the glowing knowing of the open-intelligence nature. The truth of all is known from the basic naked knowing which carries benefit, pure pleasure and all other treasures. The life of benefit, pure pleasure and of all treasure is not the life that is known if one's vantage is limited only to reified data. But in glowing knowing—in the heart essence of all dimensions—this reality is known.

Never can nature not know itself. It simply always is *as it is*, totally powerful and self-knowing. Primordial natural intelligence exhibits itself within all instants, without parts of moments, unstoppably enforcing the authentic. Not a single thing can ever stop the enforcement of nature's authenticity. Potent intelligence expands the outshining of the reification of data from within, utilizing supercharged skillful means that take control of the intelligence of human society. This natural law is one of a fast-paced evolution, rather than the slow pace we have been trained to perceive until now.

REIFICATION

"Reification" means to regard as concrete something that is in fact abstract. Thus, labels are given to data based on the assumption that they have an independent nature or identity. To reify an object is to give it an independent existence apart from open intelligence.

The practice of reification operates under the principle that human intelligence is a limited and restricted capability that networks with other separate and limited human intelligences. Reification does not allow for human evolution beyond the assumption of the independent nature of different subjects and the limited capability of those subjects.

It could even be stated that the reification of data is actually a superstition. It is a further superstition to believe that individual emotions—like anger, desire, jealousy and arrogance—have a power of their own and that they actually can control us and control our intelligence. That definitely fits with the definition of superstition: believing in something that isn't real.

However, within the past years we have started to realize how intelligent we are as human beings, and we have created incredible things: space travel, computers, telecommunications and so many other amazing technological marvels. It is open intelligence and its spontaneously altruistic nature—the most comprehensive order of intelligence and existence—that is providing for an evolution that is subsuming reification.

Certainly the idea that things *don't* have an independent nature isn't a new idea, but it has generally remained merely an intellectual idea which has never penetrated mainstream society. But now people are starting to really look into reification and are seeing that all these things we have called by this and that name do not actually have an independent nature or reality. Now we are increasingly fueled by an intelligence that is not limited by reification. There is a great interest in relying on open intelligence in order to access the unused intelligence that we have not been drawing on up until now.

We human beings hold the knowledge of the universe in a usable way, and we now know that to be the case. The thinking about ourselves as being subject to an original flaw, sin or karmic influence is saturated with the primordially pure intelligence which beneficially and inexhaustibly releases such limiting conceptual frameworks.

We are no longer living in some kind of primitive culture that existed long ago, and we do not need the same institutions and beliefs that served those cultures. We live in an information society today, and we need new institutions that thrive with benefit—new institutions where open intelligence is considered to be a prerequisite for everyone, the most sought after quality in all contributors to society.

Open-intelligence society is a seamless network where profound insight brings about powerful concepts, streamlined terminology, sophisticated methods and high-powered tools. Old ideas fall by the wayside, and society shifts to a future wherein there is no memory of society without open intelligence. The concept of using reified intelligence becomes unimaginable. It is a total shift, an exciting, manifest realization that is happening right now. All questions and doubts about open-intelligence power and the movement to be of great benefit are immediately resolved by the example and strength of those who have chosen open intelligence.

It is only within the last few years that it has become clear that the intelligence of the universe is housed in human beings in a usable way. We need to really make use of that discovery, and the way we make use of it is for each one of us individually to contribute to open-intelligence society. We contribute to the Age of Human Empowerment and Era of Great Benefit by relying on open intelligence and by being certain that open intelligence is more predominant in our perception than is reified data. Our most comprehensive intelligence—open intelligence—is the only source of beneficial open-ended knowledge creation.

THE INEXHAUSTIBLE EMPOWERMENT
OF HUMAN SOCIETY

We as a society actually have responsibility for deciding what our identity is, and then we have responsibility for living out that identity and for supporting each other while we learn to live out that identity. It is similar to feeling our way around in the dark, and then all of a sudden the sun is shining, everything is illuminated and people are able to clearly see their true identity.

The inexhaustible empowerment of all of human society is the ongoing recognition that human society is an exact explanatory model of nature's intelligence. The way human society is explains what nature is, and the way nature is explains what human society is. Nature's intelligence always provides for instantaneous open-intelligence society, and nature's intelligence is engineered into all phenomena—without our needing to do anything. Nature's intelligence destroys confusion, and so it is very important that we rely on the natural open-intelligence view. The destruction of confusion is a mighty feat as well as a natural one. Nature seems limited due to reified ideas about what it is and how it works; however, we are seeing a nature we did not know existed until now. We can only instinctively comprehend nature when open intelligence is our view—outshining all the reified data we have accumulated and allowing for a prolific outburst of our profoundly beneficial potency of mind, speech, body, qualities and activities.

Throughout history human society has been filled with great innovation and discovery, and things are constantly being discovered that can make life more beneficial. Now we are more and more discovering open intelligence, and this discovery makes life much more beneficial, because we are no longer limited by reified intelligence. We take responsibility for our commanding intelligence; we take responsibility for the power that we have within ourselves to give ourselves complete mental and emotional stability. That is what is emerging in human society today, and this is a very, very powerful moment of tremendous auspiciousness and good fortune.

We are going through some incredible changes right now, and it is a time of great opening—global unity, global community and the great possibility for global harmony. It is not even limited to global harmony; it is a matter perhaps even of multiversal harmony, far beyond anything we can imagine right now, where we are actually able to engage with other domains that we know nothing about today.

Open intelligence is becoming more and more obvious within society, such that we will reach a time where we cannot even remember what it was like to live from reified intelligence. As individuals grow to the point of total open intelligence outshining the noticing of all data, so too it is with society. A very great evolutionary leap is with us at this point in time, and that leap is now evident.

In order to unite powerfully, we need to get clear about the common understanding, language and principles which guide us to live together in a powerful way. These are found in the radical simplicity and potency of Balanced View's Four Mainstays—an algorithm designed by open intelligence itself in order to command human society to step into its exalted nature.

It starts with each one of us. We have to gain governance of our own individual politic; we look within ourselves and permit all data a harmonious flow, subsuming into open intelligence's balanced view. First, benefit becomes clear as self-benefit, and very quickly it follows that the focus of the benefit is on the benefit of all. The benefit, prosperity and generosity that are experienced directly by each individual are also experienced by society as a whole. Whatever is going on with each of us is replicating itself in society as a whole, because *we* are society.

A COMPREHENSIVE ORDER OF EXISTENCE

Open intelligence subsumes reified intelligence in a greater order of intelligence, enlivening this era. We as a human society right now are in the process of sharply releasing and cutting through all the limiting elaborations that we have been applying to ourselves. We have not been able to make any kind of breakthrough that would assure mental and emotional stability in the thousands of years of human society, yet now we are able. This is the power of open intelligence right here. Open intelligence is not another complicated solution that no one can understand. No, it is something simple and direct, yet at the same time it plays out with a brilliant complexity. It brings us into an optimal state of functioning that completely devours all of our elaborations.

We have this profound capacity within ourselves to bring forth technologies that are extraordinarily beneficial, which make all of our current models of technology obsolete, just as the open-intelligence model makes old models of dealing with mental instability obsolete. Open intelligence completely turns over all our ideas about everything.

This open intelligence that we each hold is our birthright. It is the most basic of human rights that no one can ever take away from us. It is an inalienable right; it cannot be violated or taken away. When a child is born, she or he should be educated to know that they have a right to open intelligence—just as all of us have a right. Even if we live in a country that is burdened by repression and censorship, there is no way anyone can take away our power of indestructible open intelligence or direct access to education in the nature of mind. This is due to open intelligence itself which is at the helm, unable to be controlled by human modes of burdening individuals with the internalized oppression of disempowerment. The great exaltation of human life is unendingly forging ahead.

It is a basic education that now will be trained into human society from the beginning of life. By virtue of being human, we have the right to the open-intelligence view, and it is up to us to recognize open intelligence as the core value of society; otherwise, we will have a life of ambivalence at best. There are already many people around the world who have decided that open intelligence is their core value and that it is what they hold most dear.

We completely settle into this sublime knowledge of the beautiful power, the complete enjoyment, the total restfulness and the potency and ease of open intelligence, and this is possible for each human being, regardless of culture or language. Human beings on planet Earth are brought together into a global society—for the first time ever a global culture that thinks and acts together, along with a similar basis of education supporting its thoughts, actions, qualities and activities.

One by one, at the grassroots of society, we come to see the reality of our own existence. We move from a primitive, coarse level of intelligence and instead adopt the most comprehensive order of existence. Any of us who have the open-intelligence view see that there are indeed profound insights and a sublime level of intelligence that come about, which is not at all like the intelligence we had before.

It is a completely distinct, comprehensive order of existence, and we are just getting the feel of it. Just like when one buys a new pair of shoes and it takes a while to break them in to the point where they feel comfortable, the same is true with becoming accustomed to open intelligence. It is a new order of intelligence for humankind that is completely distinct from reified intelligence—to which we must simply become accustomed.

We have adopted all kinds of ways of thinking and doing. Many of our responses to our thinking, emotions, sensations and our other experiences are the legacy of reactive drives. Reacting to our environment in order to feel safe is the legacy of reification. Now we are finding that, without adopting any kind of new gadget or anything whatsoever, within ourselves we find a treasury of incredible intelligence that we did not even know was there. It is truly right here within us, right now. How do we tap into it? By relying on open intelligence for short moments repeated many times. The basic maxim that comes from short moments of open intelligence is, "All is well." That is just how things are; all is well. Even when things aren't well, all is well. Know that to be your own circumstance.

We as human beings are completely relentless in our capacity to discover and to comprehend our own life and to comprehend the world we live in because of our very alive, active intelligence. However, we have had very little true education in the nature of mind up until this point in time, because we have been relying on a very limited vantage of the mind put forth in impenetrable ideologies and pedagogies which deliver results for all too few people. We may feel very advanced, and what we are discovering seems very advanced, but it is only a drop in the bucket compared to what we are revealing about our capacity based on open intelligence.

THE REALITY OF RELATIONALITY

The recognition of open intelligence is coming about for many, many people; however, this process will not unfold in the way that one might think. No preconceived ideas are sufficient to conceive the actual benefit that is possible.

One of the most cynical assumptions of the past has been that one should simply give up on human society in general. "We are hopeless; there's nothing that can be done, and everything will always be just like it has always been." By the simplicity of the open-intelligence view, all ideas are completely outshone, and through that outshining the great arising of benefit comes about from within human intelligence itself, whether people are actively cooperating or not.

When our inner environment is pristine, then the outer environment becomes pristine too, and both are seen as seamless and indivisible. We need to open completely to the beautifully pristine nature of our own environment of data, whatever they are. What a lovely notion it is to see that everything and everyone is just so beautiful. There is an immense possibility of a friendly attitude—the friendly feeling from within. It is possible to see this coming forth in the world today: the friendliness of all people with each other, all people wanting basic goodness for themselves and everyone else, all people wanting benefit, prosperity and generosity for themselves and everyone else.

When a human being is seen to be an open-intelligence entity rather than a closed system locked up in a world of descriptions of past, present and future, then it is easier to see that *everyone* is an open system. We all have seamless connectivity within open intelligence, and this seamless connectivity allows us to be interactive and interoperable in a vast expanse of open intelligence.

The reality of relationality and wanting benefit for oneself and others is brought about naturally through relying on open intelligence. There is no need to try to cultivate or develop it; it is naturally so. We make the one simple change, which is to choose the open-intelligence view rather than data. In that way we have a life of complete relationality. Each moment of our life is a building block of world peace and thriving human society. In each short moment of open intelligence we make an active contribution to world peace. That is how powerful we are.

There are many people who are totally interested and committed to open intelligence, so there is instantaneous community and relationship everywhere. If we want to make it our priority to come together with other people who are committed to open intelligence, we have a perfect opportunity to do so through the Four Mainstays of Balanced View.

A WORLD AT PEACE

We might never know that there is peace within if we are never taught this very important fact about ourselves. So, how can we learn it now? The answer is in short moments repeated many times. When throughout global human culture we gather together in the commitment to short moments, we, the people of planet Earth, create a world that is based on the innate leadership and problem-solving capacity of open intelligence rather than on confusion. It is as simple and powerful as that.

World peace is in self-governance. That is where we need to start—self-leadership and self-responsibility. Open intelligence is the ultimate skillful means of self-governance and self-responsibility, and each short moment taken by any person on earth helps build a foundation of world peace.

We live in a time of many conflicts and wars around the globe, as well as very serious problems in the world economy. We could perhaps blame political and economic leaders for the severe difficulties we face; however, while political and economic leaders may make decisions that jeopardize the welfare of all of us, the actual cause of the problem is much more basic. It is crucial to understand that the root of these problems is the fact that we have not been relying on our peaceful nature.

It is easy to see that we have many problems, but it is not always easy to recognize the causes of the problems or the ways to correct them. The actual cause of these worldwide problems is the way that we as individuals have thought and acted. If we do not know how to keep peace within ourselves individually, we will be unable to keep peace around the world.

We have seen many changes throughout the world over the centuries, with many governments overthrown and new governments put in place and with many negotiations and peace summits. However, all the peace negotiations, summits and changes in governments in the world have never led to true peace. We have seen people throughout history trying to bring the world into peaceful accord. we have seen wars stopped and more wars started; we have seen all kinds of violence: violence towards nations, violence to peoples, domestic violence within the home and the violence we do to ourselves, but despite all the tactics and strategies we have employed towards creating peace since people could first communicate with one another, there continues to be conflict growing into war.

The government of open intelligence, the all-ruling monarch, is the one that is most essential and the one which will lead to world peace. Our contribution to world peace is in each short moment we take. Peace is not going to come about in any other way. How could there be world peace with a world full of angry people? This direct personal experience where we outshine the war within us, where we outshine all data, shows us through our own direct experience that world peace is emerging right now. It is emerging in us as an emanation of open intelligence.

Tapping into the treasury of peace within, we find that its wealth is limitless. As each of us draws on the infinite reserves of the treasury of peace, its gems shine brighter and brighter throughout the world. As we each add our contribution of personal peace to world peace, we find there is an endless supply. We recognize that each of us has the profound power of making a significant contribution to world peace.

Every single person on earth makes a difference. How is this so? By the power of gaining confidence in our innate peace, we make our life into a precious contribution to a peaceful world. Our own peace equals world peace. This is a very powerful statement. With each person's contribution of their own inner peace, world peace is created.

We each have a contribution to make. Usually from reified intelligence we tend to think about a hero or great leader who will come in to make things okay or some kind of external event that will change everything forever. Through the insight of open intelligence, we start to see the incredible importance of the individual. Open-intelligence society will continue to grow more and more potent as we choose to live in a world of great benefit. Peace will be a natural outcome of this. We, the people of the world, are in fact the leader we have been looking for.

When the war within individuals is ended, peace naturally arises. When this occurs in many people collectively, war between people ends. The power of peace spreads around the earth. This power is ours to claim right now. What could be more important? We do not want to hold back. This total commitment to peace will ensure that access to our peaceful nature will endure for future generations, making the world rich with its greatest natural resource.

TECHNOLOGICAL INNOVATIONS ENRICHING SOCIETY

We live in an era of profound scientific and technological advancement, and as we build even more incredible systems, we find that we actually are a truly open field of intelligence and not a closed system of individuals. We see that what is going on is in fact the operation of a collective, open-networked intelligence and not the scattered efforts of many separate individuals.

In order to go forward with our technological capacity and our scientific advancement, we must do so from the open-intelligence perspective; otherwise, we will be blind to the way we need to go. The advancements in human intelligence will continue to sharply accelerate. If people continue to replicate things that are sub-valuable in terms of benefitting everyone, those will naturally be deselected from the process, and instead, the quality offerings will thrive. First comes self-recognition—the instinctive recognition of our own instinctive potency and the recognition that everything is indivisible. We do not have the proper vantage to make the best and most beneficial scientific or technological contribution until we have that instinctive recognition.

We can see that as a species we have incredible intelligence and are able to do incredible things, and with open intelligence we can make decisions about what to do that will be of greatest benefit to all. The focus may often have been simply on making more money or on some other personal agenda; however, all of this power to know and to do and all of this incredible intelligence that is presently being demonstrated is increasingly going to be directed to the benefit of all.

The turning point will be reached and the direction will inexorably be turned towards benefit. Science for the sake of science or technology for the sake of technology will no longer be the context. The context is coming to be spontaneous altruism—what will be of greatest benefit to all. The old way is not the way we are going anymore; we are now going in a new direction.

Within comprehensive intelligence, all the knowledge in the universe is available to us, not just the knowledge we know now. So, we actually have within us the capacity to cure diseases that have been thought to be incurable, whether they are mental or physical diseases. All this actually will come about through all kinds of means, such as re-engineering the physical body and through genetic engineering. We are going to see huge changes, and the standards for health are going to change immensely within a very short time.

One may be skeptical when one hears incredible things like this, but these things are actually underway. Just by way of example, at one time there were a lot of naysayers about the Internet. "Oh, that will never take off. Hardly anyone will have computers in their home and even if they did, they would have no desire to use them to connect with people they don't know." However, there are always a few that lead the way. There are the early adopters and innovators who are willing to go beyond the conventional way of looking at things, whether it be in the world of the Internet or in the newly emerging world of open intelligence.

We have gone from a time when the Internet was brand new and known to almost no one to it being something that is now being used by billions of people around the world. For some of us who have witnessed this in our lifetimes, it is easier to imagine that it is possible for incredible worldwide changes to take place that are presently inconceivable. The same kind of grassroots organizing, education, empowerment and mobilization that led to a successful implementation of the Internet are open to all people, and all these methods can now be refined and made even more powerful as even greater wonders are brought about.

Even though today we are either online or offline, it is not going to be that way in the future. Soon we will be connected all the time, and unbroken online connection will be natural, pervasive and ubiquitous. We will be able to talk to each other without doing anything other than ushering in a thought. This is what we are preparing for right now. The world of the future is one wherein we will feel an expanded sense of identity and an ease with having relationships with people we have never met face-to-face.

The Internet is a hugely open system, and we can see that our own intelligence pours into the Internet and blends with other people's intelligence into an open expanse of networked intelligence. Rather than being the closed system that we have learned that we are, we see that we are an inexhaustibly open expanse of intelligence.

With the power and insight of open intelligence, we are able to think totally outside the box. We are able to look into any endeavor and see all kinds of things about it that no one else would ever see. For example, a technological problem may have been looked at in a certain way, yet by relying on open intelligence we could look at exactly the same problem and see all kinds of parallels to other fields of knowledge that help to open up a solution to the problem that no one has ever thought of before.

We are now in an inexhaustible Age of Human Empowerment and Era of Great Benefit, in which beneficial open intelligence is emergent within human culture. It cannot be stopped and it cannot be reversed. From this time on there will always be increasing open intelligence and increasing benefit, even though it may not be totally noticeable in all of society as yet.

LIFE SATISFACTION AND FLOURISHING

Many people have longed to find emotional and mental stability, and almost everyone has asked the question, "How can I feel peaceful and happy, and what do I need to do to have that?" This is what is being spoken about here—the knowledge of how to be happy and to find mental and emotional stability. In a nutshell, if we wanted to describe the goal of open-intelligence training, it would be: life satisfaction, flourishing, mental and emotional stability and happiness for all human beings.

There are what could be called intelligence augmentation systems based on artificial intelligence being built around the world, and it is believed that these intelligence augmentation systems will help make decisions and solve problems for human beings in the future. In other words, problems that we cannot solve with our own brainpower alone will be facilitated by these intelligence augmentation systems.

To have a thriving intelligence augmentation system, it has to be a system that really works, one that ensures life satisfaction and flourishing and which operates within a spontaneously ethical framework. This is what an intelligent network is; it makes everything work together, and an optimal intelligence network makes everything work together for the benefit of all.

The reality of the work being done in the open-intelligence community is that an intelligence augmentation system has been created that is the cutting edge of all intelligence augmentation systems. Open intelligence has always been available; however, for a long time human society has ignored it. Even when it was recognized, there were not sufficient tools to access it in a way that would ensure life satisfaction and flourishing for the mainstream of human society. Now we have those tools, and the tools are always adaptable to the current condition of society. The tools are customized and are just right for the moment, and a skillful trainer is the proper purveyor of those tools.

Open intelligence is a commanding intelligence—an augmentation of human intelligence that allows human beings to do things they have never done before. For example, ensuring complete life satisfaction and flourishing along with complete mental and emotional stability has not been something that human beings could necessarily count on. However, assurance in open intelligence is resultant in life satisfaction and flourishing and in complete mental and emotional stability. These are very real facts; they are an actuality. We can see just from this that a frontier is being pioneered that is unlike any frontier we have ever pioneered before.

We find that we actually have an intelligent system—an intelligent network—that is capable of truly remarkable feats. Within just a few short years an instruction set and a technology based on the practice of short moments many times has been created; it has been tested in communities around the world and has been found to be resultant in life satisfaction and flourishing. Short moments of open intelligence are a human intelligence augmentation system that expands current intelligence and ability. It is an intelligence that is able to solve problems that individuals or teams have not yet solved. In a very real way it is the most advanced of intelligence augmentation systems.

Especially these days when there is so much misinformation and pseudo-information about the search for ultimate life satisfaction, the first thing to really understand is that the search does not end in some kind of mental state, like a no-mind state or emptiness or stillness. The "end" of the search is at the coincidence of stillness and frenzy—that is where it is! The end of the search is in the instinctive recognition that open intelligence is spread equally and evenly throughout all data. To try to arrive at a state in some future time is a misdirected effort, because open intelligence is only in the here-and-now. There is no state at which to arrive; we already are where we need to be.

THE PRIMAL WAVE

We as human beings in the first wave of the great ocean of inexhaustible benefit can be likened to tidal ripples in water far out at sea. The first enormous surge of water circles from the depths to the surface, and its mighty potency is the singular agent of all-encompassing life activity as the water burgeons all around in seamless concentricity. It is a great swell of the entirety of an immense body of water—all initiated by a single uprising. The magnificent intelligence at the basis of this and all other displays of primordial purity is known by its spontaneous presence, openness and beneficial responsiveness.

Beneficial open intelligence is primally pure, due to data being pure in their own place, like moonlight is pure from the spontaneous conjunction of sun shining on the moon. Likewise, pure benefit's super-factual truth is pure, luminous and pristine like a clear crystal ball—the most comprehensive intelligence subsuming into itself all riffs of data. That is the roused–up and potent beneficial factor, the pure luminous factor, which is pure benefit, with data shining forth unstopped by analysis. This is the basis for the shining forth of the whole variety of data—an inexhaustibly overflowing and pristine purity, which is clearly illuminating of all and totally freed of data.

Open intelligence's pure benefit is primordially pure—primordial in not knowing separation from itself and pure in the exaltation of its stainless greatness. Inseparable, naked, pristine purity is naked, pristine, dynamic energy and naked, pristine, beneficial activity.

We always already are this pure, potent beneficial condition with nothing needing to be done to keep it in place and with nothing to inhibit. The five vast openings of mind, speech, body, qualities and activities provide inexhaustible beneficial expression. In primordial purity there is nothing to be indulged, avoided or replaced. It simply is *as it is*—potent and clear.

Through education in the nature of mind, we as human entities find open intelligence to be pure; thus, it is completely absent or free of any datum with an independent nature. There is nothing else other than this single unique expanse. So, the great intelligence of pure benefit—the inexhaustible potency in which the Four Mainstays are the code spontaneously pervading an individual—is just this. Now instinctively recognized, we are known to have primordial freedom from all data. Free from data as the sun is free from sunshine, pure benefit is roused up with a factor of great intelligence to it. That, then, is pure benefit's uncontrived intelligence.

If you have not had an authentic introduction to open intelligence as it actually is, it is time to recognize open intelligence now and enjoy its spontaneous life satisfaction and flourishing for one and for all. In the swelling wave of those who have been authentically introduced to open intelligence, a core source is verified—a core source with a ceaseless flow of pure transmission of the super-factual reality of open intelligence. Now stay put in your own place and your own condition. This pure transmission will then be exponentially, inexhaustibly and instinctively obvious as your primordial, all-beneficial identity forevermore. Similarly, night bows to day.

It happens that you stay right here, never departing from it, unmoving from its entity. That is pure benefit; that is open intelligence, luminous by nature, which is indivisible with purity and benefit.

Chapter Seven

SPONTANEOUS BENEFIT AND ALTRUISM

Everyone is already inherently connected to the original condition of benefit, and thus all live spontaneously and continuously in, of, as and through the originally beneficial condition. The original condition of spontaneous benefit is an alreadyprepared, prosperous field which is issuing forth as the open-intelligence society of the Age of Human Empowerment and Era of Great Benefit. Everything is pouring out from right here, right now. We are not trying to get *over* to original spontaneous benefit that exists somewhere else. The condition of original benefit is *right here, right now*, pouring forth endless treasure, endless prosperity and endless benefit.

Spontaneous altruism is inexhaustible beneficial potency dedicated to all. Instead of living a life entirely focused on self, through the power of short moments we live a life focused on the benefit of all, and we seize our power to be of benefit to all. The focus on self slips away, and at the same time we take excellent care of ourselves—the best possible care we could ever take. Short moments of open intelligence gives true self-love and self-respect as well as true love and respect for all.

We open up to a more comprehensive order of intelligence that is quite different from the way we looked at things before. When we are totally wrapped up in self-focus, we are fixed on having pleasant experiences for ourselves and avoiding unpleasant experiences. An example of self-focus would be that if we had desire, hatred, anger, arrogance, pride, jealousy or fear, we would indulge those feelings or try to avoid them or replace them with something else. In the self-focus of desire, hatred, anger, arrogance, pride, jealousy or fear—or perhaps sadness about lack of education in the nature of mind—the whole consideration would be about ourselves and how things are going to turn out for us. The consideration might move out to include other people close to us, but it would still be essentially an expression of self-focus.

However, as we gain more assurance in open intelligence, we realize that all this self-focus is completely slipping away. It is replaced by an expanse so great that it can never be measured, named or characterized in any way—a pervasive expanse of the openhearted impulse to be of benefit to all.

With the acknowledgment of this pervasive expanse, we have the greatest power to be of benefit to ourselves and others. Otherwise, if life is focused on data, there will only be a lifetime of self-focus. By just this simple little shift to relying on open intelligence until it becomes obvious, we go naturally from self-focus to spontaneously caring about the benefit of all. The self is taken care of completely, everything is loved and esteemed, nothing is rejected and nothing needs to be abandoned. This is the all-embracing benefit of the open-intelligence view, which is all-encompassing of self and no-self.

We give up the old ways of looking at things through the reified data of being an individual person who is separate from others. We seize the power of networked and connected open intelligence, where every single moment of our life is a commitment to the benefit of all. We find that this is a most natural and urgent passion in our lives, and when we connect into this uncontrived impulse to be of benefit to all, we are then living in our natural state.

A short moment of open intelligence is the log-in and the password to a culture of gratitude and respect, a culture of openhearted, powerful participation—the culture of the Age of Human Empowerment and Era of Great Benefit. As we become more and more absorbed by the spontaneous benefit of open intelligence, the context for life is the benefit of all—naturally, spontaneously and obviously—without having to try to cultivate anything.

We break through to the unused or under-utilized potency within ourselves. This is a life of complete benefit and harmony, where human beings cooperate in all kinds of situations all over the world, working intimately together in complete peace with always greater and greater potency, greater and greater creativity, greater and greater innovation and greater and greater resources.

It is the easiest way to live—the easiest way imaginable. For example, we can come together with people whom we do not know well in complete confidence that we will easily be able to get along. We realize that not only will we get along, but also the whole circumstance will be one of enrichment and flourishing. We share an inherent connection with one another, and because of this open connection that we all have, there is the possibility to live in complete harmony with everyone—to go into any situation and know that we will flourish and everyone else can flourish as well.

THE RESOURCE OF LOVE

We as human beings have a great resource within us: the resource to love, to share love and to share belonging and community. To see all of this coming alive now is very powerful and exciting, and this resource will only grow from here. As we come together in benefit, not just as individuals who have decided on a commitment to open intelligence but as a whole society deciding on this commitment, then we begin to be able to do all kinds of things we have never done before—not only for ourselves, but for and with others.

An exalted expanse opens up that allows for endless contributions of beneficial qualities and activities. This is true for each one of us. We each have incredible strengths, gifts and talents to offer, and the ways in which we can offer those strengths, gifts and talents in an especially beneficial manner become very clear to us through the comprehensive view of open intelligence.

In open intelligence there is spontaneous ethics. One just knows what to do and how to act, and there is no need for a rulebook of instructions. It is open intelligence itself that is the source of all the rules, so we go straight to the source and act from there. In the glow of that indescribable beneficial force, there is the naturally produced support of an immeasurable treasury of flourishing. This is the force of plenty and benefit, of total potency, of being able to know who we are and who others are, to look at subjects and objects and really know what they are, how they belong together and how they are all seamlessly networked.

No one is a stranger and everyone is befriended, and by relying on open intelligence, those are the eyes through which we see the world. There isn't anyone who is excluded anywhere, and everywhere we look we feel right at home. In the greatly expansive all-beneficial nature of open intelligence, the beneficial energy once focused only on friends and relatives opens up to include everyone. Our generous display of beneficial qualities and activities for all is the very best connection we can have with our loved ones, as it offers the power of example of a human being endowed with openhearted natural intelligence. This is the greatest contribution we can make to our loved ones and to society.

We may have all kinds of afflictive states appearing, but we can still feel connected and totally at ease. Our data do not need to get in the way anymore, because we are no longer looking through the eyes of the data-description. Instead, we are looking through blazing eyes of open intelligence, beneficial eyes that cast their gaze on everything and see only benefit in what is truly an Age of Great Benefit.

PRIORITIZING OPEN INTELLIGENCE

We all naturally want to be of benefit. When we are small babies, we are already looking around to see what particular things make our caregivers smile, and so, what do we do? We do those things that make them smile! That is our natural urge to be of benefit; we want to reach out and touch someone with a beneficial attitude. So, this is very ingrained in us and is very easy to connect with.

The power to be of benefit is brought fully alive when we prioritize open intelligence. The more we know about open intelligence and its tremendous potency—individually and in society—the more beneficial society becomes. Each moment of open intelligence empowers absolute benefit, individually and collectively. Open intelligence is absolutely the key to a flourishing society, and without it we have not had a truly flourishing society. No matter how many technological gadgets or genetic manipulations we come up with, we can never have the profound instinctive recognition of our essential nature without acknowledging open intelligence.

Benefit, benefit, benefit is inexhaustibly emerging again and again in open intelligence, and it can never be stopped. Again and again the request and response for the enhancement of benefit is filled immediately. It is self-augmenting, continuously expanding forever. Everyone is the vessel of beneficial mind, speech and body merged in beneficial flow. In this magnificent Age of Human Empowerment and Era of Great Benefit, everything shifts seamlessly into prosperity's treasury and hold, and this is happening right now all over the world.

Even though this may not yet be fully evident, we in fact live in a state of great benefit. Our natural state is to live in unending open intelligence and unending benefit. Just showing up in open intelligence is the key, choosing the beneficial open intelligence identity rather than the data-based identity. This is the entrance into a particular type of vehicle, one could say. We each choose to live in one or more vehicles of contribution—scientific, technological, economic, educational, political, social, religious, spiritual or whatever it might be. All of our superior qualities and activities to operate within that vehicle come about through the power of open intelligence itself and do not need to be contrived, forced or cultivated in any way. Our qualities and activities of mind, speech and body simply need to be expanded beyond the reified frameworks of a history based on the limitations and restrictions caused by the confining definitions of data.

By the power of relying on open intelligence, we are able to truly experience the dynamic energy of data's beneficial energy as our own open intelligence! In this great singularity, the indivisibility of open intelligence and data generates beneficial energy. Yet, we must know this directly through introduction to open intelligence, wherein we instinctively recognize the productive energy in the inseparability of open intelligence and data. Similarly, the sun generates its energy by nuclear fusion of hydrogen nuclei into helium.

The full expression of open intelligence does not come from some authority figure who is doing everything while the rest of us sit there helpless and incapable. The Balanced View trainers, for instance, are noted for education in the nature of mind which naturally gives the result of open intelligence's beneficial potency. Open intelligence has command of dynamic energy. It has its own voice; it does not speak only from within the confines of structures of authority.

There is the prioritization of benefit in all circumstances—not contrived benefit, but the very benefit that is allowed by our own display of open-intelligence energy. That is the dynamic benefit of this moment. The uncontrived natural perfection of every single aspect of existence is already very clear; however, it remains a philosophical cage of labels unless it is instinctively recognized in our own life.

We ask ourselves, "Where is the focus of commitment going to be for my life?" We have to decide what those commitments in our lives will be. We live in the same society as everyone else, so we are exposed to the major life events that everyone else is exposed to—being born, living a life in all its many forms and dying—and just like anyone else our lives are filled with all kinds of influences that we can adopt or not. What is the choice that is going to be made in our lives today, right now, in this moment?

We can have many things that influence our lives in some way; however, we may have reached a point where we become extremely rigorous, cautious and careful in deciding what our main commitments would be. Being totally responsible for ourselves and the world around us is an incredibly important commitment, and this total responsibility comes from open intelligence in a potent yet effortless way. Even if we do not know exactly what we are going to do in any given moment, just by relying on open intelligence with whatever might unfold in life, we know that we can be totally responsible.

EVERYTHING RESTS IN PURE BENEFIT

If we apply open intelligence to our data, we can see that they are endowed with pure benefit. Everything rests in pure benefit and everything resolves in pure benefit. It cannot be any simpler than that. All data here-and-now are resting in pure benefit and resolving in pure benefit. That is their essential nature, and if we know that, then we know what we need to know.

Quicker than the blink of an eye or the instantaneous movement of a camera shutter, the complete display of data is always changing, even if in a minimal way. There is no way to keep it in place or preserve it. If we could look at a photograph of a particular moment from many points of view, each vantage would be changing in each millisecond. When time and space are secondary definitions of data and open intelligence is primary, its all-inclusive view allows for both time and timelessness, space and no-space to be included in open-ended knowledge creation.

There is a distinction between contrived benefit and the bliss-benefit of open intelligence. Contrived benefit involves so much hard work, while bliss benefit is supreme enjoyment, where the knowing and the doing are the supreme expression of open intelligence itself. One can see this very attribute displayed in so many people now, so it is very easy to talk about it in this way.

In order to release the powers of natural benefit, we need to let our data streams be as they are. This does not mean that we get rid of data; it means letting everything be *as it is*. Without letting everything be *as it is,* there is no way to see directly and instinctively that the data are free in their own place, as open intelligence and data are inseparable. A complete understanding of any data stream can only come from open intelligence. A major key point here is that open intelligence has always been shining forth as all the data, but it just was not recognized, because we had only been focused on the data and were not educated in the nature of mind.

Truly real open intelligence is what real benefit, flourishing and life satisfaction is; it is knowing yourself and accepting yourself as you are. It is knowing that whatever the here-and-now may present, it just is *as it is*, and your sole function is the knowing and the doing of open-intelligence benefit. That's it. It allows you to keep it really simple.

Sometimes when one is first introduced to open intelligence, self-benefit is recognized first; however, the self-benefit is just the beginning. The more we directly and instinctively recognize the benefit to ourselves of the simple instinctive recognition of open intelligence, the more we want for everyone to share in that instinctive recognition.

By the power of open intelligence, people are coming together all over the world. People learn how to work together from a base of empowered action, and by acknowledging open intelligence in that very first moment we also acknowledge our tremendous power and the power of our beneficial qualities and activities. For all of the people relying on open intelligence who are already of great benefit in the world, that benefit will only increase through continuing reliance on open intelligence. By the power of open intelligence outshining all data streams, new beneficial qualities and activities become evident in everyday action. Insights and advancements occur that no one has ever had before.

SPONTANEOUS ALTRUISM

When we are introduced to open intelligence, we are at the same time introduced to spontaneous altruism, and as we rely on open intelligence more and more, this spontaneous altruism becomes more obvious to us. Spontaneous altruism is inseparable from authentic open intelligence. Spontaneous altruism comes about without having to think about it; it is already built in, and it is present without any effort.

"Altruism" means unselfish concern for the benefit of others, and "spontaneous altruism" means an instinctive concern and passion for the welfare of everyone that arises naturally and without contrivance. This term spontaneous altruism is key, because over the years there has been so much misunderstanding about compassion and cultivating compassion. Spontaneous altruism is quite different from cultivated compassion. Cultivated compassion can evaporate at any time, because it involves effort and linking together various data streams through cause and effect. In contrast, spontaneous altruism flows naturally from the outshining of all data, and it is never absent or not available. Cultivated compassion is based on effort to cultivate positive states by replacing negative states, while spontaneous altruism is effortless life satisfaction, flourishing, benefit, generosity and prosperity based on the law of nature—open intelligence.

To want to be of benefit to all is really our natural state. Of course, we ourselves are also included in that "benefit to all." The spontaneous ability and responsiveness to actually be of benefit to all is a dynamic expression of open intelligence. Spontaneous altruism is our core nature, our natural state of mind, speech, body, qualities and activities. It is the natural response of love embedded in every single thought, emotion, sensation and experience.

In spontaneous altruism there is a natural passion present every single moment of the day to provide for the welfare of all. It is an incredible adventure to go through life enjoying the empowerment of mind, speech, body, qualities and activities. It is remarkable to see the enrichment of intimacy in all relationships and to see that there is no limit or restriction to the kind of benefit that a single individual or a group of individuals can offer to the world. This is totally amazing, especially if we consider that for so many thousands of years we have looked at ourselves as helpless in the face of all our perceived limitations, when in fact we are indivisible with the vast intelligence ruling the entire universe.

What is more, there is a realization that there are countless individuals everywhere experiencing exactly the same data at exactly the same moment. For any data stream that I might have or you might have, there are countless individuals experiencing the very same data at exactly the same time. This recognition is a great opening from self-focus into the uncontrived organic beneficial intent that is our natural state. That is where real compassion takes a stand, compassion that is really full of the true power and fire of open intelligence. Spontaneous altruism is what naturally flows forth from this total recognition and complete emphatic involvement in the whole human experience.

True compassion is being able to take in everything and to feel the connection with all the people all over the world. We fundamentally feel what people are going through: the children starving to death this very day, the war, the suffering and death, the fear, depression and doubt. True compassion is the capacity to be totally present with what is going on and to be able to allow it to be *as it is*. This is the stance from which to take skillful action. Open intelligence empowers the ability to do the right thing for the benefit of all, because there is no longer constant personal referencing, such as, "Oh, poor me; what will I do about all these horrible things?" Rely on open intelligence and you will know what to do.

Familiarity with our own data gives us great familiarity with other beings. We really know what makes us tick, and through that we really know what makes everyone tick. That makes it possible to look each other in the eye as equals. We know what life is, and we know that from looking at ourselves in a deep and thoroughgoing way. There is no more confusion about oneself and no more confusion about who anyone else is either.

By fully relying on open intelligence, we are able to face everything. We fully acknowledge the fact that anything that anyone has done, we are also capable of doing. If we had the same data streams, we would have done the same thing. It could be very extreme examples or people against whom we might have had a very strong reaction, but if we honestly look at whatever the person or the situation is, we can say, "Well, that person is a human being just like me. At a very essential level we are the same."

It does not mean that we go out and do any of the things that they do or did, but genuine compassion—spontaneous altruism—includes within it a very clear understanding. In order to have a direct cut from all systems of education in the nature of mind and to truly see that open intelligence is pervasive in all data, it really does require that we enter into this level of engagement within ourselves and with others. The more recognition of open intelligence there is, the clearer we are about who we are. When we look at ourselves or others, we see in a clearer way than we would without this honest insight.

LIVING FROM SPONTANEOUS ALTRUISM

How wondrous and remarkable that each one of us is an exact, explanatory, working model of this open intelligence. Vast open intelligence is the integrated framework that gives us the profound insight into all fields of knowledge. It gives us new knowledge inexhaustibly, and the new knowledge comes within the context of spontaneous altruism, so all new knowledge comes in a form that is of benefit to all. This will be more and more the case as the Age of Human Empowerment and Era of Great Benefit flourishes.

Living from spontaneous altruism means that we have opened our intelligence to the degree that we can do many things that we have never been able to do before. Complete mental and emotional stability—which is the inherent birthright of all human beings—is available to everyone right now through the power of open intelligence, and through fully relying on open intelligence this will be possible for more and more people.

Before we started practicing open intelligence, we may have tried to cultivate actions where we would act in a particular way in a particular situation. However, spontaneous altruism expresses itself in a wide range of responses to whatever the situation is. In a certain circumstance one response would be appropriate, and in another circumstance the response would be something else entirely. There is the great clarity of open intelligence and the incredible trust that develops in knowing what to do and how to respond depending on time, place and circumstance.

This then opens up the whole idea of what compassion is. We see that compassion does not always have to look peaceful and serene; it can be wrathful as well. The skilled wrathfulness of real compassion is the same sort of wrathfulness that we use to encounter our own afflictive states and to vehemently say "no" to the reified story limiting our education in the power of great benefit.

With one person we might sit and listen as they share all their data, and that might be perfectly appropriate, but in another situation we might respond in a much different manner that seems quite unconventional to an outside observer. In whichever case it may be, we have a much wider scope of how to respond to what is going on when we are fully trusting in open intelligence.

We continue to trust more and more in open intelligence until that trust becomes spontaneous and constant. In the context of that incredible trust, we know that no matter what we encounter, everything will be okay. Even if it seems like it isn't okay, everything *is* okay.

A simple human life with all the simple human connections and the joy, ecstasy, intimacy and sheer love included therein is vast and inexplicable. This really cannot be described. It is everything that we ever sought in our self-focus, yet it is so much greater. To know that every day will be filled with more and more of this is overwhelmingly profound. There is a consistent power to fulfill creative beneficial intent, and this is the sweetest way to live.

Your heart seems to be beating every day for everyone in the world! It is so empowering to walk down the street with a smile on your face and be spontaneously motivated to be of benefit to all—and to *really* want that. That is what spontaneous altruism is—a total feeling of intimacy and connection with everyone that comes from taking open intelligence all the way to outshining data including those of nonduality and no-self. Wherever we go in the world, there is a complete heart-connection with everyone, everywhere. Yes, truly, no one is a stranger anywhere.

Open intelligence is obvious and continuous! What a marvel it is!

HEY! ALL IS CRUCIAL AS IT IS

We are always in an unstopped mode of shining-forth beneficial potency. Letting everything flow on by, it is brilliantly clear that there is only pure open intelligence pervasive through and through.

With or without short moments, analysis or examination, all is clear and pure. Similarly, all images in a crystal ball are equally and evenly pervaded by purity and clarity. What a happy, powerful time, place and circumstance—everything *as it is*! In such a way, reified data based on extreme definition become absent; the shining forth of lively beneficial potency is obvious.

The great exaltation of what was taken to be a limited human creature is the radiant spontaneous presence of potent feats of vast mind, speech, body, qualities and activities inherent at the crucial juncture of open intelligence and its shining forth of data like sunshine from the sun. Incomprehensible to reified intelligence, upon introduction to the pure transmission of reality, education is received in the nature of mind, speech, body, qualities and activities. Yes, as it actually is, as we actually are—the inexhaustible expanse of open intelligence, perfect love and benefit.

Chapter Eight

EDUCATION IN THE NATURE OF MIND AND IDENTITY

In reality, the basis of irreversible social change that concentrates on the benefit for all is grounded in correct education in the nature of mind. In global human culture this has been made possible for the first time by Balanced View's standardization of the language for education in the nature of mind, just as in the past people have found it necessary to standardize language for writing, mathematics, science and so forth. Without these significant standardizations, all of which have been remarkable turning points in human history, cultural advancement would be impossible.

As a member of global human culture, ongoing education in the nature of mind is the most important step you can take for social change. As an individual living daily life, short moments of open intelligence until it is obvious and predominant at all times is the most powerful social change we can institute. In this way we go right to the root of mind and can see clearly from there how to skillfully enact spontaneous beneficial qualities and activities.

Unfortunately, standardization of language regarding education in the nature of mind has been detoured until now into a quandary of medical, psychological and philosophical rhetoric which has been of no help at all to people living everyday life. As human beings we must know that simply through accurate education in the nature of mind, in each moment we have access to immediate benefit and our most basic human right.

We unwittingly use the mind as a form of social, economic and political control—an internalized oppressive force that keeps us confused and groomed to work towards certain goals of a nameless worldwide economic enterprise, which has no specific interest in or methodology for the benefit of all. Often ignored are the strengths, gifts and talents of each of us and our unique mind, speech, body, qualities and activities as they actually are. Instead, we are expected to conform to a norm or be isolated or ostracized.

Everyone must be educated that the nature of mind is that of open intelligence with a data display inseparable from it. All information and knowledge are built from data which have no nature, power or influence apart from open intelligence—the vast, all-encompassing expanse at the basis.

The totality of reified data shines forth individually and collectively as the dynamic beneficial activity of indivisible open intelligence. Following on from that, since open intelligence does not move from its own self-illuminating status, it is called "great benefit," and as the display of its dynamic activity shines forth, this dynamism is unlimited inexhaustible benefit.

The profound key point, meaning and method is to allow that dynamic energy to proceed to self-release in its expanse of pure open intelligence, which brings to a complete stop the result of wrongly apprehending an independent nature in data. Thus, confusion is completely outshone; clarity, discernment and insight are established.

This, then, is the exalted basis of all-accomplishing beneficial activities—education in the nature of mind. Foremost among the all-accomplishing feats of open intelligence is the ability to introduce the authentic nature of mind and bring it to fruition through skillful means and insight specifically related to each individual's most beneficial strengths, gifts and talents.

ALWAYS AT HOME

We are fundamentally at ease and at home, and this at-home-ness is our basic identity. Knowing this, there isn't the need any longer to look a special way, to act a special way, to do a special thing in a certain situation or to assume anything else about ourselves. There are no rooms in this home of open intelligence, there is no roof and no windows, yet it provides the ultimate shelter.

Let's give our life to open intelligence one hundred percent! That is where home always is—a vast home filled with dynamic, beneficial energy pervading us and everything else. There is no way to get out of it, and no way to get into it, so we just relax. Beyond all words, names and labels, we feel this at-home-ness to be our basic identity. Just that.

The dynamic creative energy of vast open intelligence is the real me; I began as indestructible open intelligence, I live as indestructible open intelligence and I die as indestructible open intelligence. Even though I may have known at some level that this is true, I really have to become instinctively familiar with it and acknowledge it. Why do I have to acknowledge it? Because I have spent many years back and forth between acknowledging data and acknowledging open intelligence, so I now begin to acknowledge the open-intelligence view as predominant. All those twitches and twinges that I used to try to find a name for are nothing but the dynamic energy of open intelligence—the power of great benefit necessary for the social change I really care about.

More and more we come to recognize open intelligence as our own face. It *is* you and me, and there isn't any other you or me. The you that you are is the open-intelligence you. There is no need to try to make that happen; the realization just comes upon you and suddenly you recognize, "Oh wow! I don't need to worry about 'Who am I?' "

How wonderful and how powerful it is. How fortunate we are to be able to live in this incredible way—to be able to have full-fledged open intelligence as our identity, along with its beneficial qualities and activities, rather than the old way of being all mixed up with self-concern and always worrying about our own data.

A LIFELONG TRAINING IN BELIEVING IN DATA

We have been trained and we have trained ourselves to believe in the data making up a separate identity. Even though we have seen ourselves as a separate individual, all the while we have really been a network of intelligence. The totality of *all* phenomena, not just human beings, can be considered as an information society and an intelligent network. The relationship we have to the network is whatever we want it to be.

Rather than learning that open intelligence is our primary identity, most of us have learned that the body and mind comprise our identity. We have accumulated data about the body and mind and then believed that this accumulated data was our identity. We have been given a name, told we have a certain gender, and stories that are associated with the body-mind-name-gender data have come into being, and we have believed these data to be real.

This process of accumulating all the data and saying "yes" to them becomes very ingrained. "All these data that I've had all these years, that's who I am. I have a lot of paperwork to back it up: my birth certificate, résumé, personal history and all the other proof that this is who I am." That is one way of looking at our identity; however, no accumulation of data is any kind of conclusive evidence of who we are. It is interesting to consider that a newborn baby has no idea about any of these things. There is no connection to a fixed identity or any opinions about categories associated with this identity. This notion of identity is acquired over the course of a lifetime spent believing in data.

So, for years and years we have learned many ways to describe ourselves and everything else according to data. That required so much intensive training that the training could never be complete, and there was a constant seeking for more data to create a more secure identity. We used data to communicate who we thought we were to others and to ourselves. Habitual data reinforced an identity centered on being a separate individual, and most often there was almost no communication with others that transcended the centering on habitual data. Even though we may have taken positive and effective actions in life, many times those actions were rooted in uninformed data accumulation rather than in relying on the power of open intelligence.

Because we are trained in our lives to see ourselves as separate individuals, we then refer to ourselves as a subject that is different and separate from the objects which this subject perceives. We are an individual subject that is assessing objects within a world, and basically we live every day of our life through that perspective. As we believe that we are separate from others, we go on from that initial belief to the conclusion that we are better or worse than others. Then, in order to compete, show our abilities and secure our identity, we engage in a wide variety of actions.

We learn to give everything a fixed identity and to reach agreement about what those fixed identities are—in other words, what a human being is and what any subject or object in the world is. We learn that things have an independent nature that is governed by the definitions given to them. This colors our whole perspective and the way we look at everything.

We are also trained to see ourselves as a history of positive, negative and neutral data that we have had during our life, and these positive, negative and neutral data include all our thoughts, emotions, sensations and other experiences. We live within the context of waking, dreaming and sleeping and birth, life and death, and that is our context as an individual. Within that belief system we may have other belief systems that relate to what happens after life. This is what our history and identity are according to popular culture, and we are led to believe that we do not have any other identity. Through the predominance of the open-intelligence view we come to see that these sorts of identities that are supposed to be so concrete are actually fleeting, impermanent and momentary at best.

Most of us have been taught how and what to think through many years of schooling, and we were told that we would be capable of thinking correctly because of this education. Because of the conviction that this sort of conventional schooling leads to correct thinking, it is common to see in people the certainty that they are correct based on this assumed logic and reason.

However, although they have been using apparently logical reasoning processes, they have *not* been using logic and reasoning that flow from open intelligence, which is the most comprehensive order of intelligence. It does not matter how

108

much confidence we have in the logic and reason we have acquired if they are fundamentally incorrect! By relying on open intelligence, we come to see that we are naturally spontaneously endowed with the correct process of logic and reasoning.

We were told that we had certain physical and mental characteristics and that these are what constitute a human being. We were not told, "Your actual basis is indestructible, no matter what appears within it. You are the basic space of all the data. Nothing that appears has a nature independent from that basic space." To treat data as though they were something that had power and influence to possibly harm us is an incorrect perception.

The idea that identity is based solely on the flesh and blood form is dissolving, because we have many relationships online today that do not have any real verification that there is a flesh-and-blood person involved. At one time it would have been unthinkable to have a relationship with someone unless they were present in some way based on a flesh-and-blood form, but now with the digital world we have all sorts of ways to express identity. Our identification with body, speech and mind as something that is comprised of flesh and blood is loosening up completely, and these are very major shifts in the way we live, but the power of open intelligence allows us to shift with these changes in a very easeful way.

Our identity still includes body, speech and mind, but not in the way we have thought about it for thousands of years. Our body, speech and mind are expanding and extending, our qualities and activities are expanding and extending, and our whole sense of identity is expanding and extending.

We can now re-train ourselves to completely encompass everything we think about ourselves with the open-intelligence view. Instead of feeling ourselves to be fixed, concrete and physicalized, we release into the openness of space. We are not separate from the openness of space, and when we look closely we can find no clear and definitive boundary of where we begin or end.

We really have to take a look at the assumptions we have made about ourselves. Do we really want to pour our lives into a lot of psychological, religious or economic descriptions of what a human being is? If we are not happy with our life, do we need to start doing positive affirmations whenever something difficult comes up? Do we want to avoid and ignore completely what is coming up? Do we want to continue to use all sorts of antidotes to deal with the things that bother us?

Many of the things that we learn in our lives are actually defenses or barriers—trying to keep the negative feelings at bay or trying to keep the immensity of negativity away from us completely—and most of us are pretty skilled at that. Some of us may have a very turbulent emotional life, in which we cannot help what we feel or think, and it is wild and woolly all the time. Yet, something as extreme as this, which is very often considered a great disability, can be a welcome friend, because if we happen to have that kind of mind, there is so much incentive to find a way to be able to be at ease with it.

Looking at the world only from the vantage of data is very narrow and fixed, but when we are introduced to open intelligence, we are instantaneously introduced to an entirely new perspective. Just as reified intelligence had colored every single aspect of our lives, now open intelligence shines forth as every aspect of our lives. There is such a radical distinction between the reified knower and doer and the open-intelligence knower and doer. The reified knower and doer is continuously living under the limitation and restriction of their own personal history, while the open-intelligence knower and doer is living without the limitations and restrictions of relying merely on data.

Our sense of identity begins to change, because it is being nurtured by open intelligence rather than data. We no longer see life in the same way, and our characteristics, qualities and activities of body, speech and mind completely change due to open intelligence. This is the real significance of human identity—education, empowerment and mobilization through open intelligence to use the innate qualities and activities of body, speech and mind in a beneficial way. Body, speech and mind are brought to the full richness and power of beneficial qualities and activities, and in this is complete life satisfaction and flourishing. Now we are empowered to lead ourselves and to lead others.

We had not been educated before about our beneficial power, but now we are being educated in that way. Once we are empowered by open intelligence, we all join together in open-intelligence society for the benefit of all. As a human society, we are no longer living the way we have lived for thousands of years. We are establishing a new platform for the expansion of identity.

Up until this point in time our identity as human beings has been shaped around ideas that say we have some kind of original flaw that needs to be overcome. The shift from seeing ourselves as flawed to seeing ourselves as beneficial and responsible for actual empowerment of our beneficial abilities and qualities is something quite new, but we are beneficial. However, no one else can convince us that we are beneficial; we have to see it in our own experience.

How do we see that? We see it by relying on open intelligence. By relying on open intelligence we find that personal problems we could never overcome have no meaning to us any longer. The anger or the depression that used to really get to us is not a pressing issue any longer. We see that open intelligence is sovereign, and through this recognition we undergo an incredible shift within ourselves.

This very moment of open intelligence is the only conclusive evidence ever of who we are. In that there is complete freedom from all fixed frameworks whatsoever. Not just freedom, but also absolute courage—simple and complete in itself with no point of reference as to an accumulated identity.

FIXED GENDER IDENTITIES FALL AWAY

It can seem a little jarring or disconcerting if we have had a lot of fixed ideas about ourselves, and then all of a sudden open intelligence is alive and real. We thought we knew exactly who we were, and now all of a sudden it does not look that way at all. Whatever seemed to be supporting that identity isn't there anymore, so it can feel like the bottom has fallen out.

Long-held and very fixed identities begin to fall away. For example, we no longer have fixed ideas about what it means to be a man or a woman. From the moment we were born we have been called either male or female, but this is not our fundamental identity. In one moment we may be very female and in another moment we may be very male, or we may be something else; however, this complexity of ways of considering identity could not be dependent on genitalia alone. Instead of being fixed in the identity of "I am a woman," or "I am a man," we instinctively recognize open intelligence as our fundamental identity.

If we want to truly know about our femininity or our masculinity, it is already known in open intelligence. By the power of open intelligence we are a real person without a lot of trumped-up ideas about who we are, who we have been and who we will be in the future. We have learned to make everything so complicated, but we find out that it is actually very simple, and at the same time very radical, very fruitful, very fired up right now.

It is very, very important to know that gender identity is also a political matter and that whoever we think we are, that identity either plays into reification or it does not. If we really make a decision about our politic of identity by taking responsibility for our data, then we are truly in a position of power, because what we are saying is, "No matter what description comes up, it is empowered by open intelligence, and I am going to commit myself to that open-intelligence quality."

When we come to see what our true identity is, rather than having everybody else deciding what our identity is, we see that we are not weak, powerless and helpless. Truly powerful people know how to take care of themselves and the world they live in. We clearly see reality and are then able to take care of things in a real way. This is what it comes down to. We are our own authority in that, and we know where we are; no one else needs to tell us that. The authenticity of our own experience is the validity of open intelligence.

When it comes to sexual identity and how one is going to participate sexually, one can have all kinds of thoughts about things like that, but the instinctive realization of open intelligence is one of transmutation of all conduct to that of profound benefit. "Instinctive recognition" means that the recognition does not require thought or reason to keep it in place. It is instinctive, just naturally present, and that makes it simple and easy.

All conduct is brought to the highest level of spontaneous benefit. We are no longer motivated by twitches and twinges of all these sexual data; rather, we have a fundamentally clear ethic that can never be disturbed. It is without the need to gain anything for oneself—but simply to be and share with others in a relaxing way.

According to conventional thinking, a human being is limited to a body and a gender, but according to the explosion of open intelligence power and benefit, the body is equal in size to the entirety of everything. That is the actual body: the entirety of everything! That is your actual body shining forth in this very moment. Open intelligence is bodiless, yet vividly apparent as the body. Bodiless open intelligence is completely robust, outshining every single here-and-now.

EUREKA, I HAVE FOUND IT!

In light of the discussion in this chapter on the total transformation of identity, it would be quite helpful to offer a real life example that illustrates what is being expressed. What follows below is a short description from Candice O'Denver, the founder of Balanced View, of a total and immediate shift in identity that occurred for her thirty years ago.

In developing a steady familiarization with the open-intelligence view, there is instinctive recognition of the primordial inseparability of the open-intelligence view and all data. Now, when this occurred for me, it was really exciting. I was in a town called Eureka in Northern California. Eureka means "I have found it," so in the town of Eureka I could really say, "I have found it!"

In my life at that time I had all sorts of afflictive data streams coming uncontrollably, and they were even more painful than they had ever been before. They were scary to the point of being terrifying, and I knew for sure that there was no antidote whatsoever that was going to work against them.

Although I had lived my entire life with a commitment to benefit all, I had only intermittently *instinctively comprehended and realized* open intelligence and its beneficial potency spontaneously infusing mind, speech, body, qualities and activities.

So, even though I had already reached the point of knowing that there was no antidote to data streams whatsoever, I went out that day and I drank three Heineken beers with my lunch, yet the Heineken beer did nothing for me. If it did anything, it just made the data streams worsen. I felt even more terrified and more paranoid, so at that time I could know for sure that drinking beer was also just an antidote.

I had quite a few friends, and we all lived a life of service to the benefit of all. I also had a new friend who had appeared suddenly out of the blue, and he was in such incredible pain with a sense of total overwhelm and confusion. He felt he had been humiliated by his wife, and then following that she had left him. He was feeling totally bereft and not knowing what to do. He did not know how he was going to get the energy up to do the big commercial fishing expedition that lay ahead of him.

Even though I had immense terror and paranoia and a personally violent circumstance that had just occurred in my own life, all I wanted to do was to offer benefit to my troubled friend. I thought, "Well, I can just be of support to him, and that's what I'll do. I'll be of service to this person, and then that's how I'm going to spend my time, rather than thinking about all my own data streams, such as drinking alcohol." I did that in whatever simple way I could. I would be of service and hang out, make a cup of coffee or tea, go for a walk or to a movie or whatever it might be. I'd listen to him for hours and hours as he told the story about his whole life—how as a child his parents had punished him by locking him in a closet for days, pushing trays of food for him to eat in a dark space.

I listened to him and supported him for ten days, and then within that there arose the power of complete willingness, I would say, to be of profound benefit. With that power also shone forth incredible lucidity; they co-emerged inseparably. I could see that all of the negative thoughts and tremendous afflictions that I was having really had open intelligence as their core—the great willingness to be of benefit to all.

This grew in me more and more. I saw that I could go directly to the potency of lucidity and benefit through short moments, rather than to the reified description of the affliction that told me it had an independent power to hurt me or ruin my life. I could go to open intelligence's core strength of benefit, to the actual spontaneous ability and power to benefit all. So, I relied on short moments over and over again as they spontaneously occurred to me, and then all of a sudden I had a thought, "Well gosh, if this applies to the negative data, it must apply to the positive and neutral data, too." I saw this very clearly, and so I started relying on open intelligence in the positive and neutral data as well.

Then I came to a point where I was just completely flooded with that recognition; I was consumed by the outshining of all data. I was sitting in a coffee shop with the new friend that I'd spent the ten days with, and I said to him, "Well, it seems that what happened with you is that when your parents were so abusive to you, you grew up thinking that that's what love is, because they said they loved you, yet they abused you. So you've had this unconscious confusion that abuse is love."

When I said that to him, it was like all of the lights went on, and he understood his whole life completely, including the trauma he had had with his former wife. Additionally, in that very moment all of my own data streams were outshone, just as his were. Now what about that? It was a very convincing demonstration, and I just sat there saying, "Wow! Wow! Wow! Wow!"

All of my life passed before me, and I saw how each incident in my life had great meaning and purpose in bringing me to this moment. I knew I would never drink alcohol again, because I had now found what I had been looking for in alcohol. The meaning of eternity came clear as inexhaustible open intelligence. All fears of death disappeared, never to return. The obsession I had with being a perfect mother was fulfilled in open intelligence—the perfect parent of everyone. The only thing I could think to call open intelligence was perfect love. I knew that whatever people thought about God or love, this is what it is: totally perfect love, and that it is available right here. Then a powerful force moved me to share what we had realized with all people. Moreover, it was absolutely clear that I *would* share it with all people.

These are just a few comments about my own experience, so that you can understand the power of open intelligence in an actual person's life. For me this outshining allowed me to go beyond all conventional limits surrounding a personal identity. It allowed me to form associations with other people who felt the same way and who wanted to work with me on Balanced View's global organizing at the local community level. Immediately I started looking for other people, and with everyone I met, I would wait for them to offer some hint that they were interested. So, that's how all of Balanced View formed.

We knew that everyone must be educated in the nature of their own mind, their own human nature, rather than relying on the internally oppressive ideas they had been taught. Empowerment of open intelligence is the unending solution in all circumstances. Empowerment of everyone in the beneficial potency of open intelligence is spreading like wildfire. You can count on it without fail.

Chapter Nine

DISCOVERING OUR GIFTS, STRENGTHS AND TALENTS

We all have very special gifts, strengths and talents to contribute to the world, and with greater assurance in open intelligence these gifts become blazingly clear, even if we had not known what they were before. If we have not seen these talents in ourselves, it can be guaranteed that in open-intelligence community someone will be able to point them out for us! They will recognize our potential and make sure that we know what it is. That is of course a very joyful and supportive way to be together.

When the pure benefit that is at the basis of everything is potentiated and utilized as the basis of human life, we have access to the best of our innate strengths, gifts and talents, and we contribute to a human society rich with inexhaustible prosperity and generosity. Each person has their own particular disposition, and there are many ways of expressing beneficial qualities and activities corresponding to this disposition. It does not matter who we are or what our IQ is, everyone is competent in open intelligence. Our strengths, gifts and talents automatically and spontaneously shine forth in open intelligence, and when trained in open intelligence anyone can realize their strengths, gifts and talents and share them with others.

Exalting ourselves and exalting others is what human life is about, and every single area of human knowledge is exalted by open intelligence. We are able to see ways to do things that have not been done before, we are able to discover what has not been discovered before, and it is so very self-confirming when we see this exaltation of capacity occurring in ourselves.

The entire human make-up—body, speech and mind—is intended and purposed for spontaneous benefit that is completely natural and always-on. And what does that mean exactly? Well, you wake up in the morning, and it is really exciting to be alive. You are looking forward to a day that will allow you to serve and benefit in so many different ways, and you are so grateful to have all the shining, joyful friends you have who will be serving and benefitting with you.

These are exquisitely beautiful illustrations that have a total ring of truth. They have such a profound resonance, and one really wants to hear more of them and have them be a part of one's own life.

A wonderful opportunity to experience this always-on benefit occurs when we come into a community of people totally relying on open intelligence. We can see there how open-intelligence society really operates—the ease, the fun, the enjoyment, the complete relaxation, the going from day-to-day looking forward to each new day, feeling completely attended to and taken care of, knowing that all of one's strengths, gifts and talents are completely honored and will be encouraged to be liberated even beyond the point that they already have been.

Genuine benefit comes down to the very simple everyday activities we are engaged in. The context of the benefit of all is a spontaneous aspiration and motivation to benefit in every way possible with every bit of available energy. We do not need to strive for this; it comes naturally from the complete reliance on open intelligence. We are naturally endowed with a motivation to be of benefit, because we are in fact altruistic to our very core. We care about the welfare of others from the moment we are born. Just look at a new baby: a baby is all about connecting, wanting to be there with others, listening to others, taking up the ideas that others have to offer, wanting to fit in and wanting to belong.

THE CONTEXT OF BENEFIT

We each have different strengths, gifts and talents, and due to the power of open intelligence we will have the courage to utilize them skillfully. This is the power of open intelligence; it allows us to stand straight and strong and to know that it is possible to contribute in a very profound way.

The identification of strengths, gifts and talents comes about through the comprehensive view of open intelligence. Through the recognition of open intelligence we are naturally empowered to take action and to move forward without fear or hesitation. Let's say we have a new idea that goes against practically everything that has ever been said before, and yet we feel emboldened to move forward despite great opposition. It is in a situation like this where we see the empowerment and fearlessness coming into play that we have found in open intelligence.

The fearlessness, strength and courage come because we have laser-like insight and total reliance on the wisdom of open intelligence. We know what the value of the idea is, and we can fearlessly and courageously state that clearly. We find within ourselves unshakable fearlessness that can never be taken away. With that comes the courage to act from fearlessness and to set aside all conventional outlooks, approaches and ways of looking at everything.

"How can I make good decisions?" is a question that almost everyone asks. By the power of open intelligence the whole process of excessive negativity and problem-orientation is completely resolved and replaced by a solution-orientation. There is no more talking for hours about the problem and excessive negativity about this, that and the other thing; rather, a complete solution-orientation takes over which so readily supports the making of clear decisions.

With all decisions and opportunities placed before us, we ask, "What will be of greatest benefit to all?" That is an easy way to make decisions! The direction that comes from the answer to that question is the direction we want to take. All the grueling thought processes involved in thinking over a decision are outshone by the blaze of open intelligence, and then, *boom*, the decision is made in, of, as and through open intelligence with the intention of expressing the highest possible benefit. That is how simple this is, and everything about life can be that way, because everything has the relaxed attitude of its natural state.

We become powerful decision-makers in terms of how best to utilize our talents. What incredible things do we want to commit to? What mountain do we want to climb? We have tremendous capacity, and we can take that capacity as far as we want it to go. All the considering we have done about our life and how we are going to use our body, mind and speech is cleared up completely in short moments of open intelligence. The richer open intelligence is in our experience, the clearer it is to us what to do and how to act.

A PANORAMIC VISTA

Another term for the treasure that is being described here is "open-ended knowledge creation." It is a matter of knowing that we are in fact open-ended benefit and knowledge creators and then growing into that and getting used to that. This is true about all aspects of the instinctive recognition of open intelligence; it is a matter of getting used to it. We already are vast and intelligent and we already are clear about everything—it is just a matter of getting used to it!

Open intelligence and the skilled utilization of gifts, strengths and talents must be trained up fully in order to let their powers really roar. Otherwise, we cannot see beyond what is conventional and what everyone else is doing. Training up open intelligence is like any other means of familiarization with a particular skill; it must be used again and again until it is completely familiar, to the point of spontaneity. It is just like learning to tie our shoes, ride a bicycle or brush our teeth. We continue to train these things up until, over time, they become completely spontaneous abilities.

Having perfected the readily available instinctive recognition of open intelligence by not moving away from it and by remaining always in and as it, we shine forth as the power of open intelligence. We become an irresistible human being, and many other people are able to recognize that. What is more, they recognize their own irresistibility in our irresistibility! They say, "Wow, I can be like that, too."

No matter what field we are in, through the power of open intelligence we have a whole new panoramic vista. We build whatever we want to build without being limited by convention. We can build something on our own, or we can find other people committed to open intelligence who will help us in the building. The easiest and most profoundly powerful way to live life is with other people committed to open intelligence.

If we have nothing to prove—where everything is just left totally *as it is*—then there is a true connection with other people, and the spontaneity of interaction really opens up. It is a spontaneous quality that allows for the zenith statement to be made in whatever that interaction is. It does not matter what it is; it could be in sitting right wherever we are or in speaking to the toll taker on the highway or in addressing a room full of people—it is such a complete, open connectivity in which everything is very direct, precise and right on. All the unnecessary chatter settles out and the core power of potent speech that is very directed and purposeful comes to the fore. This is the expression of the enormous potency of open intelligence, and it clears everything up absolutely.

THE INNOVATIVE VANTAGE

Through the innovative vantage of open intelligence, we are able to see incredible new ways to do things that are extraordinarily beneficial to many, many beings. As we get more and more familiar with open intelligence, we find that we are flooded by new insights and ways of looking at things. In fact, we get to the point where our insights are really fantastic. We have the feeling that we would never have enough lifetimes to take action on all the fantastic insights we have had!

The open-intelligence choice is a life plan that takes over everything and directs the flow of life without any pondering or effort at all. The radical shift from being totally self-centered to being mutually aligned and mutually connected with everyone and everything is a completely different orientation. We are not making the choice any longer to go the ordinary way or to merely make ordinary decisions. We are completely reoriented to the perception of the world as it really is—the open-intelligence world—a world of constant solution, a world of piercing statements that connect, that go right to the heart, that bind everyone in mutuality, trust, collaboration and in the power to solve the problems that might come up.

There are sometimes very difficult and challenging tasks to perform, and we might arrive at a point where we say, "Oh, I cannot go any further. I couldn't possibly do any more than this." But what does it matter if we feel that we cannot do something? We just resolve to do it anyway! We show ourselves that we can do it, instead of taking the I-can't-do-it trip. We discover the resources we need in order to get it done, and we rely on all the powers of pure benefit to carry out our intention.

Everything could look like it is going to fall apart, but suddenly we might see, "Wow! That isn't the case at all. I can find a way to do this." We see that we can compose that concerto, we can solve that computer problem, we can figure out how to feed 150 people in a dining hall that only seats 70. If the point eventually comes where we are fully convinced, "I just cannot do this," then that is a good time to relax completely, allowing all the data to be as they are and to really rely on open intelligence to see how best to move forward.

In this generation of human society, for the first time in a widespread way human beings are claiming the power of their own open intelligence and claiming the power of beneficial action and of the power to be of benefit to all. It is the strongest basis in terms of any projects we are facing, especially where we might feel any kind of overwhelming doubt. Because we have gained trust and assurance in open intelligence from the successful completion of other projects, now with any new set of circumstances that we face where doubt might arise, we have trust and assurance that we will find the best solution. We use that trust to enliven the current project, knowing that what we are facing now will be enlivened and supported by the beneficial insights we gained in past projects. In the process of finding the perfect solution, it seems to be so often the case that something wonderful happens that is totally unexpected which brings such great innovation.

If we just allow the open-intelligence view to come alive within an individual and support them in their strengths, gifts and talents, the result is an incredible outcome that could not have been achieved by conventional means. We can see this over and over again in communities around the world where people are committed to open intelligence. This is the living evidence.

QUINTESSENTIAL KNOWLEDGE

The quintessential knowledge of open intelligence surpasses and subsumes all other knowledge-seeking; it is the knowledge-seeking that does not require any work. Knowledge comes effortlessly and easily, just at the moment when it is needed. Of all human knowledge at this time it is the most profound, as it presents a comprehensive map of knowledge and instruction, whereby each and every human being reaches the highest accomplishment and complete enjoyment of mind, speech, body qualities and activities.

No matter how great an accomplishment might be when using reified intelligence, it falters in the face of what it could be with open intelligence turned on. We already have many brilliant people in the world, and by putting the open-intelligence upgrade in the mix, it allows everyone to boost their natural strengths, gifts and talents to an extraordinary degree.

In letting everything be *as it is,* we go against everything we ever learned, and we can live unflinchingly. We become citizens of open intelligence in that we get to the point where each data stream is completely outshone. This is the very real experience of leaving everything *as it is;* everything is seen to be the brilliant energy of beneficial open intelligence.

We live in an era now where there are many new skillful means that can be used, and all of these are weaving together into a singular open intelligence. It is something that cannot be plotted or mapped on a particular course, as it is spontaneously and naturally evolving.

In this era of rapid scientific and technological advancement, there are changes coming about that are totally incredible. As a society we will no longer be living the way we have been living, and increasingly more and more people will live with total commitment to open intelligence. This is a totally awesome time to be alive, and each one of us is a precious resource; we are here at this time for a specific reason.

Certain people are adopting instinctive recognition of open-intelligence benefit and others are not. Those who are willing to participate do so, and others do not, but it is just like the adoption of any other technology: the more effective the technology is, the more people will want to adopt it. That is just the way it is. This is a shift that is required. Maybe before in human history the adoption of this technology was not required, but now it is an imperative.

One of the first questions people ask upon introduction to open intelligence is, "Well, what can I do that will be of benefit to all?" If that is a question you have had, it is a good idea at that point to write a paragraph about what you would most like to do, and then with the assistance of the trainer your talents can be matched up to the best service task. It could be that you will be given a task that you think you could not possibly do, but through relying on open intelligence and discovering your talents through applying yourself to the allotted task, the full potency of the open-intelligence factor is allowed to come forth. Often what one finds is that not only does one have the capacity to accomplish the task, but the capacity is discovered to exceed the projected outcome. This is a very interesting skillful means, because it allows one to be engaged in beneficial conduct while experiencing the transmission of open intelligence.

KEY POINTS AND PIVOTAL INSTRUCTIONS

If we go to school to learn math or reading or science, there are key points and pivotal instructions that must be learned; otherwise, there will be things that are not understood, and the ability will not be present to put that subject matter into action. The same is true with open-intelligence training; there are key points and pivotal instructions that are very important, and indeed required.

There are certain skillful means that evoke open intelligence in many, many people. All of the different decisions we make about the way a training is going to be presented at any given time should be based on what will be of the most benefit to all. What are we seeing that really works with people? What are we seeing that might even work better? Nothing need be laid down in stone forever; the skillful means of the training should be a dynamic process that is unending.

Whereas before we may not have had a platform for the full expression of our gifts, strengths and talents, now we do. Not only do we have a hope for this, we have the promise of it if we just follow simple instructions. That is of course a really big change, and we see in our own experience the benefit from the outset.

Potent open intelligence, when recognized as the fully evident, beneficial ground of all data, dwells as an unchanging intelligence in a mode of supreme benefit. That open-intelligence factor is right here in our own basic cognizance. We cannot really trace it anywhere; if we look for it inside, we cannot find it, and if we look for it outside, we cannot find it. We can just say that it is wide-open and spacious like the sky.

Human intelligence is now massively networked, and as that opens up more and more, the networking will not just be with human intelligence; it will be with all kinds of intelligences everywhere. Our own intelligence will expand into a power beyond anything we can imagine, settling completely into the capacity to provide all the resources we need.

By the power of open intelligence we open up to the natural resource that can never be depleted, and in it we find all the resources we need. Infinite power and capacity are already built in, and all of it is accessed in this simple moment of open intelligence. This moment of open intelligence is direct accessibility and direct connectivity to the potent intelligence of nature instantiated right here. The potencies of mind, speech, body, qualities and activities and the full expression of inherent gifts, strengths and talents are thereby empowered.

RAMPING UP THE AGE OF HUMAN EMPOWERMENT
AND ERA OF GREAT BENEFIT

In this Age of Human Empowerment and Era of Great Benefit, the power of great benefit that we as individuals contain is being ramped up, and all of the stories, mythologies and ideologies that have driven us so far are being re-examined. We are looking at things from the vantage of our own direct experience, and we are no longer so much relying on authority figures to tell us what we should do. This gives us a powerful force for change as a society.

When this power of open intelligence from many, many individuals flows into institutions, then we can build institutions and organizations that are based on a culture of gratitude and respect, where everyone is working together for the benefit of all—rather than everyone working together to fill their wallets or to get what they want for themselves. The motivation completely changes.

If you are wondering what to do with your life, just get familiar with open intelligence, and then you will know what to do. Maybe the option you are involved in right now will not be the option you will be choosing in the future. You may find out that there are a lot of things you absolutely will not do any longer. You will for sure no longer debase yourself, and you will not debase others.

You stop bothering yourself about every single datum that you have and toiling over what to do with all those data. You just stop; you will not do it anymore. The best advice would be to go to any lengths to have that as your primary project, because you cannot go wrong there.

For instance, you might leave your present job, even though it was your only source of income, because you decided, "This job isn't a place where I feel comfortable, and it is not a place that is really calling on my gifts, strengths and talents." Many people have made this choice because of their commitment to open intelligence, and it has posed no threat to them. Many people have gone completely and totally against everything their parents and all of society told them to do with the skills they had. Where did they get the courage to do so? They got it from the power of open intelligence.

Our parents might want us to live a certain way, our husband or wife may have very specific expectations for us and other people we are associated with will expect us to live a certain way. However, because of the power of open intelligence, we can see how to be a true participant in a healthy human society and how to be of benefit to all. We can see how to go beyond all the fixed frameworks that society has given us which we took on willingly before our introduction to open intelligence. We take the open-intelligence pill and let that intelligence soak into every single aspect of our life. By doing so, we end up doing a lot of things in life that we never dreamt possible.

We have the power to change the world with short moments of open intelligence. The world is undergoing a change that exalts human culture and its relation with all beings forever. There isn't a single solitary creature whatsoever that is not endowed with the pervasive spread of open intelligence.

Short moments spontaneously prolong into days, weeks, months and years of obvious open intelligence with no need any longer for moments. Yet, each short moment is an indestructible infrastructure for a human society that is of benefit to all. Education in the nature of mind is indestructible social change.

Society is shifting to a future where there will be no memory of a time without open intelligence. There won't be even a vague memory of what it was like to live in neediness, scarcity, lack, loneliness or emotional and mental instability. It is a total shift—an exciting, manifest realization that is happening right now before our very eyes!

Claim and acknowledge the open intelligence power that belongs to you. It is your birthright—the most basic human right.

Chapter Ten

WHAT WON'T WEAR OFF

In Balanced View you find what won't wear off. By letting the razzle-dazzle of temporary highs be as they are, they flow on by and you enter what you can count on—an unending increase of sheer completion. In primordial open intelligence, there are no states, levels or paths to go on. As the lucidity of the vast expanse of great benefit is already established, it does not need to be recreated.

In the spontaneous existence of pure space, there are no paths to be walked, no levels to climb and no destination. Like pure space, open intelligence has no data that need to be analyzed and understood, and that being so, there is nothing to achieve through contrived effort.

This lifestyle of great benefit is to be found in spontaneous existence—the expansion of intelligence *as it is* in its inexhaustibly open reach and range. Without so much as a speck of obscurity found anywhere—its purity instinctive, subsuming the range of comprehension and with spontaneous presence the only location—its elusive exaltation is not something to comprehend or obtain. Forever on the move without going anywhere, amazement is the name of its magical display. Here one instant, gone the next!

Attempts to contrive the great benefit of open intelligence only lead to confusion and despair. Similarly, it would be preposterous to attempt to create space through the contrivance of paths and levels. Even pointing it out would reveal only the exhaustion of so much pointing!

Complete confirmation offers empowerment of the sheer potency of utter relaxation, which is the charm! Instinctive realization, the direct experiential affirmation, is the lived reality of wondrous qualities and activities of mind, speech and body. These results alone prove the point.

In reality, that which is the totality of reified appearances shines forth individually and collectively as the dynamic beneficial activity of indivisible open intelligence. Following on from that, since open intelligence does not move from its own self-illuminating status, it is called "great benefit." As the display of its dynamic activity shines forth, its dynamism is benefit that is unbounded and unlimited.

Allowing that dynamic energy to proceed to self-release in its expanse of pure open intelligence brings to a complete stop the wrong apprehension of an independent nature in data. Thus, confusion is completely outshone, and clarity, discernment and insight are established.

SPONTANEOUS BENEFIT: A SIGNIFICANT KEY POINT

This is a highly cherished key point. It is placed here for the purpose of demonstrating once again the difference between spontaneous benefit and contrived benefit.

Spontaneous benefit is based on reality and is indestructible. It is indivisible from the spontaneous existence of open intelligence's beneficial potency, which appears as a multitude of skillful means ranging from peaceful to very fierce. Spontaneous benefit is already existent and is always a perfect fit for time, place and circumstance. Primordially here and without contrivance, spontaneous benefit is always so.

The most fundamental spontaneous benefit is that which is immediate and which pervades all—equally and evenly. This is instinctively recognized through introduction to open intelligence and through the short moments practice. As the immediate benefit of open intelligence is so very real and obvious, it confirms and affirms the relaxed potency that is our only actually-occurring identity.

It is important to note that the Four Mainstays are the easiest means to recognize open intelligence and its powers of great benefit, due to the ready availability of every kind of support for doing so within each of the Mainstays. Spontaneous benefit does not wear off; it is inexhaustibly increasing in its reach and in its evidence in mind, speech, body, qualities and activities.

Contrived benefit is based on cause and effect and is driven by conceived effort. It is a process of trying to develop or gain positive qualities and activities in order to win friendship and support and to be recognized as a good person. There is, however, no such accomplishment to be done. The roots of contriving benefit can be directly traced to the notion that has been spread throughout global culture that humans are basically flawed and must be taught to be good and beneficial.

As this conceptual framework is so remote from the reality of human nature—yet so ingrained in human ways and means—it is solely through a radical paradigm shift that human beings will join in their true reality, rather than continuing with conduct which is entirely unsuited to what is real. Right now, this shift is exactly what is occurring in what is called the "Age of Human Empowerment and the Era of Great Benefit." What a relief it is to know these are unending!

Like heat is with fire and wetness is with water, spontaneous benefit is always here and does not meet or depart from reality *as it is* in elaboration-free equality. Elaboration-free equality pervading all elaboration renders elaboration itself free of elaboration! This demonstrates that elaboration is in fact filled with the most comprehensive and inexhaustible intelligence of great benefit. Again, what a wondrous marvel this is: seeing how we have tricked ourselves into believing in the stress and strain of cultivating benefit, when in reality pure benefit is our spontaneous nature.

Immediate benefit is right here, right now.

NO-SELF AND NONDUALITY

As open intelligence is all-encompassing, it includes self and no-self, duality and nonduality. Some segments of popular culture are focused on the conceptual frameworks of nonduality and no-self as a destination or positive state in itself. However, this is a grave error caused by lack of proper education in the nature of mind. The nature of open intelligence is indivisible, all-inclusive and spontaneously present, open and pure. If we have accidentally become trapped in the data stream of nonduality or no-self, we immediately need to find a Balanced View trainer who can transmit the authentic introduction to open intelligence. Without this proper introduction, we are at great risk.

PERFECT LOVE

In open intelligence the most perfect love there is—the power of great benefit—is spontaneously present. We do not need to contrive qualities and activities in order to find perfect love; it is always already present. We were meant to have the incredible connection in life of sharing true open-ended knowledge, benefit and love-creation.

Everything we think, feel, say, do and experience in every single moment is a highlighting of the inexhaustibility of open intelligence, so there isn't any place to get to. We can look around and we can see that all data, no matter what they are, are encompassed and pervaded by open intelligence. It is just absolutely clear; there is no other way that anything would be.

Precious data are the liveliness of nature's intelligence filled with total openness. No matter what data shine forth, the data are safe and clear, just like open intelligence is safe and clear and perfect love is safe and clear. By relying on perfect love itself, we are like a rainbow in the sky: just as a rainbow in the sky is inseparable from space itself, so too our very own precious self is inseparable from perfect love, which is synonymous with open intelligence.

When we commit to love of self, we commit to the Age of Human Empowerment and Era of Great Benefit. Each moment we rely on open intelligence, we rely on perfect love itself, and by relying on perfect love itself we bring love to the world. This is what the Era of Great Benefit truly is—living from love and from perfect love-relating in all relationships.

The instinctive realization of open intelligence is inclusive of a great spontaneity of love and caring beyond anyone's wildest imagination. The full love-potency of every individual on earth is so strong and so filled with great force—meaning that love is accompanied by the great energy of action. What love actually is cannot really be explained; only through giving oneself entirely to open intelligence can it be discovered. When we seek for love in another person, it is this incomprehensible love that we are actually seeking.

We are all endowed with the perfect love that is experienced most keenly in the spontaneously felt sense of wanting to benefit all. The desire to benefit is not a matter of learning anything or doing anything, because *it already is*; it is the reality of human nature. It truly already is; it cannot be learned or fabricated. If we have lived in any way other than in spontaneous benefit, it is just a matter of slowly getting used to it through the natural expansion of open intelligence that comes about most readily through the Four Mainstays lifestyle. We find out who we are and what our power is and how to use it for the benefit of all.

We start to see that love is something much different from the usual conventional notions about it. We discover that we can find love in the depths of our own afflictive data. This is so unlike what we have learned, yet this insight is the gateway to the most comprehensive open intelligence in which positive, negative and neutral data are subsumed into open intelligence's beneficial potency. All of the data about ourselves that we have tried to indulge, avoid or replace, *that* is where we find real love, real open intelligence. It is very empowering to rely on open intelligence while letting all these data just flow on by. As our intelligence opens up, we care more, we love more and we are capable of tremendous intimacy.

NEVER FALLING OUT OF LOVE

It is only possible to find permanent comfort and happiness in open intelligence—the most comprehensive order of intelligence that subsumes all ordinary definitions of data into itself. To subsume ordinary definitions of data requires that we allow everything to be *as it is*. We go through the flow moment-to-moment as open intelligence itself and as perfect love itself, with our whole being pervaded by open intelligence. In future generations everyone will be knowingly empowered by open intelligence. We are all empowered by open intelligence, whether we realize it or not; it is just that if we know it, life is a lot more fun!

Once our profound gift of perfect love is introduced to us, then we are really clear for the first time. We instinctively recognize open intelligence empowering everyone with its potency to create open-intelligence society. How do we do this? By first of all loving ourselves freely and openly and completely and by taking care of ourselves in the best way possible by letting all data be as they are.

Falling in love with our own data really allows us to love freely and openly. When we really love our data as they are, then we love all other data exactly as they are. We are then able to look at ourselves and at other people and love them exactly as they are too, being completely open to anything they have to say or do and never falling out of love. There is no escape hatch in perfect love. There might be a change in the nature of relationship, but there is never falling out of love.

Always being totally and completely in love is truly the easy way. Let there be no confusion whatsoever about what open intelligence is: perfect love itself, and that's it—the basis and fundamental reality for everyone.

We are able to feel such a strong connection of perfect love with everyone, and no matter what people do, we can see that they are basically the effervescence of benefit and of perfect love. Even if they act in extreme and bizarre ways, nothing they do can convince us that their fundamental nature is other than the great benefit of open intelligence. We are each born this way, and it is simply a matter of nurturing our profound giftedness in open intelligence.

The spacious life satisfaction created by this perfect love is the most potent benefit we can ever give ourselves throughout our entire life. By committing ourselves one hundred percent to standing up as open intelligence, we give ourselves the greatest gift possible, and we also are of benefit to the world in the greatest way possible. If we had a life of endless trying-to-be-of-benefit without open intelligence, it would be a good, dutiful life for certain; however, it would not be nearly as powerful, spontaneous and potent as it is with open intelligence at the fore. Open intelligence is the greatest natural resource and the greatest force there is, and we are each endowed with natural intelligence, natural warmth and natural openness.

FROM THE VERY BEGINNING

As babies we were all born in open intelligence and in great completion, and whether we were laughing or crying we were completely at ease. Now, what if from the beginning of our life we had been told to let data be as they are and we had everyone around us joining in—each of us participating in loving data and knowing exactly how to love the data from others. If that were so, then whoever was teaching us would know exactly how to train us in perfect love of self, which always includes love of everyone. From the beginning of our life we would enjoy the love of self we naturally enjoy anyway as a baby.

If we were trained in self-love, then when we had different data streams in our completely open baby-intelligence, we would immediately recognize that as a shining reflection of our own crystal ball-like intelligence, which is open and spacious like the sky. Self-love is the seamless accommodation of all data as open intelligence with nothing left out. If we had such information from the beginning and saw it reflected in society, we would automatically know that we are not a victim of any data. This data would be simply seen as a self-reflection that is pure—pure exactly like we are totally pure. This is key to loving ourselves: harmonizing all of our data streams, letting them be exactly as they are and not needing to indulge, avoid or replace any of them.

We would see that our intelligence is completely open and endless, always spontaneously present in whatever is appearing and seamlessly indivisible from all data, just like the sky is seamlessly indivisible from space. When we eventually learn these things about our true nature, for many of us they take hold immediately. We know that we are hearing the truth about who we are. We feel fed, as if we were receiving the best food we have ever had. Why is this so? It is because we are nurturing and being nurtured by open intelligence.

FILLED WITH LOVE, WARMTH AND OPENNESS

Circumstantially we each have our own data streams, whatever they might be. They are unlike those of anyone else, so while we are all indivisible and seamless open intelligence, at the same time we are special and unique, and we have a specific set of gifts, talents and strengths to offer for the benefit of all. We are all born with the profound giftedness of open intelligence's power of perfect love. Perfect love is inseparable from open intelligence's beneficial potency. This self-love is also self-illumination. When we empower the love of self and of all data, we empower the illumination of self and the care of self. When we do so, we find that we are profoundly gifted in love and love-relating, and we begin to feel comfortable in all circumstances.

Each day we feel that life is a miracle and that it is increasingly blissful, although this may not match our ideas about what bliss is, because our ideas about bliss are often misguided. Bliss is the instinctive recognition that no datum has an independent nature.

We first feel comfort with ourselves—a new comfort, which we may not have felt before, because it is impossible to feel comfortable with ourselves if we are always trying to indulge, avoid or replace data. We begin to feel in love, totally in love! We are in love with ourselves and others, maybe for the first time, and our life is a life of love, bliss and brightness. This love of self allows us to love freely and openly, and only when we have this love of self that allows us to love freely and openly can we begin to have truly harmonious relationships with others as well as to build organizations that are based in love-relating.

We are not usually trained to recognize our giftedness in perfect love, and when our giftedness in perfect love is diminished by indulging, avoiding or replacing data, this compromises our desire to really live as perfect love. This diminishment instills deep uncertainties in us, which include anxieties about the future. When we do not have the permission field of open intelligence's perfect love, we have doubts about what to do in life. Without the recognition of open intelligence, we can have an anxious, subtle complaining or muttering going on—a flow of negative thoughts, emotions, images and feelings—a constant under-mutter, you could call it.

When there is a profound gift present and it is not acknowledged, and instead all we have is the constant under-mutter, then what can come up? Depression, tension, panic attacks and feeling ill at ease. By acknowledging our own profound giftedness in open intelligence, all of these naturally fall away, because we are acknowledging the gift we were born with.

We are all born naturally in love with our own self and naturally in love with all other beings. We are all profoundly gifted in love capacity, and the more that we love ourselves by allowing everything to be *as it is,* the more our life becomes a magnificent love reflection and a magnificent flow of pure open intelligence. This natural open intelligence that is the essence of everything we perceive—including ourselves—is filled with love, warmth and openness. By the simple practice of letting our own data be exactly as they are, we come into real love for the first time. The introduction to open intelligence is the introduction to truly real love and love-relating.

So, first of all we need to relate with ourselves totally and completely and exactly as we are. It does not matter what is coming up or how that is labeled; leaving it *as it is* while we bask in open intelligence is what we want to do. We relax mind and body completely in the openness of harmonious relationship. This is what a short moment is, and by this power we come into the field of allowing ourselves to be exactly as we are. We take off our "look good suit" and we are naturally naked, pure, open and clear, leaving everything *as it is*. What a boon! What good fortune!

It may seem a little unusual at first, because we have needed to look a certain way and have a certain social respectability, along with so many other things we thought we had to have. However, when we are just as we are, we really recognize that our own self is nothing but open intelligence. This infuses, pervades and fuels everything we think, feel, say or do, and we do not have to contrive our behavior any longer.

We have profound giftedness in this love-intelligence, and we really want to take it seriously, just as we would if we had a profound gift in science or sports or music. It is an area of profound giftedness that we have as a circumstance of our birth. If we had a profound gift in physics, for example, we would want to know everything about physics that we could. So, in a similar way we become very acquainted with the giftedness of love-intelligence.

No matter who we are, we have incredible capacity. The way that this natural capacity—our natural strengths, gifts and talents—can come into being is through this care of the self, the perfect love of the self exactly *as it is*. In this we find true self-leadership for the first time. We are all powerful leaders, and there need not be any confusion about this any longer. By a commitment to our own being exactly *as it is*, we naturally affect others in a very profound way without even saying anything. The dynamics of even large groups of people can change by the presence of one person who is tuned in to perfect love.

One must have an instinctive recognition of perfect love and not just an intellectual recognition; it isn't just something one could think oneself into, but it is radically and obviously present at all times in our own experience. Only then is one able to use body, mind, speech, qualities and activities in the way that they were intended. We are all intended and purposed for our mind, speech, body, qualities and activities to shine with perfect love.

TRUE LOVE-RELATING

The drive to bond and connect with others is a natural drive; however, before we make any steps in terms of bonding with others it is crucially important to allow all data to be as they are and to fall in love with ourselves by throwing open the doors to all data—overt and hidden data. For a truly intimate, real relationship it is essential that the other person or people involved in the intimate relating have the same commitment to the Four Mainstays lifestyle.

Don't fool yourself by letting your bodily and emotional data lead the way. Intimate relating comes down to everyday practicality, all day long, so all partners want to be perfectly aligned in the reality of open intelligence, and in that way the relationship will work. Without the open-intelligence commitment and alignment, the relationship will fall apart, regardless of how dreamy-eyed and certain you are at the beginning. You are really shortchanging yourself if you choose a partner who does not have a Four Mainstays lifestyle well in place.

This is the way to go if you want to have an intimate relationship with someone else. The way to ensure that there will be a perfect relationship is by relying on perfect love itself—by caring for yourself and loving yourself first before making that step. In this way your choice will be very far-reaching, and it will not be limited by data streams. Your choice will be free of all limitations and restrictions, and you will be able to truly love and commit to others.

The love we are looking for has to be given first to oneself. This is the key to romantic love and the key to perfect heart-love. It guarantees that we can carry out the commitments we make in any kind of ceremony we have to celebrate that commitment. Almost everyone has at some point been interested in falling in love, and *falling in love is rooted in perfect love of all data streams*—letting each one be *as it is,* whatever it is. This is the great outshining of all data in perfect love, in open intelligence.

Very often, though, there is a lot of confusion about love. People associate love with biological or emotional urges that are like an itch that must be scratched, but these urges that seem like love most often are not really love at all; they are a data stream that has not been yet clarified or outshone in open intelligence. Usually, for many of us, being in love involves some kind of sexual urgency at some point, and there is a sexual need and it feels like it *must* be satisfied; however, in addition to such drives being beyond the scope of intervention by good logic and reason, these sexual urges most importantly are just completely open and free, spontaneously self-releasing as they are. Just that one incredible insight allows us so much expansion and so much more freedom in the ability and capacity to love. Sexual relating is brought into a whole new arena of pure pleasure and union.

We find a true love-relating that subsumes into it irrational and rational drives for physical involvement. We see then that the love that is there is a love that is inexhaustible. This recognition allows us then to see how love can be played out in many ways, but mostly as a love that can fuel our ability for benefit creation.

Otherwise, we tend to really get bogged down by what we could call the "falling-in-love" data stream, and we may go off in one circumstance or another where we really do not belong. We hide out in our couple-ness, and it seems like it is a matter of "us against the world." But if we continue to rely on open intelligence, that will restore us to sanity on this topic. We have an innate sanity, and it is revealed through resting naturally in open intelligence. From that vantage we can enjoy falling in love much more.

When we come into contact with people, we just love them naturally, and we may really feel that we have fallen in love with many others. We may also feel that "in-love" sort of feeling for one person, and that is fine too; however, we know now that it does not necessarily require sexual follow-through.

One of the things that comes from loving ourselves naturally and resting naturally in love of self is that we become much better at choosing someone we can actually be with and enjoy. It may take a while to find that special someone or it may not happen at all, but in open intelligence we have the discernment. This is an area where each of us as individuals can learn a great deal.

Discernment means that when we fall in love, we do not need to follow up on all these urges and surges, because through discernment there is an automatic spontaneous consideration of time, place and circumstance. We do not realize just our twitches and twangs; we realize *all* the factors that are going on in what is happening. We realize the whole retinue of people that the other person is involved with and the whole retinue of people we are involved with; we realize their particular circumstance in life as well as our own.

We would never have these profound insights if we thought love was only a sexual thing and that we had to follow through solely in that way—as if we needed some kind of physical encounter to really show that we were in love. Love of others is directly related to love of self, and this actual genuine love of self only comes about in open intelligence. In open intelligence, whether we have that in-love feeling about someone or we love them just naturally in another way, we can have complete freedom of expression.

THE PRIMORDIAL HEAT OF OPEN INTELLIGENCE

Open intelligence itself is hot, and because it is hot, it burns data. In the moment of inception it burns off data, spontaneously self-releasing the data that are its own liveliness and its own dynamic energy in the here-and-now. As the data *are* open intelligence, the data spontaneously and naturally self release. The heat of open intelligence is not something we can measure or think of, as it is completely beyond all conceptual frameworks. This isn't heat in the way we usually think of heat. We could think of it as a primordial heat beyond anything that could be described through current science. It is the primordial heat of all that is and isn't. It is instantaneously burning off data, which is its own dynamic energy.

If we look at everything exactly *as it is*, we can see everything in every single moment burning off. There is no way to control the current moment or to capture it in any way. We do not need to do anything about data; we simply rest naturally and data spontaneously burn off in open intelligence.

Everything that is *is* the liveliness of that open intelligence. There isn't anything that needs to be done to make this moment burn off; it is going to burn off by itself, and through the insight of open intelligence we can see that everything is burning off moment by moment. There is no way to capture any moment and hold it in place, relive it again or do anything else with it. It simply is *as it is*, and that is the way it will always be: just exactly *as it is*, open intelligence itself.

By letting data be as they are, we do not scratch the itch—we do not indulge the data, avoid or replace them with other data. We have no need to do that any longer; we let the data streams be as they are—the dynamic, powerful energy of open intelligence. This letting things be as they are brings forth the natural beneficial potency of mind, speech, body, qualities and activities. By relying on open intelligence, by relying on perfect love itself, we empower data and instinctively recognize their luminosity inseparable from primordial open intelligence.

We need to take responsibility for all of our data streams and to not waver in letting everything be *as it is*—not falling victim to reified data streams; in other words, not blaming data streams on other data, such as people, places, things and so forth. Otherwise, whenever we have a data-stream itch, we will constantly be scratching it. Some ways of scratching the itch might be to indulge the data, avoid what's shining forth naturally or replace one data stream with another, like replacing ill-will towards others with contrived compassion.

So, in that example, if ill-will towards others comes up, to just allow that to be *as it is* will be the most profoundly meaningful scratch that could ever be given to that itch! Then the ill-will opens up naturally and self-releases in pure and potent open intelligence and in pure love creation.

All data, no matter what they are, are of the nature of open intelligence. Each datum is pure and inexhaustibly open, spontaneously present and indivisible. This is the fundamental reality in which all beings are beneficially potent, physically and mentally happy, healthy, filled with life satisfaction and flourishing.

Chapter Eleven

THE DOMAIN OF PURE PLEASURE

Pure pleasure is the basis of all of our experience. It is only the *idea* that things are otherwise that has made it seem as though pure pleasure is not the basis of all of our experience. When we are introduced to open intelligence, we see that open intelligence itself is the domain of pure pleasure. In fact, to instinctively recognize the ultimate pleasure, it is required that this self-arising, natural pleasure be actually experienced as the entire nature of negative data. To find self-arising natural pleasure as the nature of negative data contradicts all the ideologies we have learned that say pleasure is restricted to certain domains, and it lets loose our most comprehensive intelligence and beneficial potency of mind, speech, body, qualities and activities.

The clarification of data as self-arising pleasure and bliss is really the zenith of erotic experience. Each moment is the union of data and open intelligence. The idea that erotic pleasure is restricted to certain domains is just an unfounded ideology that was fabricated out of various kinds of moralistic ideas. There are many areas of repression and oppression in terms of the natural pleasure that is our real nature, so this particularly is an area of great discovery for everyone. We especially must train our young people to instinctively understand the nature of open intelligence's pure pleasure. In this way, they will be empowered by puberty rather than disempowered by joining in the crass mass of reified data.

SEXUAL DESIRE

In open intelligence we find the beneficial vitality and power of sexual experience, and by doing so we are freed up in so many ways. Otherwise, sexual desire is a data stream that is always lurking around in the background. If we just allow all of our sexual data to be and get real with them, that is very freeing and very spacious.

All data, no matter what they are, are equally self-arising bliss. In each datum of sexual experience, regardless of the description of the data, let it flow on by without further elaboration. So many times we learn that there are data that limit bliss and pleasure, such as unfulfilled desire, no desire, boredom, fatigue, lethargy and so forth. We get all these ideas about where pleasure is or where it is not. However, whatever our experience is, whether it is the terror of the moment or the joy of the moment, allowing everything to be exactly *as it is* with no special situations or special states to achieve is the real act of indivisibility. That makes life very easy.

In that is such tremendous freedom, because everything—desire, jealousy, pride, ignorance, anger—is completely freed up by allowing all of that to be *as it is*. Erotic experience is fulfilled in whatever data we are having right now. Sometimes people feel uncomfortable if they are full of desire, and sometimes they feel uncomfortable if they have no desire; however, it just is whatever it is. In instinctive open intelligence we get to be familiar with the full range of data without making them into a description of who we are. Many of us feel driven by sexual urges—as if we didn't have any control—but this is merely a data stream like any other. We might as well simply relax and enjoy the inherent bliss in every single data stream.

THE HERE-AND-NOW AS THE PLACE OF PLEASURE

We are sexual beings and being sexual is normal, and when we practice open intelligence we get to see just how sexual we really are. Sexuality is not something that has a special power. It is the domain of open intelligence, just like any other data stream. By allowing everything to be *as it is,* we are really greatly empowered in this area, and it isn't so scary anymore. Because almost all of us are products of some kind of data-driven culture or subculture, we all learn different things. We all have our fantasies, our special thoughts, our special feelings and our special sensations. We each are whoever we are in the data-driven way of that subculture, and it is really important to normalize that. By practicing open intelligence and normalizing our experience, we learn a lot about ourselves in regard to the sexual domain, and more and more this will be true in the Age of Human Empowerment and Era of Great Benefit.

We do not hide out from our sexuality anymore, and as a result soon everybody may start looking attractive! One minute you are thinking about being attracted to a guy, the next to a girl, the next to something else—you don't know what is going on! We all have these things about us in that regard that most of us do not want anyone to know. To become perfectly clear about this takes us out of the situation of being like a ping-pong ball going back and forth, never knowing what is going on because this twist is leading this way and that turn is leading that way.

Many times we restrict ourselves and restrain our natural responsiveness because we get caught up in ideas of what appropriate thoughts, emotions, sensations or other experiences are. The most intimate we can ever be is with our own experience, whatever that is. That is really the height of intimacy. Whatever our experience is, whether we deem it sexual or not, that is an offering of pure pleasure. Moment-to-moment open intelligence is the perspective, just like the perspective of a flawless crystal ball pervades all of its reflections. The same is true with our own spacious open intelligence. Whatever is going on for us, it is just the way it is, and it is all an expression of open intelligence.

Everything that is looked for in sexual associations is right here in the indivisibility of indestructible natural perfection and in whatever happens to be appearing—the perfect intercourse, the perfect union, the big erotic high or the crushing disappointment. The here-and-now increasingly becomes the place of pleasure, giving you very clear knowledge of what to do and how to act with everyone. With any kind of involvement of a sexual nature, it involves you and at least one other person, so right away you can see that there is a lot more involved than just satisfying yourself. Open-intelligence education in this area is very important, so you allow yourself to get totally grounded in that.

From the open–intelligence vantage we can see clearly; so, if sexual feelings come up, we can see exactly how acting on those feelings would play out. We can see the effect our actions would have on us and the effect they would have on other people, and we become much less likely to act irresponsibly. All the flirtatious energy diminishes. We do not need attention from others to give us self-worth; the worth comes from indestructible open intelligence and not from the attention others are paying to us through flirtation. We empower ourselves for optimal sexual relating that really is uncomplicated.

SOVEREIGNTY OVER ALL EXPERIENCE

No one need be a victim of the data that they have adopted. According to these data the urges that we have are called "sexual," and we come to believe that they have an independent nature. We come to believe that they can drive us and control us and that they are signs that we must do certain things—like hook up with someone or satisfy an urge or whatever else it might be.

All these reified data have been created by someone, but none of them have authority or sovereignty over our own experience. It is up to each person to take care of themselves in a way that derives the full pleasure of open intelligence from life. This is not some kind of clichéd idea of pleasure, but the basic pleasure of sovereignty that every individual has in their own experience—their own innate dignity and integrity that does not need to be regulated by anyone else.

Things have gotten very confused, to the point where many things that are natural parts of human experience and which should not be regulated by someone else are regulated within legal and institutional systems. We need to see that these interpretations, while they may be helpful in some regards, do not really represent a basic understanding of our experience. We need to look at ourselves as we are and then decide what our laws are going to be, rather than hauling in these outmoded legal structures that try to control what we do.

For instance, when human society does not allow reproductive rights to be an individual decision, then that is very significant. Things are very confused if people lose their right to decide what they can and cannot do with their bodies. We need to take the power into our hands and from a very clear intelligence decide how society is going to skillfully take care of everyone.

We find within sexuality the vast expanse of open intelligence extending everywhere. This is an area of our life where there are many injunctions and ethical and moral commands lurking around every corner, and to let everything be *as it is* is extremely powerful. We no longer shut down our power by misunderstanding our data related to sexual matters. The data require no action; it is surprising to see what power there is in simply letting the sexual data stream flow on by.

If we are unable to decide what to do when a sexual impulse comes up, then we might end up in a situation that can cause harm to us or to others. However, by the power of open intelligence we will not end up in a situation like that. Why? Because we are no longer led around by the primitive impulses of reified data. Sexual data are perfectly normal, but if we do not know that their nature is open intelligence, they become primitive drives that can lead us around in the same way that a puppeteer controls a puppet. We really do not want to live that way, individually or as a society.

What we are as human beings is very simple, very radical and extremely powerful. If we complicate it, we go out of control. If we simplify it to its radical core power, then in the ongoing Age of Human Empowerment and Era of Great Benefit we are able to live together powerfully all over the universe(s), really committed to a sane society.

NORMALIZING ALL SEXUAL DATA

The key is to normalize all of your experience in ever greater open intelligence and to extract the power of what you think, feel and sense by relying on open intelligence. In this way open intelligence is continuous. The sexual domain is a very powerful area for the outshining of data in open intelligence, because you get into all kinds of thoughts and emotions that you never really knew you had. "Oh, I better be doing this. Or had I better be doing that? Or maybe this is right and that is wrong, and I better not be thinking about this thing this way."

We have all kinds of different relationships to our data, depending on who we are. Some of us have a propensity to indulge, others to avoid, others to replace and others to clarify. Often a mixture is present for a while. In the immediate self-knowledge of the pure pleasure of the here-and-now, all these things get sorted out. We find that we have really been subjected to all kinds of social injunctions about erotic desire, and they come flooding in from religion, education and from society in general. But we take responsibility for their effect on us by treating them simply as data, free in their own place, the dynamic energy of open intelligence. In instinctive open intelligence everything is completely normalized—all our gender roles and everything else that we have imagined as related to erotic desire or involvement.

By normalizing all our own data in the great bliss of open intelligence, we know exactly how to proceed. We know what it means to involve another human being in our life in a sexual way, and we deal with it with great responsibility. That can only come about by normalizing all our own data in instinctive open intelligence. This is the way to be responsible.

It is not a mystery: you take responsibility for yourself and all your own data, whatever they are in this moment. That is a great act of pleasure right there.

EMOTIONALLY CHARGED DATA

Depending on our circumstances, we all have different attitudes about sexual experience. Some of us grow up feeling restricted about data related to erotic pleasure, and we feel they might be scary or even terrifying for different reasons. Or it could be the opposite extreme; we are completely out of control, and if we have a sexual desire we think we have to act on it. The assumption that we are powerless in the face of urges and surges is really absurd, but in some cases we have been trained to believe that. Whatever these data may be, they can be resolved and brought into complete accord through instinctive open intelligence.

Things come up such as, "Oh, am I going to get hurt here?" or "Am I becoming too vulnerable?" or "What about all those things that happened the last time?" or whatever it may be. These things might appear when we get together with someone else, and they will start to play themselves out exactly where we do not want them to—in sexual communication! However, with a clarified view, any kind of sexual relating that does occur can be really easeful and enjoyable, because no special set of data is required. There is complete freedom, and everything is normalized in great pleasure and bliss.

We each have our own little scenario about a perfect sexual experience, but whatever that scenario is, it will never work out! It does not matter how attractive the other person is or how ecstatic the sexual pleasure may be, that is never going to make our sexual experience unendingly satisfying. But in instinctive open intelligence, sex does become inexhaustibly satisfying—in the same way that all data are unendingly satisfying as open intelligence. Every moment becomes one of erotic pleasure.

Some people like sex a lot and some people are less interested, but it really doesn't matter which it is. When all the urges and surges are encompassed by the bliss of open intelligence, then we have real freedom individually and real freedom as a society. There is an attitude of carefree openness, and we can relax in all areas of sexual relating. We can really take it or leave it. That is the way it is supposed to be—take it or leave it—not controlled by sex, but not avoiding it either, encountering everything fully and directly until outshone by the pure pleasure of open intelligence.

SEXUAL RELATIONSHIPS

One needs to speak about things in a very frank and open way, because taboos and misunderstandings are so ingrained in society and very ingrained in each one of us. For example, from the time we were very small, most of us have been trained to have certain data about different bodily sensations and to identify those as somehow sexual; but who says they have to be sexual? What exactly defines data as sexual? We have the complete power to interpret our data in any way we want to. If we interpret them as only sexual, that is a choice, and if we get locked down in that perception, that is a choice too.

We learned society's norms about our sexual nature, and these norms are probably what we believe. We all have things we think are right, other things we think are wrong, things that are scary, things that we would never want to do, things we want to do but we never have. By the power of relying on open intelligence, we get to normalize all these data.

When the step is made to involve someone else sexually, through the self-responsibility of open intelligence we understand exactly what is happening. Our impulses and drives may have led us in all kinds of directions before, but they do not anymore. We still have them, but we do not feel driven by them. Instinctive open intelligence opens up the full range of erotic desire and the full range of pleasure as being self-evident in every data stream.

From the open-intelligence vantage, having a sexual relationship is not taken on in a casual way. The open-intelligence vantage has tremendous discernment, responsibility, clarification and spontaneity in all matters—the ability to clearly see a vast range of facts, to clearly see whether or not a situation is truly of benefit to everyone involved.

So, we can just relax and enjoy life; we take things in our stride and are no longer driven to do any particular thing. We always know that instinctive open intelligence will guide us and show us a responsible and enjoyable course of action. With the recognition that we are not powerless, helpless, originally flawed creatures, we see that we are powerful and that we are filled with tremendous capacity and potency. With that comes a new attitude. It is a different attitude from being powerless and helpless. We get used to living with that new attitude, and no matter how long we live, our familiarity will continue to grow. This is very nurturing, nourishing and encouraging in all ways, and this will become more and more evident in the Age of Human Empowerment and Era of Great Benefit.

The clarification and responsibility of open intelligence is tremendously reassuring, affirming and clarifying—giving us great strength, great ability to thrive and great ability to make good decisions. This is the greatest reassurance we can ever give ourselves: to see through clear eyes and to know with a clear mind. Then we will not run off on urges and surges, because we understand what the urges and surges are. We have clarified them and we are able to act in a completely spontaneous way—but also responsibly.

People go through all kinds of things in a relationship, and to have a fixed framework of expectation for yourself or others related to sexuality is a total dead end. If you have some kind of fixed expectation of another person or of yourself, all of that has to be relaxed. There are all these expectations, all these drives, all these impulses, all the fantasies, all the thoughts, emotions and sensations. By not trying to fix data and not trying to shove them into a certain little form, that is where the real freedom is found.

By the power of open intelligence we have real solidity within ourselves, and so we do not get into a state of needy anxiety such as, "Oh, living alone doesn't work for me; I need to find someone else to be with." A world of single people would be just fine! If your choice is to be on your own and not couple up, it is all fine. Whatever you decide, the key is responsibility. Open intelligence allows optimal sexual experience coupled with discernment and responsibility, and that is really powerful.

We no longer need to seek to be understood by other people; we have that understanding ourselves, and it is tacit and certain. That is an incredible power. Without that power we will always feel left out and that we are not understood, and we will continually be seeking people who we hope will understand us. When we understand ourselves and we make a connection with another human being who understands themselves, then we have a mutual understanding based in open intelligence.

It is very interesting to notice that at Balanced View centers where open intelligence is being trained up, it is not an environment where people have come to try to hook up with each other. That is really amazing; people are coming together for the enhancement of open intelligence, and that is how the whole space is held and seen. That is very, very powerful in its own right. It is totally relaxing to be able to go somewhere where sexual relating is not what people are focusing on. Everyone is there for the same reason—to expand inexhaustible open intelligence.

ON WANTING TO BE ATTRACTIVE

Many of us gather our sense of identification by the attention that other people pay to us. "Am I sexually attractive to this one or that one?" These thoughts come even if we have no plans whatsoever of ever having any kind of erotic relationship with the people to whom we are trying to be attractive.

Let's say there is a beautiful woman walking down the street, and the men are looking at her and maybe even a few of the women are looking at her too. So, then she may think, "Wow! This is great; they really think I'm hot!" Yet, let's imagine a different version of that scenario. What if, instead of being focused on the attention from others and taking it to mean something, she is totally at ease in this situation, taking a short moment and recognizing what is really going on?

No data need get in the way of the open-intelligence view. Open intelligence will direct the appropriate course of action, and it will always be within the context of the benefit of all. By relying on open intelligence we get to outshine all these data, and this totally frees up our energy. Instead of spending our time trying to get people to acknowledge us, we are completely steadfast in our very own space.

With all of the games—the flirtation, the needing to be noticed through looking this way or that—we need to be crystal clear in the moment. "What am I doing? Is this really how I want to identify myself?" So the same scenario could occur; the woman is walking down the street and people are really checking her out, yet now she says, "Whoa, I used to live for that, but I was a real fool." When we consider that we would live our life for these cheap tokens—to get some kind of meager acknowledgement—it seems so ridiculous. We can still look attractive, that is fine, but it does not mean that we are doing it to get attention that we desperately need so that we can feel that we are somebody.

The vast expanse is a very roomy space, and there is a lot of pure potential and energy in the purity, openness, spontaneous presence and indivisibility of open intelligence! Energy is freed up for other activities and qualities that are much more engaging, satisfying and fulfilling. They are benefit-producing and benefit-expanding, rather than being a pastime as self-focused as trying to get other people to acknowledge us in some way for our good looks.

TRUE BIRTH CONTROL

There are many sexual activities carried out that are irresponsible, and as a result human society has struggled with population growth. Why do we struggle with population growth even though we have birth control pills, condoms, special foams and who knows what else to try to control the population growth? The problem isn't in the birth control methods; the problem is in us. We have to bring ourselves into the place of indestructible open intelligence that opens up within our sexual experience. That is the only way we will ever have true population control.

The built-in birth control, so to speak, is in instinctive open intelligence. Real birth control will never fully come about from a pill or any other device. We have within us a way to control our population. No one ever need be sexually out of control; inherently, no one *is* ever sexually out of control. The basic sex education we need is education in the nature of mind, and without that all kinds of things will play out.

When we are no longer led around by our desires, we see we really do have the power to control the population naturally and spontaneously—in other words, no pill required. Through the medicine of open intelligence outshining sexual irresponsibility, we take full responsibility for our actions and are suddenly able to solve problems that were unsolvable. That recognition is very, very convincing. Yes, the nature of mind—open intelligence—is authoritative and convincing, outshining all data. Similarly, the noonday sun outshines all planets and stars visible at night.

Chapter Twelve

SOCIAL ACTIVISM IN INTIMATE RELATIONSHIPS AND PARENTING

There is pure pleasure in the spontaneous beneficial potency of social activism for the benefit of all. Pouring forth from open intelligence as the sheer brilliance that is always present and which can never be taken away, this beneficial potency is the ultimate in intimate relationship with oneself and with everyone. The ultimate parenting is also found in caring for oneself as open intelligence.

Instinctively comprehended at the crucial juncture of open intelligence and data is the reality of data as it is—pure, luminous, spontaneous, indivisible open intelligence. The kind of pleasure inherent in open intelligence—at its crucial juncture as data and the relating associated with it—is really a basic human right, because without it we cannot thrive individually or with one another. So, it is absolutely required.

Intimate relationship begins with a profound act of self-love, which means coming into full relationship with oneself through education in the nature of mind. This is an authentic introduction to open intelligence which does not wear off, and from there it is a matter of just letting all our data be as they are, while simultaneously instinctively recognizing and preserving open intelligence. Similarly, a loving mother could be with a little child who is screaming at the top of their lungs, all the while maintaining a profoundly caring love amidst all the surges of data about the child. From within that caring love grows a smile of self-care and true love for oneself.

This is the beginning of outshining data with the obviousness of open intelligence's beneficial potency. As is stated throughout this book, instinctive recognition of open intelligence as inseparable from data is the fundamental basis of all permanent, inexhaustible social change for the benefit of all.

It is a strong natural urge to want to have the sort of special love relationship that is going to fulfill us, but the love relationship we are seeking is provided through relying on open intelligence. This special relationship that we are seeking is not to be found in the love of one person or a special group of people with whom we have strong sympathetic attachments based on reified data. This love found in open intelligence allows us to be in love with all people. It becomes easy then to choose a Balanced View lifestyle in everyday life in which we are able to be with people who share that love.

One tremendous benefit of open intelligence is an all-out, generous love for everyone, everywhere. We all just want to love, we really do. We have such a capacity to love and such a desire to love. We are so often looking for an opportunity to love, and we want to be loved in return. Very often we learn that love is dependent on someone else, and we do not learn the basis of self-love. When we let data be as they are, we really see exactly how we have been programmed, so to speak, and we begin to find out what open intelligence's beneficial potency really is.

We allow all those parts of ourselves that we like and do not like to be as they are, and that leads to one of open intelligence's beneficial potencies, which is perfect love. Total love for ourselves comes first, and then love for others begins to saturate us—the great inexhaustible spread. That is the easy way. We can do this in the context of a coupled relationship as well, but if we are single, first we take on ourselves, so to speak, by being able to be potently at ease with everything *as it is*.

Unless we love from the vast expanse of open intelligence, our love for a partner will have an agenda filled with all kinds of reified data. Love that comes from self-love without an agenda is pure, and it isn't an up-and-down kind of love. If there are conditions placed on a partner that are based on reified data, then there will be expectations and agendas in the relationship along with many ups and downs. If our expectations and agendas are not met, there is often a feeling of loss of love.

However, with the power of open intelligence, solid and strong like pure space, there are no reified data to contend with.

If we start out with the self-love of open intelligence itself, which is built-in love, then we do not expect love to come from anyone else. We live in a state of pure love, and our love isn't dependent on anything or anyone else. We can freely enter into love-relating without ups and downs, and this is really the way to love someone else. That is very, very powerful, because then we really are able to make a clear choice.

TRUE INTIMATE RELATING

When we choose to enter into a relationship from the vantage of the self-love of open intelligence, we know for sure that we are entering it with complete clarity—or as much inexhaustible clarity as we have at the time. We will know that we have covered all our bases and that every step along the way we were open about everything.

Unless we know the source of love in open intelligence, we will be confused in our relationships and we will not be able to have true intimate relating. But the solution is very simple. By relying on open intelligence we know that we have the whole package ourselves and that we do not need to get anything from anyone else in order to experience that. Many people feel that they are not capable of always-on pure love, but that assumption isn't true at all. When we see increasing, overwhelming all-consuming love come alive in ourselves and many other people, we know we are all completely capable.

We can now go from one experience to another in life enjoying each of them totally. Why? Because we have no expectation that the experiences will provide happiness for us, we know where happiness is. Just like the reflections in a crystal ball recede into the purity and openness of the crystal ball, so too all our desire for special positive experience recedes into the great bliss-benefit of open intelligence.

Through short moments of open intelligence, open intelligence becomes obvious at all times, and we come to understand that experience has no independent nature that could provide lasting happiness or benefit. If we do not have this recognition, it can be very difficult because we will continue to look to special kinds of experience for our happiness. If we enter into a relationship and things do not go well, what do we do? We blame the other person. We say, "What happened to the falling-in-love feelings that we once had? Something's wrong, and you are the reason for it."

By reducing everything to pure open intelligence and its vital dynamic energy—data—everything becomes very simple. When we rely on the perfect love of open intelligence, we are taking one hundred percent responsibility for our relationships being loving, and we do not need to blame our partners for experiences that we think they are not giving us. Once we are introduced to open intelligence, we then realize more and more that the love is *in us*. We are naturally fulfilled as the living presence of love right now. Many people spend their lives looking for love in all the wrong places, so what great joy and great freedom there is in not having to do that anymore.

We grow up and we are told, "Someday you will fall in love and it will be wonderful," and we look forward to that moment. Of course, falling in love is so much fun! So, one happy day we get to the point where we look across a room and there she or he is—"the one"—and pretty soon there is the euphoric love that comes with falling in love. That euphoric love is in fact open intelligence itself, and that is what we have really fallen in love with—spontaneously presenting itself as the dynamic energy of the other person. This is a big secret out of the bag: we are in love with open intelligence and not with an individual! It is very important to know that we can be in love without anyone else involved, and we do not need to be loved by another in order to feel fulfilled.

If there are not any expectations in a relationship that the other person will provide our happiness, and if we already have our happiness and the other person does too, then we are in the ideal circumstance. We can really enjoy ourselves and each other as well. We are enjoying what an intimate partnership really is.

For a person committed to open intelligence who is looking for a partner, a good suggestion would be to seek out someone who is also committed to open intelligence through Balanced View's Four Mainstays language system—someone who speaks the same standardized global language of education in the nature of mind. Otherwise, the relationship will be a lot of work. It is a lot easier if both of you have made the open-intelligence commitment. Then you both know from the very beginning where the other partner is coming from, and both people are willing to take full responsibility for their own data. The two of you together are going to be able to be very beneficial to one another, and that is what your lives are about—bringing joy to each other and really deeply caring for each other, rather than constantly trying to change each other's data.

During the time of very rapid transition in human culture, it is vitally important to have the home base of the Four Mainstays lifestyle. There is great sadness in seeing people fool themselves into thinking that they are going to be happy forever with someone when they fall in love, when in actuality there is no Four Mainstays basis for the relationship.

PATIENCE

Even if we are initially very attracted to someone, we should just sit with it for a while and see what happens. The attraction feels so good at first, yet how long will it feel so good? If the relationship is truly right for us, as we get to really know the person more, it will feel better and better. Let's see what else comes up after the falling-in-love time, because sometimes people change—or we change—after we have been in a relationship with them for a while. Then maybe two or three years into the relationship we can begin to consider a permanent relationship.

However, sometimes when we fall in love we feel like we have to jump right into it. We think that we have to partner with the person right away, because otherwise we might miss our chance. So, when it is suggested after being introduced to Balanced View's Four Mainstays that we wait some time before entering a long term relationship, say a few years or so, it might really seem like a very long time to wait. But if the relationship is real and it really is everything that we feel it is, it will be even more robust in a few years' time. During that period we will have the opportunity to get to know the person better and to have a full examination of ourselves to see if we really are prepared to enter into an intimate relationship on this basis. This then provides a much better basis for relationship than getting carried away with the tremendous emotions that come with that initial feeling of falling in love. This is just common sense.

If we do decide that we want to find a partner to be with in a long term relationship, then we need to be able to see things clearly, and we want to be able to make a wise choice about the person we will partner with. In being wise, we will not see the person only from the falling-in-love vantage. We are able to see the things about the person that are not so strong and the things that are strong, the things that might be difficult in a relationship and the other things that might be really great. That is a much better way to go into a relationship than, "Oh, this person is so absolutely incredible in every possible way, and they can do no wrong."

If a relationship is not one based on relying on the Four Mainstays, it very often can be like a dumping ground for data. "This is the person I can talk about all my data with, and they'll listen and probably mostly agree with me." But we find instead that when we rely on the Four Mainstays, spontaneously we are called to reality with other people—one of openhearted mutual relating, one of true caring in all ways. Then when a conversation occurs with one's partner, it can be a conversation of true love, true openheartedness and true relating that is not based on data streams.

We are able to be clear about what our future together as partners would be like, for example, what it might be like when we are really old and the inevitable challenges of old age have come in. We have a broad enough scope of comprehensive intelligence to think through all those things and to really see them clearly. Especially if we are in a long term relationship, all kinds of changes might happen. Our partner might get a severe illness such as Parkinson's disease, cancer or Alzheimer's, or the same might happen to us. To bring up the issue that "anything could happen" is not meant to talk anyone out of a relationship, but at the same time we want to ask ourselves, "Is this a person (or people) I could go through challenging times with? Is the relationship I have now really that level of lasting relationship?"

We suppose that this understanding of the implications of a long term relationship is behind the original idea of marriage ceremonies and the vows to be together "till death do us part." The vows would confirm in each partner the capacity to enact all of the qualities and activities of perfect love in relation to the other individual and the children who may come from that relationship. In addition, the marriage vows would confirm the commitment to bring joy, love and happiness to the other person and not only to oneself. Ideally, along with the family itself, the Four Mainstays would also be used for support.

JEALOUSY

Now, of course, jealousy can sometimes come up in a relationship. If we get really jealous and we cannot stand it if our partner even looks at somebody else, what is the solution? Is it to control our partner's behavior? Is it to control our own raging thoughts and emotions? Rather than trying to control anything, we let everything be *as it is*. We come to terms with the jealousy within ourselves and we mine the power from it. We have instinctively realized that everything is fueled by open intelligence, so we expand the definition of all reified data to include the pervasive beneficial potency of open intelligence itself.

However, if we do not make that choice, we might take all kinds of actions to deal with our jealousy such as continuing to obsess about it or becoming hypervigilant and watching the person to make sure we know what they are doing. It could even go further. Maybe we check to see whom they are emailing, or we read the emails or we monitor the phone bill and see whom they are calling. We might follow them around to see whom they are meeting or even hire someone to follow them.

If open intelligence is not preserved, this jealous episode can spiral into excessive negativity and cause a deep wound that doesn't easily heal. However, if there is preservation of open intelligence and reliance on the other Mainstays, the whole scenario can be passed through as a tremendous expansion of the profit and power of the strong emotion of jealousy into the beneficial potency of all-accomplishing activity.

There may be an incredible data stream of jealousy, yet we can look at the jealousy at a very fundamental level. We can get down to the very basis of our feelings about this extremely strong emotion, and all the while we remain as we are no matter what is going on. We allow the intensity of these really awful data to be. To be able to attentively abide as the open intelligence that is always present in jealously demonstrates the real open-intelligence power right there. We are then able to subsume the jealousy into its root nature of all-beneficial, all-accomplishing activities.

We see that the scope of jealousy opens up completely, and we also come to see it in a different way. "Wow. I'm not the only one who's jealous. There must be millions of other people right now who are jealous too." It is a total change in perspective and an expression of tremendous spontaneous altruism when we can see that we are all in the same boat.

We are no longer indulging the data; "indulging data" means mindlessly following the data stream from one thought to another. Instead, we maintain open intelligence while we unflinchingly look into all the feelings of jealousy, and in this way they are known to be the surge of open intelligence's beneficial power. Indulgence in jealousy is just a mindless regurgitation of data with no escape. Instead, we can use the negative data as a support while maintaining open intelligence, which is inseparable from the power surge of data.

We could make all kinds of assumptions about open intelligence not being present, but where exactly did it go? If we decide to rely on open intelligence, *that* is fueled by open intelligence; if we decide to *not* rely on open intelligence, *that* is fueled by open intelligence; if we feel ourselves to be in a downhill spiral of jealousy, *that* is fueled by open intelligence.

As was explained in prior statements in this book, the way to outshine jealousy completely is to preserve open intelligence all the while during the course of the jealous episode—from the first data stream to the last. Regardless of the storm of jealousy that we are undergoing, we can carry on with simple, openhearted love-capacity of mind, speech, body, qualities and activities.

THE SKILLFUL MEANS OF PARENTING

There are big changes that are coming about in society that will alter so much about the way we live as human beings. From a balanced perspective we can see things as they actually are, and we can envision a future which will look very different from the present. We understand that, among other things, parenting may not be done in the same ways it has been in the past.

We know, for instance, that it might be possible for a fetus to come to term somewhere other than inside the body of a woman. Additionally, we may be able to download our mind at death, preserving all of its open-ended knowledge creation and benefit. These are just two examples of the enormous changes that science and technology are making in our lives.

We as a human culture need to rely on our vast open intelligence and the other Mainstays to form a stable, united human culture to handle these matters well, and we need to augment this intelligence to the point where it is equal to or surpassing our scientific and technological ability. In an Age of Human Empowerment and Era of Great Benefit, with increasing reliance on Balanced View, the clarity to make the proper decisions in these crucial matters will be available.

Decisions having to do with whether to have a child or not need no longer be driven by acquired data such as, "Oh, I simply must have a child in order to be a complete woman." We are no longer following urges and surges of data that are commands from a primal evolutionary drive that we are not aware of, and we are not powerless in the face of our hormonal or primal desires. We are not helpless in the face of a strong urge to have a child, and we can make a wise choice in this matter. Open-intelligence power holds sway, and whether or not to have a child is given serious consideration, rather than it only being the byproduct of a reified data surge.

Once we have made the choice to have children, we should be clear that the way in which our children are going to live their lives will ultimately be their choice. Perhaps the child isn't at all interested in relying on open intelligence; then of course as a loving parent it would be important to give them training in replacing negative states with positive states. If they are unable to rely on open intelligence and have no interest in that practice, then we can at least give them a positive basis for living their life. At the same time, a child who starts out indulging, replacing or avoiding data may eventually be able to rely on open intelligence at some point, especially if they are in a family where there is a clear open-intelligence example for them.

If the parent maintains open intelligence, the beneficial qualities and activities will shine forth, at first gradually arising and then becoming more and more predominant. Parents may at first be uncertain about how exactly to raise their children, yet it is just like doing anything that we are not familiar with. When we learn a new skill we approach it a bit hesitantly at first; however, then we grow to feel comfortable with it over time. Becoming comfortable with it does not happen all at once; we gradually gain a bit more experience and carry on from there to assurance.

Many parents may have had the experience when their first child was born of, "Oh dear, what do we do now?" There are probably many parents who feel that they do not know what to do with their children. Here the parents are all of a sudden with this little baby in front of them; they are totally in love with their child, but they may have little idea of exactly what to do. The parents may read lots of books and learn everything they can about good role-modeling and parenting, but in real life situations it often is a matter of moment-to-moment interaction where one has to go with one's instincts, so to speak. It is in these crucial situations of not knowing exactly what to do that relying on open intelligence can be of enormous value.

As spontaneous benefit is inseparable from open intelligence, we can be assured that all is well. Parents simply have to become accustomed to becoming a parent, and they also have to become accustomed to allowing open intelligence to shine forth as much as they can as they move along as parents. They may have learned some things about parenting before, and they may want to continue on with some of what they have learned; yet, through open intelligence the vantage becomes much broader. The more attention that is paid to open intelligence and the more it is acknowledged, the more predominant it becomes as the entire space of life. The Four Mainstays provide an insurance policy of life satisfaction and flourishing that helps sustain a parent in raising children.

Let's say that your child has done something completely inappropriate that totally pushes your buttons, and you begin to get all sorts of powerful data streams. The thought might come, "I'm supposed to be the ideal parent, and not only do I not know what to do, I am having all sorts of out-of-control thoughts about my child." Through relying on open intelligence, there is no need to go into the soap opera scenario that is playing out mentally and emotionally. Everything is just allowed to be *as it is*, and through this the knowledge of exactly how to handle the situation from that place of total potency shines forth spontaneously. So, you are responding from a place of total potency rather than from chaotic frenzy.

In this way your very presence is a teaching to your child. You do not have to say anything; the child is already being provided for. Your commitment to open intelligence is definitely the best thing that can ever be done for your child, no matter how old they are. All the other parenting contributions that can be given to a child are minimal when compared to the skillful display of your own open intelligence. Your own open intelligence is evidence to your child of what a real human being is, and it is the greatest gift you can ever give them.

For us as educators and parents of our children, we need to see what the capacities and abilities of our children are, recognizing that each one of our children has the foremost capability of open-intelligence competence, as well as all of its beneficial potency. There isn't anyone on earth who does not have this inalienable right available to them. As parents we acknowledge this from the beginning, and we can instruct our children accordingly. To show a child their open-intelligence potency and vitality is such a great benefit for a parent to offer.

The focus of all the skillful means of parenting is to bring out the talents that the child has. It is not a matter of drowning them in conventional data, but bringing out the power and the potency of open intelligence as the core education—fueling and vitalizing all strengths, gifts and talents to be used for the benefit of all.

The role of every parent is to guide and protect. to truly be the best guide and protector possible, a parent must be able to let all of their data be as they are. In becoming a parent to ourselves in a sense, we know how to parent the children we have. By entering into full love relationship with ourselves, we are able to enter into full love relationship with our children—and with our own parents as well—rather than living only in the field of sympathetic attachment and all of its many shoulds and shouldn'ts.

A parent is involved in many skillful means, and there are new skillful means around every corner. Parenting never stops! Our children may be grown up and have children of their own, and we may think, "Okay, now they are on their own and they won't need me anymore," yet most likely our children will continue to share joys and sorrows in which they will turn to us for mature, beneficial support. The parenting relationship with one's children is an always-on relationship, as anyone who is a parent of adult daughters and sons knows, and the best possible basis for a loving relationship is our ever-increasing recognition of open intelligence's beneficial potency through the Four Mainstays lifestyle.

EDUCATING OUR CHILDREN

So often the question comes up, "How can I best educate my children?" The best education for a child is the best education for everyone—to rely on and claim the power of open intelligence through a Four Mainstays lifestyle. As a parent, your primary skillful means and the most powerful educational tool for your child is your own example.

The education of our children is of course a crucial part of our overall education. For each of us living as open intelligence through a Four Mainstays lifestyle, we naturally communicate to our children their own nature through being exactly who *we* are. Within the flow of that, the natural responsiveness of knowing when and how to contribute to a child ensures that they will grow up with a vast and open intelligence that is all-inclusively present in all the decisions they make and with a beneficial potency that is always-on in all qualities and activities.

As a parent one sees the incredible responsibility of actual love, service and joy, as well as the responsibility to bring love, service and beneficial potency to all children, no matter what kind of circumstance they are facing. Our duty as parents is to pour open intelligence's beneficial potency into our children, knowing that it is most important for them to receive a direct transmission of it through our own lived example. We contribute to our children through the Four Mainstays lifestyle, particularly by fulfilling open intelligence's beneficial potencies of mind speech, body, qualities and activities.

In terms of how children were being raised, there were many changes that occurred in the 1960s. The world was in the throes of actual revolution at that time, and there was a vast activism ignited globally and also at the local level: student rights, reproductive rights, free speech, anti-war activism, civil rights, migrant worker rights, the economic right of women to join the work force and be paid equal wages for equal work and so forth.

All kinds of social activism came bursting forth from within the generations of humans living at that time. This was the time of the first generation having easy access to convenient and inexpensive transportation, which helped lead to, among many other things, the forming of the Peace Corps over fifty years ago. These newly created circumstances of modern travel also allowed people to go and live in places around the world and to get to know people in other cultures. This direct experience led many people to want to support all the world's people in attaining basic human needs such as food, clothing, shelter, health care and education.

This was all part of the vast movement of social change that began to occur at that time, and this social change continues on to this day. The things which were begun then are crucial elements of the infrastructure of society today and must be protected and guaranteed. The generation of the baby boomers and flower children has made a pivotal change in the way human beings live, and the Balanced View Training is essential to that ongoing change. The change in the way we educate ourselves in the nature of mind—and the way we empower and enact that in ourselves—ensures and guarantees that the next generation will also be empowered in open intelligence's beneficial potency through a Four Mainstays lifestyle.

Open intelligence is inexhaustible and just keeps flowing, and why does it flow continuously? Due to its inexhaustibility it flows continuously. Beneficial potency is all about inexhaustible benefit—listening openly to everything and everyone, no matter who they are, what they are saying or what they are doing. How do we develop the ability to do that? We simply rely on the Four Mainstays, wherein we have the great freedom to express our own unique strengths, gifts and talents empowered by open intelligence's beneficial potency of mind, speech, body, qualities and activities. By relying on open intelligence, we see everything *as it is*.

As we see everything within ourselves *as it is,* we no longer experience internal divisiveness, and we no longer experience constant war within. We begin to feel united within, as well as empowered and filled with beneficial potency. Without even trying to understand what is happening, we begin to feel indivisible from everyone and everything, totally natural, powerful and at ease. It is just a natural process of events with no special tricks or trades—just life as it simply is.

When it is that way for us as parents, then it can be that way for our children as well, and then for their children and then on down through countless generations. Through simply living life as it truly is, we have a world filled with people who are bright, beautiful beings endowed with open hearts and open minds, who are full contributors to society in all aspects of life with nothing left out—relaxed, restful and alert, potent and beneficial, easily identified as leaders simply by who they are.

Interacting with children is just like interacting with everyone else; in each moment with our children we know what to do and how to act, and if we don't know what to do, we have a whole community of people to rely on. In a Balanced View Four Mainstays community one has a large group of people that represent open intelligence and its beneficial powers, so a child is surrounded by that. A child needs support for who she or he is, and that is provided by the parents and the entire community worldwide as well.

Today it is easier to have an educational process that is really top notch for a child, and it will be increasingly that way. We do not have to put our children into conventional schools and other institutions that train them to reify data. The educational setting should be extremely high quality, with everyone having equal access to the finest education available.

Such settings are in place right now and eventually all schools will base all education on the most pivotal training—education in the nature of mind in Four Mainstays community. The Four Mainstays are the open-intelligence algorithm of the best training in mind's nature.

Education has usually been set forth in a very standardized and conventional way, and so generally children all over the world leave home and go to a classroom in a school located somewhere near their homes. There are of course home schools as well, but it is often a matter of teaching the same set of reified data, just in the setting of a home school. However, schools and schooling will look very different in the coming years. Children will not need to go to a special place called "school" anymore; a lot of the schooling will take place wherever there is an online connection and teachers or other caregivers to give support. A much more rigorous and challenging curriculum will be possible, because so much more of the education will take place on the Internet.

For example, each child in a Balanced View school receives a customized education that is based on open intelligence's beneficial powers of mind, speech, body, qualities and activities, and the schooling is relevant to their own particular strengths, gifts and talents. It isn't a matter of everyone sitting in a classroom together doing the same thing at the same pace or a similar setup with a different name. The students have special mentoring relationships that are cultivated with teachers around specific topics, and the learning proceeds according to the child's interest and capacity. Students may be involved in learning the same basic material, but for each of them the homework is different. The course material is tailored to their strengths, gifts and talents, and the child's natural interests are nurtured and evoked by all the resources that are available in person and online. Competence and fluency in technology is emphasized, because that is a very important skill in today's world.

Of course, all parents want the best teachers for their children, but up until now those excellent teachers were only available in the classrooms in which they taught. Now children can have a very high quality education from excellent and motivated teachers online. The best of online resources and other resources can be employed. These are actually only very small shifts compared to what will be going on in education in the future.

This is only the beginning of a revolution in education in the Age of Human Empowerment and the Era of Great Benefit, where there will be so many incredible and unimaginable changes.

It is a very simple matter to provide a fantastic education to everyone on earth through very simple technologies that we have available today. What an exciting turning point, and to be able to package that together with open intelligence's beneficial potency—wow!

CARING FOR OUR PARENTS

By the power of open intelligence's beneficial potency, we move from having a possibly disharmonious relationship with our own parents to having a mature adult relationship, a relationship in which we are actually of service to our parents. We learn to really care about our parents as actual people. We care about their needs and care about what is important to them; we have an interest in their friends, respect them for who they are and the benefit they have contributed to the world.

No matter who our parents are, they have done their best to support us in whatever way they thought was best. In their role as parents to us, they did what they could do. It is important for us to recognize the fact that if we had had the exact same data they had, then we would have led the same life they did, and we would have done exactly the same things they did. With this gentle acknowledgment we have less reason to criticize or blame our parents when data about them come up.

The recognition of this is extremely essential to our own life satisfaction; otherwise, we will drive ourselves crazy with all the accumulated data about what could have been or should have been. If these data are going on about parents or anyone else, the negativity, chaos and confusion are happening *right here and now*. This is very, very important to understand.

We need to confront these emotions directly and extract the power of love by encountering all of our negative data openly. We need to face it all and avoid nothing. In this way we come to a deep understanding of our parents and a total openness and love that is very soothing to them. This actual demonstration of our loving and service-oriented lifestyle will bring great happiness to parents and friends.

It is good to look for small ways we can serve our parents. For example, when we are together with them, we can take pictures of the visit and later send them the pictures with a short note or email. We can make an arrangement to see them once a week if they live nearby or at least call them once a week if we cannot see them in person. There are many simple commitments we can make that enhance our relationship with our parents.

When we can be at ease with all our data, old grudges come to be resolved, and an openness to have a new relationship with our parents is created. It is actually very helpful to be direct with our parents about this and to say to them: "I've done some self-reflection and made some changes in my life. I see now that I have had some complaints, and I want you to know that I have resolved those complaints completely, and I feel a sense of openness, and I would like to develop our relationship further."

Through Balanced View's Twelve Empowerments, we learn to completely harmonize and empower the relationship with ourselves, our parents or caregivers and everyone else. It is a very simple thing to do, and then the whole relationship will evolve from there. It is very beautiful to harmonize relationships and to come into right relationship with our parents. When we have developed a right relationship with ourselves, we can come into right relationship with our parents and with everyone else in our lives.

Chapter Thirteen

THE BENEFICIAL SPEECH OF SOCIAL CHANGE

All uttered sounds spring directly from the primordially clear and indestructible sound. The tremendous potency of brilliant benefit powerfully circulates everywhere and in everyone and in all of the sounds that have ever been heard. All sounds are pervaded by the primordial sound that is filled with nothing but love, empowerment and benefit for all. It is forever expansive as open intelligence. Even if one has no sense of hearing, the primordial sound is forever present.

In the Four Mainstays lifestyle, indestructible, beneficial and stainless speech pours forth, and the old, limited context of speech is rendered forever obsolete. All the ways of using speech that only go this way or that way, such as power trips, put downs, sarcasm and so forth are subsumed into the most comprehensive open intelligence and its beneficial potencies, through which speech provides benefit, prosperity and generosity for all. The speech that is used shines through everything with the lucid, potent quality of pure benefit for all with no one and nothing left out.

The speech of open intelligence is inconceivably magnificent, and its quality is so profound. It is speech that soothes and empowers all at once. It reflects all sound clearly in infinite aspects, so an end to its expression cannot be found. Since its speech is indestructible, its beneficial power is unending.

We have learned that some sounds are good and some sounds are bad, yet by the power of open intelligence everything is known to be equal and even. Everything is subsumed into a greatly beneficial intelligence more comprehensive than opposites of right and wrong. All sights, sounds and sensations are then an exalted expanse. By knowing this, the way human beings perceive things is altered forever.

Whatever is encoded in data of any kind is the shining forth of open intelligence. Appearances and sounds are the precious expression of natural perfection. Everything is totally pure and free of anything of a different kind. To recognize sights and sounds as data of open intelligence is crucial. Holding to sights and sounds as positive, neutral or negative is freed in natural open intelligence. The great benefit of open intelligence is free of the need to alter or create a story about the flow of data.

COURAGEOUS ELOQUENCE

We come to have a courageous eloquence that becomes boundless. To realize that we actually have courageous eloquence at our disposal can be both illuminating and terrifying. First of all it is illuminating because we know we have it and can make use of it, but it is terrifying because the only way we can use it is to claim responsibility for it. The Four Mainstays lifestyle gives us the opportunity to come into the spontaneity of skillful and beneficial speech. We have been brought up to believe that only some people have courageous eloquence, but the courage that shines forth after truly realizing the great algorithm of the Four Mainstays ensures that we are totally unafraid, and because of that lack of fear courageous eloquence is naturally available.

Assurance develops, and we know that we are incapable of taking the wrong direction. Whatever comes up, it is going to be something that we will be able to handle, and we will be able to draw on the power of open intelligence's beneficial potency to face that situation or circumstance. From this alone we feel great courage and immeasurable and boundless fortitude, as well as a conviction that says, "Yes! Yes! This really is pure benefit, and this is something that would help other people too." This realization is so powerful that we cannot help but share it.

As we live our lives day-by-day, we see that we really do have these qualities. We do develop a courageous eloquence— sometimes a quiet one and sometimes an active one, depending on what is needed. We become very profound innovators of social change and truly capable of building an Age of Human

Empowerment and Era of Great Benefit, where we can live together peaceably in a way that could not happen before. This is not an abstract philosophy, but very real and tangible.

In the pristine environment of open intelligence, its beneficial speech is unable to be destroyed in any way. This beneficial speech restores the mind just through hearing and places it in an irreversible state where there is no return to the confusion and fear of data. This is the power of the indestructible sound of beneficial speech.

When you hear the indestructible sound of beneficial speech, you know it is *you* it is talking about. That indestructible sound rings deeply and truly within you in a way that makes you know exactly who you are. This form of exalted speech is not just speaking *about* open intelligence; it actually transmits the instinctive recognition of open intelligence's beneficial potencies. This manner of speech has a powerful impact that can never be taken away. It has an authenticity to it; it isn't like other modes of speech which fade into insignificance.

We have looked at our body, speech, mind, qualities and activities in a certain limited way for a very long time, but through the instinctive recognition of open intelligence we begin to see the overarching aspect that pervades every aspect of our being. Our body is the body of open intelligence, our speech is the resonance of open intelligence, our mind is alight with open-intelligence insight and our qualities and activities demonstrate open-intelligence benefit. Always present is the unborn simultaneity of open intelligence and potent benefit— the simultaneity of open intelligence shining forth all data.

When we discover the enormous potency of the primordial sound and the indestructibility at the basis of our own nature, we really start to hold ourselves to account for what we say. "How am I going to use this sound-producing vehicle called speech that I have, and how am I going to use the written word in the best way possible?" These are fundamental questions that people usually don't even think about, but the response to these questions can dramatically shape every expression of a person's life. As open intelligence becomes spontaneously obvious, so do its beneficial potencies of mind, speech, body, qualities and activities.

Conventionally we think, "This is my body, speech and mind, and that's your body, speech and mind," but really the ultimate body, speech and mind is open intelligence, which includes everyone and everything. It is all-inclusive, and all sound emanates from its primordial sound. All sound whatsoever is pervaded with open intelligence, like an echo in a canyon pervades the entire canyon.

WORDS OF EMPOWERMENT

There are certain words that, when heard, allow all false ideas to just slip away like broad daylight easing away the depth of night. Such is the song of pure benefit. As soon as the words are heard, the recognition is instinctive and simultaneous, and confusion is eased into open intelligence. There are special words that, when heard or read, have great power. Even though they might look like other words, they are not like any other words. They are words of empowerment; they completely clear up doubt and confusion.

When we see the essence of what these words mean in our own experience, we no longer focus merely on our individual self. Instead, the even flow of open-intelligence benefit pervades everything as we go about our day. It takes us away from habitual self-focus and directly towards always-on and potent open intelligence.

Words can be a temporary diversion or distraction—a moment of entertainment—something to ponder once in a while or to call up in recollection, or the words can be words that enter in and forever change the body, speech, mind, qualities and activities of a person. There is a distinction between those kinds of potent words and the words of entertainment or information. What kind of speech is going to be coming out of us? What kind of connection do we want to make?

We can go on and on our entire lives babbling about so many things, or we can enter into true connection where every word we speak is imbued with the resonance that directly enters in. The words have an effect way beyond the syllables; they have a permanent resonance.

By the power of our own open intelligence, our speech is expressed in a brilliant way. This sort of speech isn't just another dull drone; it has the primordial ring of truth, and that ring is infectious. It has a way of working that is much different than other speech. It works from within to verify the actual nature of existence.

When understood without confusion, words provide a complete and instinctive confirmation, and the words serve to increase open intelligence's recognition of beneficial potency very naturally, without having to do anything other than instinctively realize open intelligence. There is an absolute sense of augmentation and of increasing vividness of the vast expanse of benefit. This is just the way it is.

To merely know words is one thing, but to know the profound meaning of something is another. There is what could be called "word-open-intelligence," and then there is "factual-open-intelligence." Word-open-intelligence means to only understand things intellectually. Factual-open-intelligence on the other hand means to fundamentally comprehend the profound meaning of all data as the lucid beneficial energy of open intelligence.

So, to take an example, one could say, "Nothing has an independent nature," and to only be aware of this intellectually would be word-open-intelligence, but we would not be able to fully understand the true meaning only through word-open-intelligence. We can only know it through factual-open-intelligence, whereby we have the fact of the profound meaning instinctively impressed in us and it permeates our lived experience.

By becoming familiar with the basis of our speech—all the ways we have learned to describe everything about our life and the world—we come to rest firmly in lucidity and indestructibility, and that is where we always reside. Lucidity and indestructibility are our nature, and from there we live our life. We find that we cannot be affected by language systems, because there is no way a language system can affect innate lucidity and indestructibility. This recognition gives back to us our basic dignity and integrity, which had been stripped away by the sort of language that diminished and marginalized us at every turn.

A COMMON LANGUAGE

The essence of life is to spontaneously recognize all data streams as the beneficial creativity of open intelligence, to hear all sounds as sounds of open intelligence and to recognize all words as open intelligence. In this way all these data streams are outshone by their innate beneficial power and the indestructible powers of open intelligence's great benefit to all are recognized.

The nature of everything just *as it is* is pure benefit, and things in themselves are pure and simple. We learn to describe the world in terms of dictionary definitions, and we learn diverse and myriad ways to describe everything. We come to believe that the reified definitions are true, and we enter into a state of confusion and tension. We believe that if we learn all the right words and we put them in all the right places, then everything will be properly ordered and in its right place. But it never comes about, and so we feel disappointed and confused.

In the conventional sense, when we see something, it is translated into language—"table," "chair," "person." We have then put the perception into a code that we can share with others to account for things in the world. The sounds in the form of language filter all of our perceptions about everything we see, and we account for subjects and objects in the world according to these sounds.

When we find the power of open intelligence within our speech, we see how important the sounds are that we make or the words that we write. Through assurance in open intelligence we become true speakers and true writers who impart the instinctive recognition of open intelligence and its beneficial potencies through a global standardized language for education in the nature of mind. We each have a superb capacity to describe everything, and now we have the capacity to really understand it as it actually is. It is the beneficial energy of a profound intelligence ruling all of nature, and that intelligence is present as our own power to know.

There is now a standardized Balanced View common language to describe open intelligence and its beneficial potencies, and not merely a common language but a piercing language that directly outshines misunderstanding. Whether this standardized language is used between individuals or in organizations and communities, it is a language that people everywhere can understand, regardless of the national language in which it is employed.

Human beings want to feel connected. What is more, we want to know how to transition successfully to the world we are creating together right now. The way the world is shaping up is so far beyond our present imagination, yet we can transition to it successfully through the power of open intelligence. When open intelligence informs our language, science and technology, then we are truly expanding our intelligence and our scope to support the transitions that are occurring.

It is important to know what specific language is the most suitable for the people being spoken to. If there are people who are involved in a certain constellation of data, then there is a suitable open-intelligence language which is developed by Balanced View to meet the needs of that group very precisely. However, the language that would be suitable for this particular group might not necessarily be the same language used for people who have a completely different take on things.

Hence, the words of a skilled training have to be adapted to many types of people, and it can be adapted to any specialized field of language. If one is working with a team of engineers, for example, the Balanced View Training can be adapted to the language they are using to show them exactly how to progress in the development of their project, particularly overcoming challenges that seem to lack solution. Because of a comprehensive overview and the ability to understand the relationships of all data, the Balanced View language can be utilized to quickly and easily meet the requirements of various people whose needs are different.

UNERRING TEXTS

In Balanced View's authentic trainings and texts for education in the nature of mind, we will not find anything other than a single unerring message of great simplicity. All that is needed for human society to enter open intelligence's beneficial potencies of mind, speech, body, qualities and activities is communicated. The texts are never off-message; they always will be a precise guide to enhancing open intelligence. In reading them the experience will be one of always-increasing open intelligence.

The words of the texts allow pure benefit to grow familiar in its inexhaustibility, so the ring of truth that is so strong throughout body, speech, mind, qualities and activities grows more and more resonant, real and alive. By reading these texts, by listening to them and by writing them, the instinctive recognition of open intelligence is evoked. The Four Mainstays provide the reality environment for this display of spontaneous benefit, and the words in the text are an actual invocation of benefit.

The entire body of texts is very much informed by what people actually want to hear, rather than being the ideas of one person that are then foisted on other people. The texts are always flexible, immediate, powerful and directly relevant to what the concerns are of people living today. All of the Balanced View trainings are up-to-the-moment in terms of time, place and circumstance.

The words of the texts offer that which is wordless—an intelligence that subsumes all data whatsoever and makes sense of data completely. This intelligence gives us the ability to think and reason in a totally precise manner, to be able to dispense with all theories that have explanations with a huge amount of variants, and to be able to understand all data in a very clear fashion.

These direct transmission texts are like the song of this Age of Human Empowerment and Era of Great Benefit. They are a combination of poetry and prose that does not really sound like anything else; they also do not sound like they are written by anyone. With most things we read, we can find the presence of the author in what we are reading, but in these texts we do not find an author evident anywhere. The power of open intelligence is the sourced force that writes all the texts that are an endless flow of expression of our actual nature. Open intelligence is spontaneous; hence, these texts just come spontaneously and are then written down. The only purpose of the texts is to completely nurture and support us in gaining assurance in open intelligence.

The Four Mainstays are the indestructible vehicle of open intelligence itself. The purpose of the Four Mainstays is to highlight and illuminate the pure benefit of open intelligence, and these texts that are a part of the Four Mainstays belong to all beings and are the treasury of all beings.

The texts are not meant to be memorized; they are not commandments to act a certain way or do a certain thing. There is no need to study them or try to figure out what they mean. These texts are the words of complete release into open intelligence's comprehensive beneficial potencies. Just to sit and read or listen to them is all that anyone would ever require in order to recognize complete open intelligence and its beneficial qualities and activities. These texts have an incredible power. For example, if the phrase "complete perceptual openness in all experience" were to be read aloud from the texts, just the sound of those words would transmit the introduction to the actual experience.

We have tried so hard to learn so many things, and the reason it is very difficult to learn many things is because the ideas we are learning are not really grounded in reality. If something is grounded in reality, then there isn't even a need to learn it. There is a space of non-learning that is instinctive and so pleasurable, which does not require thought or reasoning or mental and emotional analysis. Because we may have learned to read and write and think in terms only of data, it is really important to give ourselves an opportunity to listen to, write and pronounce our actual nature. It is the right of everyone—absolutely the right of everyone.

When it is said that a text is a "direct transmission text," it means that it relies primarily on nonverbal and non-symbolic means to directly transmit reality, which cannot be understood only through the intellect. One can partly understand and comprehend the text intellectually, but it is only through instinctive realization that the message of the text becomes real and obvious to us.

When the phrase "non-verbal and non-symbolic communication" is used, this means that something is being imparted that is not limited to words or symbols. We receive it as the truth, and we know it is the truth. Even if we cannot understand it or describe it, we know it is what we have always been looking for—even though at the same time we might have all kinds of data come up.

The easiest and quickest means of benefit to all is transmitted through a nonverbal, non-symbolic communication. Introduction to open intelligence as well as recognition, intense trust and dedication to it must occur. These stir up the openness for nonverbal empowerment of pure benefit that comes from understanding that the trainer of open intelligence is an embodiment of open intelligence's effusion of pure benefit throughout past, present and future.

Again, it is important to repeat—these kinds of texts are not meant to be studied or memorized. They are not like some sort of compulsory school work. They are a balm; they are an opportunity for us to hear about what we really are, maybe for the first time. No matter how long they are listened to or how often, there still is nothing to memorize. Each time a text is heard there is inexhaustible increase of open intelligence's beneficial potency.

In the beginning the words might sound foreign and unfamiliar, but by just setting the text aside and coming back to it some time later, all of a sudden it is found to make perfect sense! There is no rational accounting for that. What does it matter how it happens? This is evidence of the very real and raw potency we have within us. It is a whole order of communicating and connection that simply isn't like the reified way we have been going about it up until now, and it is discovered in the Four Mainstays lifestyle.

The literary devices that are used throughout the text are spontaneously employed. So, for example, in conventional forms of writing, it is not a good idea to be repetitive, and one would be considered a bad writer if one repeated things over and over again. However, the goal of texts like these isn't to be a good writer or a bad writer. These texts are meant to be spontaneous pronouncements of education in the nature of mind, expanding the mind into inexhaustible comprehensiveness and beneficial power of speech, body, qualities and activities; they are the infrastructure texts of reality. The repetitive nature of the texts is a powerful literary device that actually instantiates innate beneficial power in the reader or listener.

The power of word and sound to evoke our potency is enormous, and these texts have that sort of potency. The texts are a cultural document of rare order in that they unite all of humanity in the domain of benefit and bring forth an Age of Human Empowerment and Era of Great Benefit, prosperity and generosity.

QUINTESSENTIAL TRANSMISSION

Mere words are not sufficient; they need to be coupled with the instinctive recognition of what the words describe. There has to be the transmission of actual open intelligence, and the transmission has to open you in a recognizable way to the vast expanse of benefit, where you say, "I am not the same as I was before, and I never will be," and that transmission is brought on by openhearted dedication to reality.

Impressing instruction so that it does not wear off is what transmission is. It is a communication that cannot be forgotten. Due to the slogan-like nature of the instruction "short moments many times," the learning and retention process is made much easier through this amazingly uncontrived nonverbal and non-symbolic transmission of inexhaustible open intelligence's beneficial potency. We easily transition from introduction and recognition of open intelligence to always-on, unforgettable open intelligence through the incisive power of the algorithm of the Four Mainstays.

When we hit upon the direct transmission of naked open intelligence, whatever ways we have described everything before are erased in pure benefit. All we can find anywhere is pure benefit, and it is very reassuring, completely confirming and exalting. It places us in the proper disposition by the empowerment of beneficial qualities and activities which are innate to us.

The quintessential transmission is provided through the combinatory pattern of the Four Mainstays instruction and lifestyle, resulting in open intelligence's beneficial potency. The proper instruction is the one that makes each day better than the last, no matter what is going on. A great trust in life is instilled through instruction such as this.

In order to be able to be open to the quintessential transmission, we must leave everything exactly *as it is*. Key points, pith instructions and nonverbal and non-symbolic communication join together as detailed levels of explanation evoking the powers of great benefit that are beyond a personal recognition of open intelligence. Here the Four Mainstays enter in and are the combinatory pattern of instruction or algorithm that effortlessly and potently brings about the powers of great benefit. Openness to quintessential transmission is based on introduction to open intelligence, increasing recognition of open intelligence, intense trust in the Four Mainstays and great esteem and respect for the trainer and trainings of open intelligence's beneficial potency. Each of these Mainstays represents an essential formula for the complete outshining and illumination of all knowledge in spontaneous altruism and pure benefit.

If someone's mind has not opened to the possibility of open intelligence, very often it can open through a nonverbal transmission from one person to another. If a person has never before been exposed to another person living from the powers of great benefit, transmission such as this can be extremely potent. It is a very powerful form of communication that permanently introduces the person to open intelligence. It does not need to have any words; yet when words come in the form of open-intelligence speech, the words are certainly quite different from reified speech.

Key points and pivotal instructions plus the pure beneficial power of the trainer have the power—the moment they are uttered—to be alive in the person who is receiving them. This is a true communication—a true transmission and the most intimate kind of communication one human being can ever have with another.

The moment we are introduced to open intelligence, things start to happen fast. One could call it swift-acting transmission, because we go through really significant changes in all aspects of mind, speech, body, qualities and activities, and we cannot understand or recognize how it is happening through reified definitions.

Upon arousal of the truly real beneficial nature of mind, speech, body, qualities and activities, the force of the trainer's benefit as well as that of all of the benefit fruited by the entirety of open intelligence become available for access and display. The door to the treasury of great benefit flies open and a resultant array of beneficial qualities and activities ensue. The illumination of knowledge is complete. The full display of great benefit has become obvious through profound transmission and foremost instruction, bringing all beings to the fruits of the Age of Empowerment and Era of Great Benefit.

All of these things—profound transmission, communication and foremost instruction through the Four Mainstays—are the best education in reality human beings can ever have. At this point in the history of our species, it is not a voluntary education. It is coming forth as an evolutionary process, and we just happen to be here realizing it.

As of yet we know very little about nonverbal and non-symbolic communication, yet in the next few decades we are going to learn a great deal about both. A lot of what is going to come about is going to come through non-symbolic communication. Open intelligence and its spontaneous beneficial potencies of mind, speech, body and qualities are subsuming humans into an evolutionary imperative, the likes of which we have never seen.

The transmission of pure benefit is shown to be the actual intelligence of our mind, which is primary to our speech, body, qualities and activities. Without a single word spoken, the Age of Human Empowerment and Era of Great Benefit is opened up by the introduction to society of open intelligence and its beneficial potencies. Innovators and early adopters of the full power of these beneficial potencies are enacting the greatest social change to ever come about.

Education in the nature of mind which is assimilated at the crucial juncture of open intelligence and data is the very powerful transmission force. You just get it, and you know you've got it.

Chapter Fourteen

THE SOCIAL PROFIT OF EMPOWERED DISCERNMENT

There are countless instructions to choose from about how to live everyday life, and some of them bring incredible capacity to human beings. As regards which one is most helpful, it really depends on what people want for themselves. To take one example, there are people all over the world from many different cultures who are very devoted to cultivating beneficial beliefs. There are very direct parallels and bridges between the cultures, and there has continuously been an aspiration for benefit in the world—people really wanting to be beneficial in their individual everyday life and then to come together to provide benefit to each other, to the planet Earth and to all of its inhabitants.

Yet, in the entire history of humanity, until Balanced View, there had never been an instruction set developed that produced spontaneous benefit as its predictable result. This statement is actually quite startling, as humans are beneficial by nature. In actuality, almost always we are trained in mind, speech, body, qualities and activities to be self-centered (whatever will benefit *me* in this situation). Everyone and everything else comes second. Even if we try to be beneficial, very often it is self-centered as well.

What does it mean to be naturally beneficial? It depends on our motive. What is influencing us? Do we want to feel better? Do we want money? Do we want prestige or for others to look up to us as beneficial? Are the beneficial actions used as an antidote to guilt about something?

We must be strongly motivated to align with reality, as it is naturally beneficial. We must *discern* reality. We must *instinctively* recognize or become aware of it. How do we do so? Again, first the introduction to authentic reality must take place. Upon introduction to open intelligence, synonymous with reality, benefit is obvious. Although initially open intelligence may feel self-beneficial, increasingly it is realized to benefit all. Examining reality *as it is* has never been easier. We can get to the basic state of anything or anyone quite easily, if we really are motivated to live from reality.

The linear particle accelerator shows us that, in reality, everything and everyone is pure space. This "space" that is being spoken of is not the common notion of space, but the space of space—the most basic reality, indeed, the reality of time and space. Though scientists continue to look for the smallest particle, it will not be found because the "small particle" they are seeking is the vast expanse of reality itself—open intelligence—that is the basis of everything.

Thus, everything we see is a multicolored projection of pure space, lively with intelligence and benefit. We have trained ourselves to see a world based on the secondhand beliefs of others; yet, now through Balanced View we have the basis of excellent discernment—the ability to establish the real from the unreal. Firstly, we can state with authority that not a single thing has an independent nature separate or apart from the pure, lively, beneficial expanse. It is naturally illuminated by the light of light. Even darkness is seen via light.

The exact instruction-set for gaining assurance in open intelligence has been attempted many times, yet we as a human society often did not have a great deal of clarity about what the best one would be. But now we do have a powerful instruction set, and people are coming together *in reality* for the very first time. "Reality" means the state of things as they actually exist. Reality is the foundation for beneficial society. There is no way to get out of reality. In fact, it can be stated, "Wherever you go, there it is."

It is fairly easy to look at people, places and things (data) and see their true state as it actually is. It is more important than ever to do so right now.

POTENT MEANS OF INSTRUCTION

The means to realize the power of the universal intelligence that we are all a part of is standardized in this book. A standardized language that can reach all human beings has been created, and it is extremely helpful to bring forward this standardized language and set of instructions that can give the different traditions—and all people—a means for coming together in a precise definition of human nature. To have a standardized means and standardized language for sharing the commonality of the human experience is a very powerful achievement in the evolution of human knowledge.

Throughout human history people have believed in gods, angels, benevolent deities and supernatural helpers, but compared to the gods and goddesses and other deities we have had in our lives, we humans have always seemed ineffectual, powerless and helpless. It is definitely a position of feeling "less than" and "not as good as." Very often we have projected all of our power onto the gods that we believed in, and we have not recognized that the gods we project our power onto are actually projections of ourselves. What is more, the way that we have treated our thoughts, emotions, sensations and experiences is really informed by religious beliefs, even if we feel that we are not religious.

When we recognize our own open intelligence, God comes home, so to speak, and to the original place—the originally beneficial condition of our very own open intelligence. We completely understand God for the first time. All of the power that we have given to a being other than ourselves is to be found naturally within us, and so we gradually become accustomed to resting in that beneficial empowerment. This is the profound meaning of all teachings about God.

The kinds of teachings developed down through the ages that have not had such positive results for everyone are frequently based on a basic misunderstanding of overall existence, and until recently a lot of the instruction-sets have been based on superstition. For instance, it is a superstition to believe that data, our own or anyone else's, have the power to take away our open intelligence. All data are the shining forth of lucid open intelligence. There is no datum that has a special meaning, and all of these data are equal and even in being nothing other than open intelligence. Their secondary definition is only for purposes of communication and knowledge-creation.

There are ancient symbols and images that are extraordinarily meaningful, and there is such deep and profound significance in the metaphors from the knowledge created throughout human history. But often people are caught up in dogma and doctrine and they lose track of the essential, profound meaning. However, people who come to an instinctive recognition of open intelligence can immediately understand the meaning of all these powerful symbols. They will not be distracted by the layers of confusion that have been added over time through the intrusion of incorrect logic and reason. There is also not the compelling data of wanting to have an original voice that is better than that of anyone else, which is such an immature approach to benefit and knowledge-creation.

A hidden assumption in many teachings is that there is a need to get out of the realm of ego or the fundamental condition of lack of education or one's bad karma and so forth; however, if there is nothing to get out of, you are already out! This is a very powerful distinction borne of empowered discernment. These old patterns of thinking and emoting that have been ingrained in us are not our natural state. These are learned messages, but they say nothing about who we really are.

Many times we learn a lot of things from our cultures that limit our choices, and some of those things might be very deep-rooted in us. For instance, in a culture where there is a fixed hierarchy, there will be the chosen people, the not-so-chosen people and the not-at-all-chosen people. The idea may then arise, "Oh, I'm doomed. By an accident of birth I'm not a chosen person," or, "I have the wrong karma," or whatever it might be. We may not even recognize these forms of internalized oppression until we actually become aware of their deep presence in us.

All data shine forth from all-pervasive open intelligence and have their basis in open intelligence, and to recognize this creates a great equalness within us. We can see how we have adopted all these data in a way that may have been damaging in some way and which may have lessened our assurance within ourselves. These ideas can be great sources of oppression, yet by relying on open intelligence all of the internalized oppression that we have used to put ourselves down and to dampen our assurance and innate confidence are all set free. It does not mean we necessarily need to change data streams; it means that we see them clearly as they actually are.

FREEING OURSELVES FROM INTERNALIZED OPPRESSION

Because so many of us have been trained to think that we are sinners and originally flawed, many of us are actually drawn to scientific, technological, philosophical, spiritual and religious systems where we get the confirmation that we are flawed. The fundamental and often unconscious belief is that we need to be fixed, so there is an attraction to systems that say, "This training has a way for you to overcome your innate imperfection."

This assumed imperfection takes many forms and is called by many names. Many of these forms of internalized oppression state that human beings suffer from an original sin or karmic disposition that we have been carrying for countless eons. It could be called human nature, ego, lower self or any number of terms, but all of the internalized oppression we have about this original flaw are just that—internalized oppression. It is simply a matter of what we have been trained to believe; we are trained to believe that we are flawed and to focus on getting out of our situation of being flawed. This has involved a lot of micromanagement and adjustment of all our acquired data in an attempt to free ourselves from this perceived flaw.

We have also learned along the way that things have to be complex and difficult. We come to believe that anything that is worth having involves a significant challenge that includes a lot of effort. Instead of this, now we are learning that all these ideas can be blown open with a blast of open intelligence, swift and sure. Bright open intelligence shines forth free of allegiance to confusing data—an open intelligence that is fully obvious like a clear sky, open intelligence that asserts, "There is only this."

One pervasive form of internalized oppression carried down through the ages has been that we are all marked by sin because Adam and Eve were forced out of the Garden of Eden. But if we become intimately familiar with our own deepest experience, we see that no one was ever kicked out of anything. The Garden of Eden is just a metaphor for our place of primordially pure and potent benefit in open intelligence, and we are still very much in that place. It is up to us to find what it is about our internalized oppression that makes us believe that we are *not* in the Garden of Eden. We are able to do this through the boldness of the Twelve Empowerments.

There isn't any hell realm to get out of or some heavenly place to get into. Instead, one instinctively recognizes everything *as it is* with nothing to get oneself out of or get oneself into. The seamless resolution of this one datum frees up profound beneficial energy of mind, speech, body, qualities and activities that would have been unavailable from the vantage of, "I am an unworthy sinner."

Another assumption in some teachings is that of some special person being "the One" who will make everything okay for everyone else. There is an aspect of hypocrisy in the inference, "Everything and everyone is equal, but you are not yet qualified to be like me," which is sometimes unspoken yet present in such cases. There is usually one standout person and then all the rest of us who don't quite catch on. However, the Age of Human Empowerment and Era of Great Benefit is about teaming, with everyone standing together for the benefit of all.

From the time we were born we have looked to our caregivers, authority figures and to other people around us for role models or even iconic figures who would make things all right, but it is not a matter of merely emulating some kind of iconic figure. Rather, it is *our own* beneficial energy that is the most convincing for us. We do not need authority figures or big institutions to determine how it should be for us.

When we have an authentic introduction to open intelligence, plus the free support of the Four Mainstays community for all of our life, we begin to sense something new within us that we have not recognized before at all. We as a global human culture have claimed the power of our own open intelligence. We take back the power we have projected onto authority figures, institutions, organizations and others, and we rest in our own natural place of totally beneficial power. We, the people of the world, have created our own standardized language and our own worldwide movement. We have created our own mentors and trainers and we have created our own training. We decided to call these the Four Mainstays. This is one of the dynamic expressions of open intelligence—being the source of beneficial power to re-invent the way things are done.

ORIGINAL BENEFIT

There is an element of negativity that we bear in our minds that is due to social and moral injunctions handed down through religion and philosophy. This negativity is what has been role-modeled for so long and has crept into all institutions of the past. It is internalized oppression, plain and simple. Whatever these expressions of negativity may be, they do not speak directly to what the essence of a human being truly is. The fact is that within everyone there is a core of complete mental and emotional stability, despite all the philosophical, religious and sociological half-truths that have filtered into so many beliefs.

If we had been trained in open intelligence from the moment we were born, we would not be experiencing pervasive negativity, but we were trained in negativity to the extent that we saw ourselves as fundamentally flawed. We could take the news media as an extreme example of this negativity: doom and gloom, argument, competition, attack and conflict. The data-program running through this discord binds tightly the identification with negative data rather than simply allowing open intelligence to be as it is.

All these problems and political issues that everybody is arguing about and trying to solve are solvable—not by having shouting matches about them—but by allowing open intelligence to be as it is and getting down to the basic intelligence through education in the nature of mind which shows us the course to overcome negativity of all kinds. Original benefit is social action which makes obsolete the program of data that provides only struggle and strife rather than the all-encompassing benefit, prosperity and generosity which are our birthright.

It is good to keep in mind that, regardless of how pervasive negativity may be, this stance of negativity does not represent the way things actually are. If we want to know the way things are, then we have to find who *we* are. By the power of open intelligence we have both the comprehensive view of everything as well as distinct knowledge about every aspect of what is occurring in life. Having a comprehensive view such as this makes it impossible to any longer buy into the datum of internalized oppression.

We no longer live in a state of doom and gloom and overwhelmed by the negativity of society. Even though society at this point can be grossly negative, we are at a tipping point, and things are changing dramatically from within. An evolutionary sweep is occurring in which peoples' minds will change without any effort required. We are being swept up into the comprehensive intelligence that will not allow us to go on the way we have gone before. It is beyond our present understanding to be able to predict what exactly might be possible in the future, except for a prediction of beneficial prosperity and generosity.

Whatever it is we are thinking or feeling right now, that is our relationship with the entire universe, right there. To actually allow ourselves to feel the excessive negativity of the media— and yet to not be swept away by it—is a powerful release from popular perceptions and from the extreme despair that comes from hearing the negativity over and over again. None of that negativity ever changes where we really are or who we are, which is open intelligence—the nature of mind.

By relying on our own state of original benefit we can see things with clarity, because we are no longer burdened by the excessive negativity that has been so much an expression of society's internalized oppression until now. It is time for a change. Each of us can choose; we can choose to be caught up in the misperceptions which have caused so much confusion over time, or we can choose to introduce ourselves to open intelligence and to rely on it for short moments many times.

AN ENVIRONMENT FOR OPEN-INTELLIGENCE ENHANCEMENT

From the first moment of the introduction to open intelligence there is profound benefit, and then it is simply a matter of having the right setting for growing familiar with the increasingly beneficial qualities and activities that serve to benefit all. We can choose this option if we are aware that it is available.

The right circumstances provide an environment for open-intelligence enhancement that leads to a lessening of the internalized oppression that has so pervaded much of life until now. By being trained correctly using the pith instructions of a trainer—rather than being bombarded by all kinds of philosophical or psychological jargon—it becomes possible for people to see very clearly that authentic open intelligence is possible in life.

We have acquired whatever knowledge in life that we have, but when we acquire the knowledge of the open-intelligence view, then it brings all other knowledge to a complete stop, and we begin to examine all knowledge with the open-intelligence view. Rather than relying on secondhand knowledge passed on to us from others, we rely on the potency of open intelligence.

It does not matter what we have thought or done in our life, each of us has an equal opportunity to recognize the open-intelligence view. People who are in prison for life, even some who are on death row, have been introduced to and gained confidence in the open-intelligence view. Within the prison they live in they have been able to find freedom from the prison of data. To hear people who have been gang leaders and criminals and who have been involved in extremely harmful behavior say things like, "I've never felt so free," is very powerful.

By recognizing this potency through our own simple open intelligence, we get to see what we are really made of. We see that we are not a big stockpile of descriptions related to our background. What we think we are now and what we might be in the future are only data within the open-intelligence view.

Open intelligence subsumes all the accumulations of data that we have about ourselves and our identity. These accumulations of data are completely undone in the super-factual reality of the here-and-now. It is like pressing a reset button in every single moment; everything is reset to the core in every single moment. A truly piercing intelligence is revealed that knows what to do and how to act in each and every situation.

The demonstration of open intelligence is full-on indivisible benefit, prosperity and generosity. Once open intelligence is instinctively recognized, open-intelligence conduct spreads great benefit unceasingly. Truly real open intelligence turns on the power of benefit so that it is really obvious in all circumstances. Ease and potency are the disposition of a person who is endowed with open-intelligence realization.

We already see this fully alive, emboldened, empowered and mobilized in open-intelligence community. In this most profound activation of benefit, society shifts dramatically, first in small groups and then in a widespread way.

THE WILDFIRE OF THE AGE OF HUMAN EMPOWERMENT AND ERA OF GREAT BENEFIT

Without a single word being spoken, an Age of Human Empowerment and Era of Great Benefit is opened up by the wordless introduction of open intelligence to society. The open-intelligence empowerment—which is the actual introduction to open intelligence—is wordless. It comes about through the transmission of pure benefit. But "transmission of pure benefit" is just words for something that is so vast and so expansive that it could never be described adequately in language. It can be called a direct communication of the nature of mind from one being to another without using any words.

For thousands of years human beings have been focused on the shortcomings of our nature, but now we are moving into an era where we are expressing the powerful beneficial qualities and activities that are innate to us. Everyone has equal access to these powerful beneficial qualities; no one is left out. Young or old, rich or poor, man or woman, it doesn't matter—all of us have equal access.

There is now a quantum leap out of data-definitions into an expansive connectivity and relationship with the entire universe. By relying on open intelligence we really start to see how things fit together. We do not need any kind of prefabricated education to tell us about the way things are, because we are able to see things clearly and distinctly for ourselves. When we draw on the power of this moment, it lets us see how to move in a fluid way. We do not have to have a fixed plan. We can sketch out a basic plan and then grow powerfully into it.

We have to seize the power of our mind, because that is the key to the other four modes—the body, speech, qualities and activities—coming into the full force of benefit. All this comes about, amazingly enough, through this simple practice of short moments. The short moments grow longer until one's entire life is consumed by the ever-present power of open intelligence.

The first time that the first person ever tapped into the first pure moment of open intelligence, it set off the wildfire of the Age of Human Empowerment and Era of Great Benefit, and each person who adds in a short moment of open intelligence increases that blaze of inexhaustible great benefit. We can look at ourselves now and say, "Well, enough of this past history. Now it is time for us to demonstrate that great benefit in our own experience."

Conventional means no longer need to be relied upon. Totally innovative skillful means are now being used that allow people to be able to do things they never thought they could do. The practice of short moments unleashes incredible power and benefit in our lives. All kinds of prohibitions and taboos—

however subtle they may be—are completely dissolved, and something is created that never would have been thought possible.

We have the power to solve our individual and collective problems through the power of open intelligence. All knowledge is already present, and it is rich and ripe for our discovery. A beneficial world of prosperity and generosity is right here. Complete mental and emotional stability and a healthy life are our birthright, and the realization of that birthright is the full-fledged commitment of open-intelligence society in the Age of Human Empowerment and Era of Great Benefit.

Chapter Fifteen

A SKILLED TRAINER

The Four Mainstays are the heart of Balanced View life. In the Mainstays the trainer is seen as essential to training up open intelligence in the face of the challenges of life; the training is seen as the actual solution, and the group of participants worldwide is seen as a movement and community who apply the solution. Because the Four Mainstays are so fundamental to the Balanced View lifestyle, participants learn the key point of how to see themselves in relation to the one hundred percent commitment to the fourfold Mainstays.

Trainers are participants in an open-intelligence training who have actualized the one hundred percent commitment to open intelligence; hence, one sees the results of the training in the trainers themselves. A trainer role models the remarkable evidence of what can occur for those who have a total commitment to open intelligence.

A trainer is an ultimate friend who never misses any chance to help point out open intelligence. This is a very exciting kind of friendship. It is a friendship of mutual enhancement, relishing and flourishing. It is a way of being together in a very strong, stable and solid manner that can really be counted on. In life there are a lot of things we cannot count on, but having support in relying on open intelligence is something we need to be able to count on, and that is what a trainer provides. A trainer's only job is to empower others completely in their enhancement of open intelligence.

Through the support of the trainer we relieve ourselves and others of unnecessary hardship. Strong data streams sometimes produce very strong impulses to act, and when we are unable to fully rely on open intelligence, we can consider these strong impulses with the trainer. Very often the simple willingness to rely on the trainer for support completely resolves persistent data streams. The willingness indicates a voluntary release from the isolation of self-focused data streams.

Whenever we have strong afflictive emotions that do not readily resolve in open intelligence, it is suggested that we rely on the trainer. With the support of an experienced trainer, it is possible to instinctively comprehend and recognize open intelligence. The trainer can expedite recognition of open intelligence through suggestions that are custom tailored to each person's particular situation.

In some countries and cultures there is a very pronounced focus on being a self-starter and on remaining totally independent, so in that case there can be some reluctance to invite this kind of intimate and committed relationship into one's life. But when we take advantage of the relationship with a trainer, we can really experience what it means to be truly intimate with another human being. We do not need to be the lone ranger any longer. We make ourselves known and just show up, and the relationship is ours to enjoy.

THE RELATIONSHIP WITH THE TRAINER

Having a relationship with the trainer is like being given a treasure box. When we open the treasure box there is endless wealth inside, and no matter how much we receive, this treasure box is always completely full. There is power in the trainer's own example—in their being willing to take a stand for who they actually are rather than pretending to be something they are not. When we can see ourselves reflected in the trainer, that is a very powerful transmission. It is as if we were looking into a mirror, and the trainer is there reflecting us back to ourselves.

The trainer isn't meant to be seen as some kind of icon of privilege. The trainer is there solely to transmit the open field of permission of glorious open-intelligence receptivity. This is their only role. Ideally, the relationship with a trainer is lifelong, and the deepening of the relationship comes through allowing them to know us completely through direct contact.

The trainer is someone who has the presence of continuous open intelligence. They have been willing to enter into all their own afflictive states, and that is the only reason a trainer can support someone else in *their* afflictive states. The natural authority of the trainer does not come about through assuming some kind of special state that is different from other people and then protecting that position and pointing out to everyone else how they are wrong. Rather, this natural authority comes through their own deep dive into the afflictive states—all the ones that one would want to avoid like greed, anger, pride, desire, envy, jealousy, confusion—and letting them be as they are.

The participants can see in the example of the trainer something that is true. They see a bright shining face; they see the ability to move through different situations and circumstances with skill and ease; they see the insight into all situations; they see the ability to keep a cool head; they see the alertness and power; they see the ease in every situation, knowing just what to do even if it isn't always the conventional thing to do.

Seeing the glowing example exhibited by the trainer, people become convinced that they can be the same way. At some point the recognition comes: "Well, I'm a human being just like they are, so whatever they're endowed with, it's likely I'm endowed with that too." The trust that comes to rely on the trainer is often a result of examples such as this; it is not through some kind of abstract framework. We see the life the trainer leads, and we see the living evidence of something that we did not know how to claim before in our own lives. This example is very powerful indeed.

By having gone so deeply into all the thoughts and emotions, everything opens up into complete love, true intimacy and connection, and this is the space created by this empowering relationship. How lovely it is to encounter another human being who accepts us exactly as we are—acceptance not in an intellectual way, but in a deeply felt and intimate way. It eventually becomes quite normal to feel joyful, easeful, beneficial, intimate and connected with everyone!

The love of life, the love of each other, the willingness to be close and to open up and to no longer avoid relationship with ourselves or others is really a huge step for each individual and for society collectively. When we can all come together in that way, it is an honor and a privilege to share that relationship. It is a shared experience that is also a lot of fun!

The relationship with the trainer is always by direct invitation; it is never an intrusion or an aggression from their side. At the same time, it is important to invite the trainer into your life and not to make the invitation ambivalent or vague. Invite the trainer in and seal a one hundred per cent commitment to the relationship.

As the relationship opens up more and more, an excellent trainer can provide a range of wealth to you that is beyond anything you have ever imagined. The trainer is completely devoted to our aims of great benefit. Because the trainer has outshone data by relying on open intelligence, they can see a lot of things that are not ordinarily seen, including things we don't see about ourselves. The trainer, sometimes appearing in the form of a person, is simply pure beneficial energy stirring up empowerments, explaining the potent teachings of open intelligence. They can make recognition of open intelligence a lot easier, because they have already been through many of the things that you are having difficulty with in your own life. So, naturally the trainer is very beneficial in that regard.

THE BENEFICIAL POTENCY OF THE TRAINER

The trainer has opened up into open intelligence, and she or he can transmit the factual meaning of open intelligence's crucial juncture with all data so that it is seen in direct perception. The trainer has the skillful means to put us in the right situation to do that, and they know how to nurture us so we can move towards making instinctive recognition of this crucial juncture our whole reality.

Upon arousal of the truly real beneficial nature of mind, speech, body qualities and activities, the force of the trainer's benefit as well as that of all of the benefit fruited by the entirety of open intelligence—past, present and future—become available for access and display. The door to the treasury of great benefit flies open and a resultant array of beneficial qualities and activities ensue. The illumination of knowledge is complete.

The great treasury of inexhaustible benefit is brought to life in the visible form of the trainer, the ultimate friend who introduces us to a realm of treasure that is available to all beings. Aligned with reality, we recognize the indivisibility of all. In the relationship with the trainer all kinds of things occur, just like in any relationship: life changes, sickness, old age and death. The relationship with the trainer is always very profound, whether the trainer is alive or deceased. It is in fact the easiest of jobs—the trainer does not even have to be present for the work to get done! That is what is provided by skillful means.

It is to be recommended above anything else to totally rely on open intelligence and to have this profound relationship with a trainer. Whatever we have looked for in relationships altogether will be fulfilled in the relationship with the trainer, and it will allow us a depth in all our other relating that may not have been possible before this relationship occurred.

Genuine trainers of open intelligence play a most crucial role in the Age of Human Empowerment and Era of Great Benefit. Such a trainer demonstrates exceptional potency and benefit in their body, speech, mind, qualities and activities. Only with those qualities in hand can a trainer really say to another person, "I have something to share with you." What the trainer really has to share is their own experience of the release from indulging, avoiding and replacing data and their total reliance on open intelligence.

Each human being has an irrevocable right to a complete set of the trainings on open intelligence and its benefits, and these are now available. Furthermore, each person has a right to an open-intelligence trainer who demonstrates the exceptional potency and benefit of open intelligence in their body, speech, mind, qualities and activities. Most important of all is that each of us shares with one another the tremendous potency that we have realized for ourselves. When we realize the potency that exists within us, then and only then do we have something to share with someone else.

As in any profession there are all kinds of different skills and abilities, and that is true with open-intelligence trainers as well. When we look for a trainer, we want to get the most suitable trainer for us. We want to get someone who is a good fit and who can really deliver the goods, so to speak. What we are doing is entering into a contract of sorts. We are saying, "I would like to have one hundred percent recognition of open intelligence to the point of outshining all data, and I would like your help with that." That is basically the proposition, and then really it is up to us to take full advantage of that.

The trainer is an amazing support when afflictive states come up. The relationship with a trainer is a tremendous refuge of complete and total safety, and in that relationship there is enough relaxation to let everything be *as it is*. We know we are okay, no matter what comes up. By the power of relying on open intelligence in the face of these afflictive states, we really find out that we are not the only ones who have that afflictive state and that we share that afflictive state with countless other individuals.

In this way the relationship with the trainer pulls your bedcovers! Let's say you are in bed feeling very cozy with all your data, but the trainer comes along and pulls the covers and reveals things as they are. This can only happen in an intimate and trusting relationship like this one. Without this sort of trusting and decisive relationship, it might be easy to go along believing that these afflictive states are unique to you or that you are relying on open intelligence in the face of all that arises, but not ever being really totally clear about whether you are or not.

This incredible relationship that people allow themselves to have is the most empowering, fulfilling, satisfying, pleasureful relationship that can ever be had in life, because it allows for a direct, naked encounter—naked in the real sense of being willing to be completely real and not getting detoured into any thoughts, emotions, sensations or other experiences.

In the practice of open intelligence it is easy to see how these detours have been made: being overly intellectualized, overly emotionalized or overly driven by the senses. This is why it is absolutely essential to practice open intelligence in relation with a trainer. The power of open intelligence naturally reveals itself in a way that is so much more profound than anything that would have come about without reliance on a trainer.

THE TRAINER'S SKILLFUL MEANS

The focus of all skillful means is to bring out the potency of the actual strengths, gifts and talents that a person has. It is not a matter of overwhelming the person with data-based instructions, but rather bringing out the power of open intelligence as the core education—fueling and vitalizing all talents to be used for the benefit of all. The natural state of a human being is full-on potency of all strengths, gifts and talents, and when the person is given the core education in simple open-intelligence training, this potency can come forth.

Through the power of open intelligence we can see what we are capable of in life. There are all kinds of skillful means for bringing forth comprehensive intelligence and eliciting the hidden strengths, gifts and talents in participants. Because love is the most powerful force, then the skillful means that come from love and that are woven entirely of love are the most powerful skillful means. If skillful means are to be used, then how about having a training and a trainer that only use perfect love as skillful means and nothing else!

Perfect love always exalts the individual; it never harms them. To eliminate the possibility of harm ever occurring, the most effective skillful means should be based on love-action, respectful relating and expert ways of showing people how to actually live a life based on open intelligence—and to love them through that entire process.

Most people grow up never knowing what their strengths, gifts and talents are, but a highly skilled trainer can determine the key points and instructions that are directly beneficial for each person. What is a highly skilled trainer? She or he is someone who has resolved their own data. The trainer can remember very clearly what it was like when they were themselves besieged by data, and they can understand totally the situation you are in. They relate deeply, compassionately and lovingly to the situation, and they are not going to make it worse for you by prolonging your data streams with instructions such as, "Yes, it's really awful that your partner has rejected you once again. Something is clearly wrong here, and you need to do something about it."

The trainer's skillful means—woven together with one's own skillful qualities and activities of body, speech and mind—will completely resolve these sorts of data streams. Instead of being lost in the data, one gets a sense of humor about the whole situation. There is good cheer and grateful relief for no longer getting dragged around by all these data streams. So, the highly skilled trainer isn't going to be talking for hours and hours about your data with you. Rather, they are on the transmutation train that opens up all the data into comprehensive intelligence.

You would purchase the best software and hardware available for your computer in order to perform your job well; similarly, you should choose the best trainer and instruction that is most effective for you. Once you have done so, you then connect with the trainer, make use of them and befriend them just like you would make friends with someone else. When something comes up that you cannot quite deal with, you can call on them and let them know what is going on with you. Getting to know your trainer is a very beneficial act, because it will bring forth the very best in you and will allow your gifts, strengths and talents to flourish. What is more, this is a wonderful, wonderful way to live life!

The trainer is simply beneficial energy stirring up empowerment, explaining the potent trainings of open intelligence and giving profound instructions which pointedly show that naked, uncontrived, super-factual, immense benefit is primordially present, innate and ready to be demonstrated in profound gifts, strengths and talents.

THE BENEFICIAL QUALITIES AND ACTIVITIES
OF THE TRAINER

The trainer is someone who instinctively recognizes open intelligence along with its beneficial qualities and activities of mind, speech and body. The totally complete trainer is fully empowered with open intelligence and directly transmits it through skillful means that are both symbolic and non-symbolic. Thus, open intelligence is expertly explained and transmitted to participants, allowing them to instinctively realize it in an easeful and simple way.

In the totally complete trainer, the blatant data streams obscuring open-ended knowledge creation have been totally outshone. Negative aspects have been burned off, leaving only qualities and activities of benefit to all. The totally complete knowledge of open intelligence is suddenly introduced, or there is empowerment in which the genuine introduction is given in immediate perception.

Thus, a truly complete trainer indicates a person who has instinctively realized open intelligence in a way which is truly complete. They have clarified all the reified data that were preventing total knowledge, and in doing so they have become beautiful, filled as they are with the amazing qualities and activities of open intelligence.

The trainer has gone pleasantly to the full empowerment and unending auspiciousness of open intelligence. An exceptional trainer makes a remarkable contribution to society, because they have the capacity to train up instinctive realization of open intelligence in themselves and also in participants who rely on them.

The trainer knows exactly which methods to use to train participants up in open intelligence. The trainer is unsurpassed in this way. Because of the spontaneous altruism which is integral to that knowledge, they do whatever needs to be done to be of benefit to all. The trainer completely confirms the nature of reality, demonstrating the introduction of open intelligence, the one hundred percent commitment to it, and the assurance of the beneficial empowerment of mind, speech, body, qualities and activities that is arrived at.

THE TRAINER AS A SOURCE OF EMPOWERMENT

The unending fruition is empowering in many ways, and it has no disempowerment connected with it at all. It is final and requires no more effort; it is naturally beneficial to oneself and all others. The trainer solves their own problems through totally complete empowerment of the potencies of open intelligence and is committed to bringing others to the same place.

The trainer provides a training that is fundamentally workable and which has an excellent fruition because of it. The training first fulfills one's own aims or purposes because it brings personal release from problems, and then it fulfills the aims and purposes of others because it naturally responds to others with the needed confirmation and empowerment to bring them to their beneficial potencies of mind, speech, body, qualities and activities.

The trainer is steady and constant. The methods of the trainer in open intelligence are always used in a way that pronounces inexhaustibility and unending empowerment. The superb qualities and activities of the mind, speech and body of open intelligence unendingly produce empowerment of totally complete knowledge and benefit. Open intelligence is an immeasurably large collection of open-ended knowledge creation for the benefit of all that never ends.

The trainer is a rich source of empowerment because of what they have instinctively comprehended and recognized, and these beneficial empowerments of mind, speech and body are the obvious demonstration of open intelligence. Therefore, the trainer brings great benefit through continually empowering the introduction, one hundred percent commitment to and assurance of open intelligence.

The appreciation for the trainer, which manifests itself in respectful relating and true love, leads to a very beneficial relationship which is so very strong. These events of relationship with the trainer grow with the introduction, commitment and inexhaustible assurance in open intelligence to overt gratitude and joy. The relationship with the trainer is increasingly expansive due to the unending treasury of beneficial qualities and activities that are evident in mind, speech and body.

Even during extremely afflictive states, the trainer is able to bring qualities and activities that are perfectly fitting and just right for outshining affliction with its fundamental reality—the pure benefit of open intelligence. The insight and skillful means of the trainer are relentless due to instinctively comprehending, recognizing and realizing totally complete knowledge of all data. In other words, the trainer has perfect certitude of the non-independent nature of data, information and knowledge. This spontaneous authority and conviction at all times is the source of non-symbolic, direct transmission of the potency of open intelligence. Through a one hundred percent commitment to open intelligence and the relationship with the trainer, one realizes that the authority and conviction of the trainer is a reflection of one's own authority and conviction; thus, a person is always empowered to rely on their own power of great benefit.

The trainer empowers, educates and mobilizes us to be of greatest benefit to all. The trainer ensures that each person is doing well, supports them in resolving challenges in the empowerment of beneficial open intelligence and completely confirms its fruitional potencies as the reality of identity.

A beneficial rootedness in open intelligence is one that will grow into a beneficial result, unendingly producing the pure benefit of all. Open intelligence is a treasure of benefit that never ends, and it is the basis of the inexhaustible Age of Human Empowerment and Era of Great Benefit.

Chapter Sixteen

AN AUTHENTIC TRAINING

Throughout all of history, pure, direct and authentic trainings have existed in human culture, and the simple practice of relying on open intelligence for short moments many times has been ceaselessly present as well. The continuous appearance of this practice throughout human history extends like a chain of golden mountains stretching into the distant past. It is the primordial wisdom that is the basis of authentic trainings.

"Relax body and mind completely and let all data be as they are": that is the direct revelation of pristine wisdom. This is the great insight of humankind that requires no doing. This wisdom isn't born between the pages of a philosophy book. It is born in the capacity to be at rest in all the circumstantial appearances of our own being—our own thoughts, emotions, and experiences. It is a wisdom that cannot be gotten by changing or doing things.

An authentic training is one in which this is pointed out over and over, and exactly the same thing is said in a thousand different ways that enrich and soothe our being. What is already present has to be easily accessible, and to be able to know this in our lived experience is true discernment. It is the nature of our own wisdom qualities that, if we do not rely on authentic trainings, we will not be able to so easily recognize those qualities.

Direct and authentic trainings do not refer back to an author or to a personal experience. Surely, if the training is in fact pure, direct and authentic, then open intelligence is the only author of that training. Such a training may appear in the mind stream of a contemporary individual, and if that training appears in, of, as, and through the perfect purity of open intelligence, it is not the accomplishment of an individual person.

Trainings such as this are an appearance of the highest wisdom of body, mind, speech qualities and activities and are equal to open intelligence itself. They can also be called *epitome* trainings. In the past, before humanity had writing, things were passed along orally, but with the advent of writing, these trainings have been documented and written down in different forms.

In this Age of Human Empowerment and Era of Great Benefit, authentic trainings continue to be written down. The writing is done in such a way that the core message of how one recognizes, realizes and lives as the genuine nature of being can be easily understood. Whenever trainings like this appear and are then written down, they are pure and authentic trainings of genuine being; in other words, they are completely uncompounded, unfabricated, simple and direct.

SPECIFIC AND UNERRING

There are some things that are written which point to what is only partially true—the kind of writing that is about a topic from one author's vantage. When we read it, we might feel a little spark and that there is something true to it. Then there is another kind of writing from an authentic training where, when we read it, *boom*, the self is completely undone. These are two very distinct types of writing! One is concerned with data about somebody's experience, while the other is the majestic lion's roar of the infinite vast expanse of open intelligence. This type of writing is not mere philosophy; it is the direct experience of authentic recognition and realization.

Trainings written in this way are completely uncontrived, and they all say exactly the same thing, no matter when they have been written throughout time. They state confidently that the most fruitful method for becoming familiar with the nature of genuine being is to rely on open intelligence for short moments many times.

Different practices work for different people, but it is also important to find a commonality. Can we find something that works for everyone? What is the common denominator, and

211

how common can that denominator be made? Trainings in open intelligence must be precise, specific and complete and contain a complete set of all key points and pivotal instructions. These trainings are the right of all human beings and are made available throughout human society. The same skillful means work not only in a standardized way but also in a very highly customized way, allowing the very special, unique and particular potencies of each person's strengths, gifts and talents to shine forth.

All the crucial key points and pivotal instructions that show open intelligence to be alive right now can be provided to people. The training that results is so specific and so unerring; it leaves no stone unturned. The training is for people to share with each other—not just for one authority figure to share from a position of power, but for people everywhere to use to empower themselves and one another.

An authentic and pure training never veers from complete simplicity, authenticity and directness, so it never adds anything else in. It does not say that one must develop virtue or perform different activities in order to be pure enough to understand and recognize one's true nature. Rather, the pure or authentic trainings—the epitome trainings—say that who we truly are is already fully present and available and that no effort need be made towards acquiring what is already present.

A direct training in open intelligence continually empowers inexhaustible open intelligence, because it outshines all data reifications on its way, having always arrived at its destination, and because it is present in a way that allows one to have an effortless confirmation of open intelligence in its fruitional potencies.

When simplicity is the only message of the training, it becomes clear very swiftly and surely what the true nature of life is. If there is anything else added in, then there is something imposed in what has never had any imposition of any kind. There is no intermediary anywhere in open intelligence, there is no effort to achieve anything, there is no cause leading to a result and there is no destination or anyone going there. This can only become glaringly obvious through relying on open intelligence without seeking or describing anything.

When we rely on open intelligence in a completely uncontrived way, there is no need to change anything about what is appearing. Everything is allowed to vanish naturally and freely like the flight path of a bird in the sky. In this way, all data that appear within the all-encompassing pure view of open intelligence are vivid appearances of the basic space of open intelligence and nothing else. An authentic training continually points to this, and this alone.

NO SPECIAL CIRCUMSTANCE

To benefit from a truly direct and authentic training does not require any sort of previous lifestyle or preparation. One need not have lived in any special circumstance or visited with gurus or done yoga or chanted anything or done any practice. Nothing special has to be done. One could be from any walk of life—software engineer, businesswoman, student, prison inmate or whatever it may. One could have been absolutely miserable, depressed and wanting to end one's life, or one could come from a Pollyanna background in which everything looked rosy and sweet.

Whatever our personal circumstances may have been, easefulness and openness are all that are required to be ready to receive the training. When there is unerring instruction given, conviction naturally dawns, and when conviction begins to dawn, then one knows what gaining assurance in open intelligence is, because a natural settledness is felt.

Trainings that are direct and unerring about how to rely on open intelligence are available and are spreading all over the world. What is different about this era in human history is that for the first time these kinds of trainings are available to billions of people rather than just to a few. A uniform message can be shared by all human beings—a message which is very easy for any human being to understand, whether educated or not.

There are all kinds of trainings for all kinds of beings, and a truly authentic training is from the very beginning based solely on the direct perception of the natural state. The training is customizable for each person, and that is one of its beauties. The training really supports the enhancement of the beauty of everyone, so it is that which really shines through.

One of the incredible things about a training such as this is that it can be scaled into a worldwide movement that isn't focused on any particular kind of person. There may be people involved in the training from many backgrounds, but by becoming familiar with open intelligence in their own particular way, they will be able to see how to take care of whatever problems arise within their own situations. What is seen clearly about solving problems is that it always involves a very spacious, open and balanced vantage.

A skillful and direct training of the modern day is inclusive of all mindsets and cultures. The whole scope of the undertaking is focused exclusively on the benefit of the whole, with people all over the world coming together in a grassroots way with a training that anyone can understand, no matter where they live or what their life circumstances are. In order for it to be in a grassroots form for all of humankind, it requires a simplicity of understanding whereby everyone can receive what is being said.

For the first time in human history these very direct trainings are open to everyone and spoken in a language that isn't culturally exclusive. Everything everywhere is totally wide-open, and that is the way it is with these very direct trainings too. They are complete trainings with unerring instruction on how to completely realize the potencies of body speech, mind qualities and activities to be of benefit to all.

THE IDEAL DISPOSITION

The ideal disposition of a person who wants to rely on open intelligence is to simply be open to that; that is all. You simply remain open enough to listen to the trainings for a while and remain willing to be contributed to. To do so allows you to see that the conventional identity you have taken yourself to be is very limited. You also see that there is a wisdom identity that is naturally present, which can only be recognized and realized by fully relying on open intelligence.

In this simple way it is easy to know that the genuine being of open intelligence is naturally ensured in a simple and sure way. Be simple and plainspoken in all your words and be at ease. To try to hold on to the data that appear within the pure view of open intelligence is like trying to grab the reflection of the moon in a pond. There is nothing there to hold on to; there is no need to make something out of nothing. Just relax and enjoy the precious beauty of your own being.

This isn't a philosophy or a religion or spirituality in any of the limiting ways that those terms have been understood. Rather, what is being spoken of here is the optimal way of being human, without distortions of culture, tradition or dogma. If one wants to be religious, that is surely possible, as long as the true meaning of "religious" is understood. The epitome of any religion is the absolute freedom and unity of everything, and within all religions there is an epitome training that states that everything is equal, unified and free.

Complete assurance in the genuine being of pure and vast open intelligence can come about in a number of ways. One way would be that suddenly and spontaneously one's mind opens up to encompass the sublime knowing of the nature of genuine being. A second way would be to have an introduction to open intelligence through a trainer who communicates its direct expression. In that way open intelligence is recognized by the person who has contact with that trainer.

A third way is to hear pure and authentic trainings, and merely through the hearing of those trainings to have complete recognition upon hearing them. The person is already naturally easeful and open, so then when they hear about relying on open intelligence, this just makes absolute sense to them, because they are already totally open and settled. A fourth and more common way is that one hears an authentic training and gradually over time settles into the assurance that naturally comes from committing to and persisting in relying on open intelligence.

For many people today, conviction dawns just by hearing about the true nature of who we are. So, when we look at a training and want to know if it is authentic or not, we ask, "Does the training speak of unerring truth, and does it create assurance and certainty in the person who is committed to it?" The training should unerringly state over and over again the truth of what *is* in myriad ways, so in reading it and hearing it, it becomes more and more evident in one's own being. Many of us may not have received direct trainings before, but when we hear them we can say, "Wow! I've always known this."

For some very fortunate people, conviction dawns with absolute, incontrovertible certainty about the nature of being merely through listening. Again, one could call this "complete recognition upon hearing." What does this require? It requires an open mind, but everyone already has an open mind! There has never been a mind that has been closed up anywhere. The clear light of wisdom is always open everywhere, without being anywhere. It has never been flawed in any way, so there is nothing to do. If we believe that we have to be deconditioned, then we are in a trap, because what is unconditioned has never been conditioned and thus does not need to be deconditioned.

SWIFT, SURE AND DIRECT

If people have never received direct trainings, then they may not see how it could be possible that a change in their lives could swiftly and surely come about. However, it has always been true that there have been very swift, sure and direct trainings where there isn't lots of complicated maneuvering involved. From the bottom of the mountain, the summit cannot be seen so clearly, but from the summit everything can be seen all around, and all the paths leading to the summit can be seen as well.

When we hear about a training that is based upon complete recognition upon hearing, then we might object, "Oh, this couldn't possibly be the case. No! I couldn't possibly be qualified to get that!" The reality of what we are is so simple that it can be liberated into full evidence simply in hearing about it. But in order for that to occur, it is important that we *do* hear about it from someone. Then, once we have heard it, it is up to us to be open to it. If we have had the good fortune to be placed in an auspicious circumstance where we are being guided by an epitome training and trainer, we just need to keep showing up until conviction dawns.

It often occurs that new people come to a training because they have seen a huge change in a friend or family member. They want to know, "What happened to them?" so they are very motivated to look into what brought about that change. In this way, the training is best based on attraction rather than promotion. The people who want to listen will just show up naturally, and that is simply the way it is.

People may agree with what is being offered and will want to stay around, or they may not agree and then they can go somewhere else and do what suits them best. In an authentic training it does not matter what choice is made: a person would always be supported in any way possible, and if they wanted to return at some point, they would be welcomed back. Even if a person has left that training but returns and asks for support, they would be well received and rigorously supported in every way possible.

People all over the world are living lives that they never dreamt possible, and they are inspiring others to dare to dream in the same way. Each person who has been nourished by the training of short moments has a different story about what brought them, but once they are there, through their shining examples they will attract others.

HOW AN AUTHENTIC TRAINING IS ORGANIZED AND PROVIDED

Today we live in an era where information is increasingly free, including this kind of information. Not only is it free in the sense of not costing anything, but it is timelessly and spatially free and cannot be unfree. Because it is natural for information

217

of all kinds to be timelessly and spatially free, in the Age of Human Empowerment and Era of Great Benefit this will become more and more the direction, rather than a movement towards restriction of information.

To offer an authentic training is not a casual affair, and the offering should not be done in a disorganized or careless way. When the phrase "benefit for all" is used, it is not just a manner of speaking, but a guiding principle of service. So, how does an authentic training express itself in a way that it does in fact provide benefit for all? First of all, there should be a formal series of trainings available all over the world, written in a simple language which is easily understood. The target language could be different, so the written texts can be translated into many different languages. The trainings could be given face-to-face or through many electronic means, such as tele/video-conference systems or through digital facilities that the Internet provides.

The core training would be one in which participants are empowered to recognize that data are the dynamic energy of the open intelligence of fundamental reality and that open intelligence restores our naturally beneficial power of mind, speech, body, qualities and activities. Because we may have been blindsided our whole life by data streams, it would be extremely important to identify very specifically what our own personal data streams are.

It is similar to a person who has a bookstore with 10,000 books, but who has no inventory of them and does not know where anything is or where it came from. Obviously, it would serve greatly to be able to know what exactly fills the bookstore so that it can be run easily and profitably. In a similar way, we all need to know what our major data streams are and how to resolve those data streams in open intelligence.

A standardized training is needed that anyone can participate in, and at the same time one that is structured so that each person can address all of their own data—past, present and future—and get a clear, all-inclusive perspective on them. The training would be a permission field to bring up everything that has ever gone on in a person's life and to normalize all of it in open intelligence. The participant would be taken step-by-step along the journey, accompanied by supportive trainers, so that all data are subsumed in open intelligence and all relationships in everyday life are harmonized.

It is really a very empowering way of instantiating open intelligence so that no one is blindsided by any data that come up. Very carefully, in each aspect of life, one takes a look at what the data really are. It brings everyone and everything out of vagueness. There isn't any imprecision; it becomes very clear what the different data are and how they have ruled different aspects of life and disempowered all of us in so many different ways.

Trainings should be offered continuously to enhance and support the growing assurance in open intelligence. The entire body of texts and media would be very much informed by what the people of the world actually want to hear and read, rather than being the ideas of one person that are then forced onto people. The training would always be flexible, immediate and powerful, directly relevant to what the concerns are of people living today. There would be an inexhaustible supply of training media, and it would just keep pouring out in a powerful call-and-response relationship with the people who are participating.

A very skillful training is a trainer to all. This skillful training does not have limitations on who or what it can train, because it provides a most valuable, comprehensive approach to intelligence, data, information and knowledge. Thus, its endless data array, as well as its definition of the data array, always pool into open-ended quality information and knowledge creation for the benefit of all.

An authentic training enriches our life in a way that is really unimaginable. To think that we could have a life built on the open-intelligence view and that we could have many beautifully supportive resources which we can share with each other is a great joy to consider.

The power of the training media belongs to everyone. The training media reveal the expanse of open intelligence more and more and have exactly the same message, because this repetition of the same basic message over and over again is a source of incredible nurturance.

THE MOST BASIC KIND OF KNOWING

Open intelligence is a superior or superb intelligence and refers to the very precious and empowering beneficial mind, speech, body, qualities and activities possessed by those who have trained up open intelligence to the point of outshining data. That intelligence is superior to an ordinary unempowered intelligence. The super-facts that appear within open intelligence are superior compared to the facts that appear within intelligence that is not trained up into inexhaustible open intelligence.

Through the indestructible vehicle of a highly skillful training, open intelligence is trained up in an unconventional and very direct way. It is called "indestructible," because it utilizes the uttermost super-fact of reality of one's own intelligence as the vehicle of open intelligence. Open intelligence is the actual nature of all data and is the reality which allows a person to go to outshining or potent intelligence, which is the blissful, empowered state subsuming all positive, negative and neutral data—empowering a new and most comprehensive order of intelligence with beneficial mind, speech, body, qualities and activities.

This fruition of mind, speech and body is assimilated at the crucial juncture of open intelligence and data, in which data are outshone in great benefit. The fruitional forms of beneficial insight and the qualities and activities that serve it are spontaneously present in open intelligence, and they then function to benefit others.

An authentic training gives rise to the profound view of reality *as it is*. Open intelligence and its pure benefit—or a training that reveals open intelligence—are reality itself. This reality constitutes the most basic kind of knowing there is, as well as the qualities and activities associated with that reality.

In an authentic training one effortlessly and instinctively recognizes the perfect benefit of open intelligence. Through symbolic and non-symbolic skillful means, open intelligence is completely confirmed again and again. From the beginning the benefit of open intelligence is of such fundamental greatness that commitment to it and inexhaustible assurance in it are spontaneous.

The ever-increasing, spontaneous qualities and activities of beneficial mind, speech and body demonstrate that no contrived effort is needed for this ongoing accomplishment. Reality is comprehended and realized through an authentic training that elicits satisfaction, flourishing and benefit that come about without conceived effort. Reality means turning to the pure benefit of open intelligence, which of itself is already present in its own place. Resting in its own place, there is no need to seek it elsewhere.

An authentic training is understood as the foundational platform of open-ended knowledge creation and conceptual engineering in all areas of knowledge. It explains and guides the purposeful construction and support of beneficial knowledge creation for humans as intelligent entities who are in rapid transition into an inexhaustibly beneficial future.

The innovation of open intelligence in human self-understanding is part of a single process of reassessment of human nature. This reassessment of human nature affords the Earth and its inhabitants optimal adaptation to pioneering scientific, technological and social advancement within a cosmos which has many worlds.

A balanced view secures a human being in complete mental, emotional and physical stability, life satisfaction and flourishing; it is the singular basis of open intelligence—totally complete knowledge about the nature and workings of reality. Furthermore, it is the source of skillful qualities and activities, including the consistent ability to fulfill creative intent of benefit to all. This balanced view alone brings universal unity, empowerment and peace. Through empowerment, education and mobilization in the open intelligence view, the universe has entered an unending Age of Human Empowerment and Era of Great Benefit.

For human beings to arrive at the point of instinctive comprehension of open intelligence is a breakthrough of utmost import and significance. It is a complete breakaway from the primitive, superstitious ideas about what a human being is and what a human being does. The empowered fruition of human nature is instinctively comprehended and recognized.

In an authentic training, there is direct relationship to the special feature of indwelling benefit and its qualities of body, speech and mind that are always present and manifest. This is the indestructible vehicle, the vast expanse of reality's body, speech and mind, which establish the human entity *as it is*—an open-ended intelligent entity, an inexhaustible expression of open intelligence and its purely beneficial fruitional potencies of always-expanding benefit. Just this is full and complete bliss-benefit; thus, there is assurance of not needing to obtain anything.

Instinctively know the total benefit that is inexpressible by speech or thought. If that great reality is known through direct transmission— non-symbolic super-factual realization of open intelligence's pure benefit—one is completely situated in the great equality of pure benefit, shining forth as anything at all. The unending miracles of the splendid pool of data, which are outside or beyond the limit of thought and action, arise inexhaustibly.

This singular pure intelligence appears as all data, information and knowledge. It is the only holder of knowing, of totally complete intelligence for the benefit of all, and is expressed through all intelligent entities endowed with the aptitude for utilizing the actual situation of inexhaustible intelligence demonstrating pure benefit. Open, spontaneously present and indivisible, only abiding as itself, regardless of its data flow, the reality expanse of all kinds of intelligences is evident. The pure benefit of open intelligence is not one thing appearing as something else; it is in all ways a vast singularity.

Chapter Seventeen

A LIFELONG COMMUNITY

The fourth Mainstay is the worldwide community online and in all places where people gather together to rely on open intelligence. Within open-intelligence community we see how it works for everyone to create potent solutions for change—individually and collectively. This is the actual empowerment of society from the grassroots. Everything that we see in powerful communities all over the world is due to the potency of connecting with others in a way that brings about this empowerment. The best education we can possibly get is right here within ourselves. If we do not have this education in open intelligence, we will be unable to truly take advantage of any other education we have.

As regards to finding solutions to problems, we suggest solutions that we ourselves can implement rather than merely focusing on data. People do not sit around and criticize and complain; everyone contributes whatever solution they can to making the whole team work. Things flow together seamlessly, and it all works in a very powerful way. We suggest solutions and then we implement them; there is no need to suggest a solution without being able to implement it. If we have a solution, then we think through what is needed to implement it and then formulate a plan of action. Once that preparation has been done, that is the time to present a solution and get it into action.

For example, if we want build community in our local area we bring it about ourselves with the support of other people who can help us, and people connect to make it happen. Beauty and harmony arise out of a way of being together that is completely comfortable and at the same time very powerful—totally enacting change that really works within ourselves and collectively.

At the local community level each individual has complete responsibility for maintaining the vitality of the community by relying on the Four Mainstays. If everyone is relying on the Four Mainstays, there is no data stream that can take over. There is no one who can arise to bully anybody else in the group or loud voices that get to talk about everything while no one else gets to say anything. There should be an actual process for allowing the voice of every single person to be heard and to have that enter into the way that the whole organization actually unfolds.

Unified, harmonious and flowing community arises by the power of the Four Mainstays, where everyone can contribute their strengths, gifts and talents. This is very important and an absolute key. There is an indestructible culture of gratitude and respect which is quite distinct from the way society usually operates. We may have had a lot of notions about how society could be, and we were right! We actually see it in action: people living harmoniously, peacefully and powerfully together. This is really convincing, and it all comes from within ourselves.

First we allow the community of our data to be in harmony. It flows along effortlessly in a culture of gratitude and respect. That is the culture of open intelligence: one of gratitude and respect within ourselves. We are not trying to turn anything on or off. Everything is allowed to be as it is. From being at rest with the data within ourselves, we are able to really extend ourselves to others in a beautiful way and to contribute our strengths, gifts and talents in a very powerful way.

Thus, when we enter into the indestructible open intelligence-community, the commitment to the power of community is found in these Four Mainstays. We utilize the Four Mainstays to engage in action that exhibits the power of open intelligence to create revolutionary change in human society.

This is the meaning of a "grassroots" organization: it comes up from the heart of human society itself into reality. It is built from the grassroots of human society by individuals who together show the world a powerful new human identity— indestructible open intelligence. In open intelligence one finds the perfect family—the indestructible open-intelligence family. Open intelligence maintains and sustains everything, no matter its label.

SAFE AND LOVE-FILLED COMMUNITIES

There is such life satisfaction and flourishing that comes from living in community with people who are completely committed to relying on open intelligence. No one ever need be alone and isolated. The feeling of isolation that so many people have felt is removed in a community such as this. There is the opening up of a lifelong community of giving, of sharing, of caring, of intimacy, of connection—a lifelong community where no one can be kicked out for any reason.

When people rely on open intelligence together, they are capable of forming communities that are safe and love-filled, in which the usual goings-on do not go on. If these sorts of things do come up, they are rectified immediately in a loving way. This is the sort of place where you can be as often as you want to be, even for your entire life if you choose.

We are going to be dealing with people wherever we go in life, and to have a community of people who have all made the one hundred percent commitment to open intelligence is enormously supportive. When we become capable of this total, complete, accurate, authentic and genuine love of self, then we are able to enter into love-relationship with others. Truly beneficial relating with others comes when we are really willing to leave everything *as it is*.

A very important aspect of the empowered open-intelligence community is the environment of safety and clarity found there, which contains a permission field in which to normalize all of our data. For most of us this may be the first time we have ever had that kind of permission field or normalization space to be with all our data exactly as they are.

Newcomers who come to a community such as this are automatically introduced to open intelligence just by being in a room filled with people who are already enjoying open intelligence. The newcomers are benefitted by being with people who are already deeply and spontaneously involved in the practice of love of self and love of others, and who are already naturally benefitting themselves in the most significant way possible by relying on open intelligence and therefore spontaneously benefitting others.

Everyone is completely welcome in a community such as this. It is completely open, warmhearted and inclusive, and no one will ever ask you to leave. But if you want to leave, you certainly can, and if you choose to do so, the response will be, "Oh, we love you and we will miss you. Please come back whenever you want."

This really undoes many of the old models of being together and working together as a group. It allows for so much vitality, so much splendor and so much wealth within each individual and within the group. There is the ability to be with people and to genuinely care and love very deeply with total heart in every single moment.

Some people are young and some are older, but no matter what the stage of life, if you are just getting familiar with open intelligence, give yourself the opportunity to be together with other people who are getting familiar with it as well. Give yourself that time to enrich yourself totally and completely with open intelligence and the way that it operates.

The way we can be together is so simple, because it is so simple to love. We love ourselves and others by totally relying on open intelligence. What an incredible way to live: where love does not have to be contrived and where there is no fear that love will be lost. Most of us have lived a life where we were afraid that love would be lost somehow, but what a tremendous joy it is to become accustomed to a love that will not be lost—a love which is in fact impossible to lose. What is more, we have the opportunity to share lifelong community where love such as this is present for each one of us.

LIVING LIFE TOGETHER IN OPEN INTELLIGENCE

One of the most important aspects of provisioning lifelong community to everyone in the world is allowing people to know that there is a safe ground and safe connection in which to live. It deserves confirmation in very strong terms: we are never alone. No one is ever alone. There has been so very much longing for understanding—hoping that we could find people who would understand us but then never really finding those people. Gone are the days when we said, "No one understands me and no one will ever understand me. I'm just too complex, too out there; I will never truly belong anywhere."

But now, look at the communities developing around the world where people so thoroughly understand each other! This is the power of the dynamic energy of benefit. It completely changes the whole way of being in relation to each other, where we go from not really comprehending our existence to complete comprehensibility. We go from not really knowing where the bedrock is within us that we can count on to absolutely knowing what that is. We go from not understanding ourselves to completely understanding. We go from not understanding others to understanding everyone, no matter what their motivations and actions might be.

That is a quantum leap in human intelligence—so simple, so direct, so easy, right here and available to everyone. No more complex schemes. We just return to basics, each one of us, back to total basics.

These are examples of the tremendous capacity without limit or restriction of any kind that is available in open intelligence. These are major changes that have occurred within the paradigm of what it means to be a human being. In the flourishing of a worldwide group devoted to open intelligence for all, there is the evidence and demonstration of this intelligence, and it will only further itself in this Age of Human Empowerment and Era of Great Benefit. The instinctive liveliness of open intelligence is the empowerment of clarity bursting open as fully beneficial everyday living, the empowerment energy of potent benefit in action without ever thinking about it or trying to contrive it.

We have only one life to live, and we have the choice to live it in the way we want. If we want to live our life hanging out with people who are only interested in talking about data, we can do that, or we can really dive in deeply to open intelligence and see what its bright vista has to offer to human culture. The bright vista of open intelligence has all kinds of really incredible things to offer that are completely inaccessible within the context of reified intelligence alone.

Anyone who wants to live a life in open-intelligence community can do so; it is a matter of making a commitment to it, just like the one hundred percent commitment that is made to relying on open intelligence for short moments many times. We see within ourselves that we actually have the power to design our life to be as we want it to be. If we want to hang out with other people committed to open intelligence, we can hang out with them. If we want to work only with people committed to open intelligence, we can find a way to do that. In open intelligence itself the power and courage to make changes we never dreamt of come about.

Community-building today is vastly different than it was twenty years ago. The tools and skillful means of community-building that are available now are being used on a variety of levels to potentially reach almost everyone on earth. It is really important to see what is happening and to acknowledge that and be grateful for it. There is incredible technology and very advanced systems for connecting people together in open intelligence available now.

Community-building is not just having some people come together in a room. Yes, it may include getting people together in a room, but most of community-building is invisible. It is the invisible, indivisible hand of open intelligence reaching everyone. It is a commanding system of augmenting human intelligence that has a penetrating reach, and that reach is extending up from the grassroots, expanding everywhere. When any community or organization is spoken of as being "grassroots," it involves the education, mobilization and empowerment of all the people involved rather than merely complying with the dictates of a hierarchical authority.

Training up the potency of open intelligence with one another in community is such an incredible support. All around the world people are teaming up in open intelligence, seeing that what has been talked about for a long time—global unity and the possibility of a governance of the world that far exceeds the current forms—is truly possible, and that it starts with us. Yes, it starts with us. Each moment that we rely on open intelligence, we make a significant contribution to the Age of Human Empowerment and Era of Great Benefit. Each time we rely on open intelligence we join all of humankind together in the potency of open intelligence.

RADICAL CHANGE

This radical change cannot come about through one person; it has to be through everyone. Conventionally it would be only the authorities or the notable people who would be given the responsibility; however, it is people from throughout the world helping each other very directly and very powerfully that has the most lasting impact.

We see many people from all over the world joining together at the grassroots in the potency of open intelligence, seeing that government starts with *self*-government, which is the powerful government of our own data. The body-politic begins with each of us. Every individual has the power to bring forth beneficial qualities and activities, and people around the world are seizing the power of benefit. By giving ourselves completely to our own natural perfection, we can contribute insights that are otherwise inaccessible.

There is no way for human society to advance in a way that is completely beneficial unless we ramp up our intelligence into open intelligence; that is all there is to it. Open intelligence has the answers we are looking for. No matter what our field or profession is, open intelligence has the answers to the challenges that profession is facing. It just requires one person in that particular profession who is totally committed to open intelligence to build a team related to that profession and to innovate it completely.

This is exactly what has happened in communities around the world where the people are committed to open intelligence, so we have solid examples that it works. All kinds of mixed-up ideas, vagueness and misunderstandings are completely cleared up due to the empowerment of a team of people committed to open intelligence.

When challenging circumstances arise in ourselves or in our groups, we have a choice to go with all the afflictive emotions or to continue to know ourselves as we truly are. We can choose to not act on any of the impulses or urges associated with the afflictive emotions, to continue to rely on open intelligence in a natural way and to seek the support, refuge and ease of our trainer, training and the community. By relying on open intelligence rather than continuously relying on data, more and more power will come into our lives—the power of incredible benefit—and we will see clearly and succinctly exactly how to share that power with the world.

If we have integrated our data, then we can really be a support to someone else, and providing support is one of the many ways that a community can be of great help. Open intelligence has complete sovereignty over all data, and we start to see this in ourselves, and we see it at a much larger level when we come together with others. It is clear: if we are really interested in relying on open intelligence for short moments repeated many times and we are surrounded by people who are themselves relying on open intelligence, that is clearly a very helpful situation to be in! Just in a very simple human way, if we have friends and work colleagues who are living in the same way we are, it makes things a lot easier.

In a community where the basis is open intelligence, there is no competition or blame; everyone can cooperate without these issues coming into play. This is real relationship: allowing everyone to completely thrive without any hideouts, without dodging this way or that way or hiding out in pretentious notions about oneself. It is about getting very real in everyday life, moment-to-moment, interacting with each other, living together, working together smoothly and effortlessly and expanding the power all the way along.

How do we find out how to do that? We do it! We show ourselves that it is real. There isn't some future to get to or some great plan to enact. Whatever is, is right here, right now, very alive, very real. We extract the power from every single moment just *as it is*. It really does not matter what we think or feel; we just stay put in open intelligence, and we will know everything we need to know.

The opening up of a community of people within human society that is completely relying on open intelligence is part of the incredible offering of this present age. Everyone is included; no one can be left out or excluded. The more we realize this total inclusion within our own body, speech and mind, the more we realize it to be present in everything. This is why it is so important to allow data to be as they are. The manifestation of our individual circumstance is a microcosm within the macrocosm of everything. Within ourselves we encompass the whole universe.

The Age of Human Empowerment and Era of Great Benefit, in which the precious treasury of the way of great benefit abounds, is the demonstration of great accomplishment arising from this commitment to relying on open intelligence. But this current era is not an individual accomplishment; it is emerging because many people all over the world are making the commitment to live as open intelligence. This global view takes the practice of relying on open intelligence out of the context of an obsessive involvement with self or as an achievement for the purposes of an individual self into the context of the benefit for the whole of humanity.

Chapter Eighteen

REAL CONNECTION, REAL INTIMACY

What is happening right now is the emergence of open intelligence as the basis of society—open intelligence that is pervasive, where no one is isolated. Open intelligence puts us completely in touch with the reality of who we are and who everyone is. By making a total commitment to open intelligence at the basis of reality, we come to find that bliss and joy are always-on.

In order to find that innate bliss, we have to be able to not turn away from or avoid anything. Instead of avoiding the things we previously have hidden from, we explore them and go into them. All kinds of data streams could occur, but instead of pushing them away, we look into them. We see it all. The most intimate we can be with any experience is with *our own* experience, whatever that experience is.

Open intelligence is always present, and it is recognized when we are not always pushing our data streams away or trying to change them. Open intelligence is always comforting and it will always provide the right direction. After a while the trust grows, and to the degree one is committed to open intelligence, to that degree one will notice its brilliantly shining evidence. Just as this is so for the individual, it is so for all of society as well. When we really see the strength and benefit of open intelligence within ourselves, then that is what we automatically see in everyone else.

A deep inner connectedness opens up, and we see that we really are networked with all. The entire expanse is one fluid, networked, interactive and potent open intelligence. We do not need to try to become one global family—we already are! We are really hardwired to feel the sense of completely networked belonging and intimacy with others, with the planet we live on and with all its inhabitants.

It is no longer a matter of remaining self-focused and trying to get into some kind of better state of mind for oneself; rather, we open up naturally into an intimacy, interconnectivity and interactivity with all beings. That which is looking out of all eyes is the same "what's looking" in all beings, and in that very real way we are all seamlessly connected.

Rather than all the thoughts, emotions and sensations being about "me," our experiences can instead be related to the benefit of all. What a relief! It is good to finally become bored with the constant obsession with "me." What a tedious project that is! Instead, the mind is aflutter with all kinds of wonderful thoughts and the emotions are rich with deep connection. We feel a tremendous sense of connection and responsibility, because we have discovered the way to resolve our own woes. We know how others can resolve their woes too, and so our heart opens up. We say, "Oh, I can see your pain and trouble, and if you would like, I would be happy to help you in any way I could."

It does not matter what kind of circumstances we have had; everyone has equal access to the power of open intelligence. There isn't anyone left out. Whatever the data stream is, that is where the power of open intelligence is. The only way to expand the power is in this moment—in what we are thinking right now, in whatever emotion we are wracked with right now. The only way to benefit others is to first benefit ourselves in this way. So, if we really want to be of benefit to others, first we have to be of benefit to ourselves.

Open intelligence extends everywhere, and there is a great openness of connection—really knowing what everyone feels in a deep, deep way, knowing what inspires different thoughts and actions and knowing the same thing about oneself. As we move about in our lives, we come into contact with many, many people, but when we rely on open intelligence, it is so easy to understand one another. There is an instant connection where we recognize that we are all tied together—not in some kind of abstract way, but in a real way. Right now, in this very moment, there is the ability to live this instant of life in open intelligence, which is total connectivity with everyone and everything.

In a life filled with benefit to oneself and others, one has a natural, cheerful disposition and a deep connection of friendship and unity with other human beings. It is not just with other human beings, but with any kind of being or creature that might exist anywhere. It is a natural affection for everyone and everything, and this is a very special way to live.

We do not have any need to try to "get to know" anyone, because we already know everybody! The knowing of ourselves or anyone else is simple and comes from understanding the complete non-separation of open intelligence and data. When we know what is going on with ourselves and others, there is a sense of dynamic knowing and robust interconnectivity—a real connection and intimacy and caring.

It is not a contrived or forced intimacy, like when we are sitting around in a circle and letting all our data fly. "Now it is my turn to talk, so let me tell you about all the terrible stuff that has happened to me." These types of methods show that we want to connect and to belong and affiliate, but true intimacy and connectivity come through the power of open intelligence. To rest in the total potency and power of open intelligence and to live life from there is a life of complete openness and true relation, complete connection and interactivity with everyone and everything. A life such as this does not become static or stale.

We are naturally meant to feel connected and relational, but that does not mean that we always respond in the same way. It could be that one time we might be present in a loving, tender way, and in another moment it might require us to be totally fierce, ferocious and wrathful—pushing everything aside for the way of open intelligence. It provides us an insight to which we would have no access without open intelligence, and we are able to do what we have never been able to do before.

There is a total openness and intimacy. How is this provided? It is provided by the basic state of everything. It is natural; it is the way things are. True intimacy and connectivity come through knowing ourselves. At first it seems like a personal project, as if it only applied to us, but by the power of open intelligence, without contriving anything, we start to feel really connected and truly intimate.

One sees people living year after year with more and more love, more and more harmony, and more and more benefit. It is not some kind of neutralized love, but the full force of love-benefit, not only for one's family, friendship group or other sympathetic attachments, but for all beings.

What one might call "sympathetic attachment" is having a relationship to certain people that excludes other people from its domain. It could take the form of, "These are my family members, friends and community, and outside of these relationships nothing else of importance really exists for me." However, the release from sympathetic attachment opens up the beneficial domain of our energy from self-focus and intense sympathetic attachment to the benefit of all.

INTERDEPENDENCY

Unhealthy dependence or co-dependence on people or circumstances breeds all kinds of data that are disempowering. Co-dependency—unhealthy enmeshment with someone else's data or supporting another person in indulging their data or our own—is a very painful constellation of data in which to get caught up. Co-dependency is disempowering, while healthy interdependence is very empowering and life-enhancing, love-building and love-providing. There are lots of ways to trick ourselves into obsessing about data, but the easy cure-all remedy is to rely on the total simplicity of open-intelligence benefit.

It may be rare for us to see truly healthy relating in the examples we have before us; however, one of the important aspects of the Four Mainstays is the modeling of how human beings can live together in a healthy, productive way, where there always is an increase of open-intelligence empowerment and benefit. We want to be able to come together and give each other support for our strengths in open intelligence, instead of having dialogues that are about many other things that have nothing to do with our strengths, such as, "How can I fix myself so I'm more appealing to you?" or "How can I fix you so you're more appealing to me?" That is a very difficult way of being with each other and isn't really a supportive relationship.

It is so much more helpful to rely on open intelligence, where nobody is wrong and everyone is included. In this way, first of all, we build a healthy relationship with ourselves, and then based upon this healthy relationship with ourselves that outshines all of our own data, we are able to engage in healthy interdependent relationships with other people. That is a totally worthy motivation: we really want to benefit ourselves and others at the same time.

In mutual relationship there is always greater harmony, love, satisfaction, gratitude and respect—so all of these are always increasing. If we are lucky enough to have that kind of relationship in our life, it is very, very precious indeed and a real honor and privilege.

To really thrive we need to have a basic sense of ourselves, then with that basic sense there is no great mystery anymore. If something challenging comes up, we know exactly what to do. There isn't any longer a fear that something could take us down. Every person who is relying on open intelligence knows that each of us is responsible for our data. We are not running around blaming our data on other people; that trip is over. In the past we might have worried about a return of one emotional state or another, but now we have a sense of mastery and sovereignty over our own condition. This is very, very powerful, because this sovereignty is an expression of our resilience and our ability to thrive in all situations and circumstances.

Your ability to thrive is the model for everyone thriving, and not only that, it is the exact explanatory model of how everything survives in indivisibility. You are yourself an authentic expression of how everything whatsoever thrives in indivisibility. These could just be a bunch of philosophical words; however, if they are true in your own experience, then they are an experiential reality expressed in your own life. If that is so, then you become a living example for others. People look at you and say, "Wow! That is a powerful person. They're so clear. I really want to be like that."

When we are talking about ourselves in terms of the labels for our data, then we are boxed into those labels, but by the power of open intelligence all those labels loosen up and each label becomes totally spacious. We feel the actual expansion out of ourselves, but including ourselves as well. By opening up our intelligence we come to find in our actual everyday experience that data do not have an independent nature and that they do not have any power or influence to make us feel one way or another. We have trained ourselves in the past to feel that they do have a power or influence over us, but they do not!

KNOWING OURSELVES AND KNOWING OTHERS

Through the technology of the present day, people are very connected and can follow what is going on with other people all over the world. This has not always been the case, but now we live in a world that is really open and connected. Now through the Internet we can so easily see our own and other people's data, and we are able to see how so very many people share the same data streams. For whatever data stream there is, one can find other people who affiliate with it.

Different people have different data, so we each have that flavor of special, precious uniqueness, but at the same time we are extensive and expansive, which means that any kind of intelligence that is represented in nature is very definitely represented in each one of us. In every single one of our data is a statement of nature itself. That is really marvelous—one could even say miraculous.

We are trained to think that when we have an afflictive state, it is ours: "It's all mine, my hideous little world." But by the power of open intelligence we begin to see that this afflictive state represents the same afflictive state of many, many other people. The realms of fear, anger, revenge, anxiety and depression are all a direct reflection of the afflictive states of countless beings.

If we come together with another person, then it is a matter of mutual allowance and mutual respect, knowing that we are so much alike. We are an open-source for all data, and only through knowing ourselves in that way can we really know other people. If we are clear about our own data, then that really lets us connect with other people.

We have been educated to be self-focused, so one of the most powerful parts of the opening up of comprehensive intelligence is the feeling of indivisibility with everyone. That indivisibility only comes about by really feeling what everyone is feeling and expanding our whole emotional life to the feelings of everyone. If for instance we feel all burnt out or manic or depressed, instead of focusing just on ourselves and our own situation, we can turn the focus to include everyone. We open up that data point by seeing how many people in the world at this moment are going through exactly the same thing—*exactly* the same thing. We really feel open connectivity with everyone, where it isn't any longer so much about *my* stuff. When that is clear, we really get into a flow of giving and receiving that is inseparable.

Our angle of vision also changes as regards extreme occurrences of suffering or harm. Instead of instantly condemning the person who has caused harm, we can really go into the depths of the act and ask, "What could have been the motivation for this; what brought it about in the person? How unbearable that this person was pushed to such a point that something like this would happen." By the power of open intelligence we find not only the depth of our own experience but the depth of the experience of all beings. In doing so, we become much less focused on our limited ideas about things, and then our real intelligence really gets turned on. The beautiful force of open-intelligence benefit presents itself and prevents any kind of error in terms of conduct.

At first there is an understanding: "Wow, nothing has an independent nature!" and just that simple intellectual understanding alone is such a boon. By the power of introduction to open intelligence in short moments, that intellectual understanding slips naturally into instinctive recognition. Then, to be completely and absolutely present with these afflictive states in their arising is to see that shining forth from within them is total power, total indestructibility and total sovereignty. There is then nothing to be afraid of in oneself or in others. Power comes from allowing everything to be *as it is*. It is such an incredible good fortune, and this good fortune will be more and more in evidence.

DEVOTION

There are many ideas associated with the word "devotion," and for some people the word brings up negative connotations of disempowerment, insufficiency and confusion. In short, the word can suggest a dysfunctional relationship in which great faith and trust are placed in an authority figure who may prove to not be completely worthy of that faith and trust. What is more, there can be a lot of resistance in certain people, countries and cultures to any sort of devotional relationship.

But there are some people who do have an affinity for devotion, and these types of people feel naturally devoted to expressions of esteem and respect. One could say that it is a form of head-over-heels love. There is a complete openness and willingness to be in fully empowered relationship. There is no avoidance of relationship; neither is there any sort of powerlessness, victimization or dependency in relating to others. Through the sort of devotion that is being described here, there is complete openness to other human beings with no need to have them be any different than they are. One of the other wonderful aspects of this type of devotion is a commitment to the benefit of all—really living life from the context of what will be of greatest benefit. That is what open intelligence is: spontaneous devotion to the benefit of all.

When we look at things from the vantage of wanting benefit for all, it is easy to see that in the past we usually have made decisions based on what would be of greatest benefit to us alone. In actual fact, it is quite difficult to make decisions from the outlook of self-focus, but the outlook of greatest-benefit-to-all is really an easy way to make decisions, especially after one has had open-intelligence training.

In order to really ramp up open intelligence and all of its powers of benefit, it is essential to outshine all data, and the easiest way to outshine all data is to enter into deep and engaging relationship with a person with whom there will be no escaping into data. A full-on, totally trusting relationship—in which all data are honestly disclosed—is the sort of relationship one would want to have with a trainer. The trainer wishes the very best for you, is totally unflinching in their devotion to your well-being and is completely filled with love. She or he can spontaneously offer heartfelt advice or circumstances that will greatly enhance the outshining of your own data as well as the recognition of your beneficial qualities and activities.

In this sort of wholesome and loving relationship, there is the complete willingness to allow oneself to be contributed to by someone who might have something to offer. Along with that is the respect and gratitude for that person and the willingness to help them in whatever way possible. There is the acknowledgement that the good fortune one has had of being introduced to open intelligence and its astounding benefits is due to having met that person. There is a natural desire for the well-being of that person, and there is also the wish that, whatever the benefits are of having a relationship with that person, lots more people will be able to have those same benefits.

When a person is committed one hundred percent to relying on open intelligence, she or he will be entering into very deep relationships with people. This is the most beautiful way to live life and is a complete honor and privilege.

There can be all kinds of pretty words about these things, but unless they are instinctively recognized as alive and real, then they do not have much meaning. When these things *are* truly real and alive in one's life, all of what is being described here really comes into being in the most beneficial way. To be able to live in connection with each other with so much love and so much openness is a priceless gift, and it is the most precious thing anyone could ever have in life.

DEDICATION TO THE TRAINER

We could illustrate the type of dedication to the trainer that is being spoken about in the Four Mainstays with an example, and that example would come from a Tibetan man who was a monk in a monastery in Tibet some fifty years ago. He had left his family at a young age and was raised by the monks in the monastery, and that is where he lived his whole life. He had a guru in the monastery whom he completely revered, who had given him many, many wonderful teachings, and he had been very close with his guru all of his life,

In 1959 the Chinese invaded Tibet, and it was clear to many of the Tibetans that they would need to flee to India, just as so many others had fled between 1949 and 1959. It was very important to this young monk that he be able to bring his guru out of Tibet with him, but the old guru could not walk very well and was a huge man, while the monk was quite small. A solution had to be found in order to get the teacher out of a very unsafe environment. First they tried to hire eight mountain men to take him out, but that plan did not work; then they tried to use yaks, but that plan did not work either. The mountain men and the yaks collapsed from the weight of the guru.

The situation with the Chinese invasion became very dangerous, and it was absolutely clear that everyone needed to get out immediately, but this young monk would not leave his beloved guru. So, the young monk decided that he was going to carry his guru with him on his back from Tibet to India. We need to stop and consider this for a second: carry someone on one's back across the high mountains of the Himalaya through freezing cold and death-defying conditions and crossing deep abysses on narrow tree-trunk bridges.

It was a long and dangerous trip done on foot. Many of the monks from this monastery died on the way; one thousand people left Tibet together in that particular expedition and only thirty-one arrived alive. However, those who were able to do so

241

continued on. In the case of the young monk, he did in fact carry his guru the entire distance, and they both made it safely to India.

This young man who carried his beloved guru on his back all the way to India had completely embraced defenselessness, dedication and devotion to open intelligence and his own mainstays—a very good combination of traits to have for living life! He considers carrying his guru from Tibet to India to be the greatest accomplishment of his life. He said that if he had not done what he did, then he would have been leaving teachings behind that people would never be able to receive, because his guru was the only one who could impart those teachings.

This act of selflessness and love exemplifies complete dedication, devotion and defenselessness. Only because this young monk was fueled by complete devotion, dedication and defenselessness was he able to carry his guru from Tibet to India. The love and selflessness he showed are quite different from the traits that come from self-centered devotion. We are the wielders of great power, but we are able to embrace that power only through this complete defenselessness. Once we get infected with openhearted devotion and defenselessness we want to suffer from it forever, because it is a pure pleasure!

This young monk risked his own life to make sure that other people might be able to receive the teachings from his guru. This shows so much love and caring for everyone and everything. The teachings he was saving for the world give the greatest gift any human being could ever give—the great open heart of open intelligence—the beneficial potency at the basis which ensures the benefit of all. This is the great open heart that has felt every feeling and beyond, not only one's own feelings, but every feeling that has ever been had by anyone in the past, present or future.

The gift of truly loving relationships and intimate relating, as well as always-on open intelligence, is embedded in the dedication described in this story. This is a great story, for it shows how one person's extraordinary devotion could benefit so many. We are all human beings just like the monk; if he can realize open intelligence's beneficial potency in this extreme circumstance, then we can certainly do the same in our own.

Chapter Nineteen

BENEFIT IN EVERYDAY LIVING AND DYING

The ideal disposition for practicing short moments of open intelligence is one where, more than anything else, a person wants all beings to recognize open intelligence. The passion for this can become so great that the person is willing to dedicate their entire life to making this come true. This devotion to all beings is what really gives passion to a person's life, and this is the most powerful way a human being can ever live in the world.

We do not generally think about employing scientific methodology when considering open intelligence, but scientific methodology looks for truth, and truth is based on an explanation that does not vary. There is a very prominent truth in what is being stated here: any person who is devoted to the recognition of open intelligence for all beings and who has this kind of fire and passion will have the most wonderful of lives and will be of the greatest benefit to themselves and others. Even though we may not have learned about this passion for life in our culture, that does not mean it does not exist. It exists as a universal truth, in everyday terms and also in a way that is describable in scientific terms.

This passion is a total gift of the heart. It is an uncontrollable urge and desire to share, to love and to connect—and the willingness to go to any lengths to do that. It is a passion that fills every thought, emotion, sensation and experience. Foremost in every moment is the passionate desire to benefit. This passionate devotion to the service of all is quite a bit different from the mindset where one is thinking, "I wonder how I can earn the most money and have the most success."

Even if personal concerns continue to arise, there is the great power of open intelligence that is sovereign over all worries and concerns. As we gain more and more assurance in open intelligence, this great power will continue to emerge brighter

244

and brighter, to the point of outshining all the worries and concerns with which we have previously identified.

The dynamic creative energy of vast open intelligence is the real you. You began as indestructible open intelligence, you live as indestructible open intelligence and you die as indestructible open intelligence. Indestructible open intelligence is what you always are. This may be something that you have already heard and thought about, but you really have to become familiar with it and acknowledge it. Why do you have to acknowledge it? Because you may have spent a lifetime acknowledging data, so now instead you are growing accustomed to acknowledging the open-intelligence view.

With this acknowledgment you have the greatest power to be of benefit to yourself and others. Otherwise, if life is focused on data, there will only be a lifetime of self-focus. By just this tiny shift to relying on open intelligence until it becomes obvious, self-focus naturally slips away. You go naturally from self-focus to spontaneously caring about the benefit of all. The self is taken care of completely, and everything is loved and esteemed. Nothing is rejected and nothing needs to be abandoned. This is the all-embracing benefit of the open-intelligence view. Your real nature is to always abide as open intelligence. Always!

We have been trained throughout our lives to see our identity as a complex combination of descriptions, and then because we treated ourselves according to those descriptions, we treated others as their descriptions as well. However, when we no longer see ourselves as our descriptions, we no longer see other people as their descriptions either.

Once we begin recognizing open intelligence, we see through all of the descriptions we have taken ourselves to be, and we can begin to recognize the innate mental and emotional stability we all carry. People naturally stop talking about themselves and others as pathological conditions weighed down by all kinds of ideas. We are no longer talking about having to get to another place or to a more improved condition; we are talking about what is available right here and now through the vantage of open intelligence.

Some of the people we meet may have radical mental and emotional instability, but to meet those people with the complete assurance and confidence that their mental and emotional stability is innate is the greatest healing method that anyone can ever possibly bring to another person. This is a very powerful way of touching another human being without ever saying anything. No one is their data, and the confidence in that fact comes from one's knowledge of oneself and complete clarity about the way things actually are.

BENEFICIAL ENERGY BEYOND ANY DESCRIPTION

We could know about all the sensations in our body, name them all, decide whether they are positive, negative or neutral, but a more comprehensive order of understanding about the energies in the body needs to develop. If we do not understand the basic nature of our intelligence, we will never have perfect health, because perpetual perfect health is found only in open intelligence. This is the land where there is no birth, life and death. It is the land that subsumes all other lands and orders of knowing. It is not a land as we think of "a land," but one could say it is a landing spot, a space, a location that doesn't have a location.

We recognize that everything we feel in our body is beneficial energy beyond any description that could be made of it, and open intelligence is the essence of it all. This is really important to know about oneself. We allow ourselves to rest completely and totally in our primal power. That primal power is always on; it will never go away and it cannot be shut down. The more we have a decisive experience of that as our living reality, the more expansive it is to us. It never goes backward and it is inexhaustible.

In each moment of our lives we are dealing with issues of living and dying. The fact is that from the time we are born, we have all kinds of minor pains and annoyances with our bodies. If we were paying attention to the pains and annoyances, every single moment would provide some kind of murmuring over here or little ache down there. By the power of open intelligence we start to recognize not only these things that are going on, but we also see what has been our ongoing emotional resistance to them as well. However, when we have the open-intelligence view, we know that the basis of all data is open intelligence, and we are very fortunate because having that open-intelligence view gives us sovereignty over data.

Even if we are dealing with intense pain in our body and with the accompanying worries regarding that pain, there is always a great power present that is sovereign over all pain, worries and concerns. In a kingdom, the royal monarch has sovereignty over their subjects, and in the same way open intelligence has sovereignty over all data. With greater and greater reliance on open intelligence, the brilliance of that sovereignty emerges brighter and brighter to the point of outshining all the worries and concerns—even outshining altogether the focus on our physical being.

There are all kinds of things we could do about physical pain, but among the many choices is the one of relying on open intelligence for short moments many times. Within the context of short moments we are going to deal with this physical pain one moment at a time. If we spend all day focusing on our physical pain and thinking about all the data associated with our physical pain, then by the end of the day we would feel pretty depressed about this physical pain, because we would have thought about all the different things the physical pain could be—from cancer that is going to kill us to a disability that will keep us from doing the things we want to do in life. It is important to let these data be as they are.

We cannot fully understand the data or any kind of response to them without open intelligence. There is no practical reason whatsoever to give credence to the data alone, as the only good information is going to come from open intelligence. So, open intelligence is what we want to rely on within ourselves. This will lead us to skilled action in relation to the data surrounding physical pain, whether it is an action we actually take or taking no action at all. But we will be absolutely clear whichever we choose; the decision will not be made only from a muddle of confusion.

By relying on open intelligence, we will know what to do about health problems and all the worries that go along with them. We move from being obsessed with all of our sensations, emotions and thoughts to being totally clear within all those data, and it does not matter to us whether they are occurring or not.

There is a shift that occurs from being all involved with ourselves to feeling expansive. When issues come up concerning our physical condition, those issues do not take over our entire perspective. They are a spontaneous appearance of open intelligence, and whatever our circumstantial data are, they are the expressions of potent open intelligence, so we might as well get used to that!

RESPONDING TO ILLNESS

If we have some kind of health issue, it is really important to empower ourselves in open intelligence as the healing basis of that issue. Whether we are cured of an illness or whether we eventually die from it, we always exist in the ultimate cure of ever-beneficial open intelligence. We will always be taking the best medicine by understanding open intelligence as the entire basis shining forth from within all these medical labels. By the power of this assurance in our own experience, we get to see that the afflictive states of our own body and mind really are the potency of open intelligence itself.

If there is mental affliction or physical sickness, regardless of which way it is happening, the fact that it is happening is skillfully identified, and open intelligence is relied upon as the cure-all. Maybe in the past we had all sorts of ways of responding to illness: we might spend hours on the Internet researching the illness, we might talk endlessly with others about our concerns, and then we might go to several different doctors seeking help. We can certainly do any of those things if we wish, but first we should go directly to the open-intelligence cure-all and allow the best course of action to arise there, instead of frantically responding from fear and worry.

Having relied upon the pure knowing of open intelligence, the data involved with indulgence, avoidance and replacement of sickness, suffering and affliction are examined—not superficially, but very precisely to see where they come from, where they dwell and where they go, just as we examine the nature of all the data.

This kind of examination can only take place in the context of open intelligence; from that vantage we see what to do and how to act. Within conventional notions of health we only have so many options, but in the realm of pure knowing we have many more options for what we could do.

We might end up in a doctor's office or the hospital or having surgery or chemotherapy and radiation, so that is what is going on for us, but in a more expansive way we have the ability to de-physicalize our focus. We are acquainting ourselves with pure open intelligence and are not focusing so totally on the body alone. We have a knowing that is beyond all conceptions and frames of reference, including the frame of reference of being limited to a physical body.

We have so much more power than we think or believe that we do. It is only by placing ourselves in the pure open-intelligence cure that we can actually see what our powers are; otherwise, we will think we are limited to the dimensions of the hospital, the retirement home and the burial ground.

Thus, the brilliant cure-all of pure luminosity shines forth at the most profound level, and the preservation of its state will cause all data about physical or mental illness to go into self-release and to no longer be noticed. Now, that is a very powerful way of life. That is a life of no complaint, and it is a life of no limitation by physical affliction of any kind. No matter what is going on with us physically, it isn't who we are at all. We realize this not just in an intellectual way, but clearly, directly and instinctively.

What is death? Like all data, it is the great acknowledgement of absolute perfection. It is the direct experience of the vital principle of indivisibility, overpowering the myriad descriptions of data. Lucid open intelligence is equally present in birth, life and death.

By the power of open intelligence we are completely indestructible and secure, as well as fearless in the face of all data—even in the fear of death. By training up open intelligence during life, we are prepared for death to come at any moment. Open intelligence is an always-on, indestructible expanse in which there is no death. It is deathless, yet it encompasses death.

The whole way of living, the whole way of decision-making and the whole way of handling every aspect of life and death is influenced by the shift in one's identity from taking oneself to be an individual to being the living evidence of nature's intelligence in which there is no death. Whether it is life or death or any other datum that comes along, we know that we are going to be okay. We are always learning more about who we are; we are always feeling more empowered, even if we are very sick or even dying. We are able to flow along with everything.

If we can fully rely on open intelligence, then when death comes, it will truly be seen as just another data stream; otherwise, it would be seen as a total threat, a disaster, a final end and exile forever—but exile from what? What exactly are we trying to hold on to from which we would be exiled? In relying on open intelligence, we come to rest in the stronghold from which we can never be exiled, the stronghold that can carry us through all situations of life and death with steadfast ease.

It is important to really recognize in our own experience that open intelligence is very potent and powerful. Even though a lot of these same words about life and death have been written down in a lot of different places, when the words are seen to be true in *our own experience,* then they are revelatory.

Often people have very charged feelings about death. There is frequently a sense of not knowing how exactly to deal with it and having feelings of powerlessness and helplessness in relation to it. These things are generally not talked about openly because there is so much resistance to and avoidance of the subject of death. Often when people face death, they are afraid of what is happening, and everyone else around them is afraid, too. When one goes through the dying process, there are a lot of completely new data that come up because of the circumstances. "Oh, I'm losing my sense of touch. I can't see anymore. I can't taste. I've had my last meal. It is all over for me now." These data can be very shocking if there is no context for them.

All of our conceptual frameworks and ideas about everything are going to become particularly vivid to us when we are dying. We are going to find in that moment that all the descriptive frameworks that we have built and the assumptions about our physical well-being cannot be relied upon. We can no longer count on the things we counted on before. When we reach that point and we realize that the constant seeking to make something out of ourselves has come to an end and we are headed towards death, it can be very frightening if a person is not clear about what is actually occurring.

We relax in the evenness of what is appearing, as there is no way to control what is going to happen. If we think we have control, at some point we will learn that there isn't any control. Rather than seeking to control the experience, we identify the basis of all appearances and then enjoy that as our identity. Even if we have fooled ourselves about what is going on for a long time, now we can begin to see clearly.

Each situation is different, but open intelligence gives dying people—which by the way we *all* are—a clear sense of where they are and what is going to come next. Dying is really just like living life. The actual process of living and dying is one short moment at a time. In a short moment of instinctive open intelligence, everything is known about what to do and how to act. By the power of being with ourselves as we see data appear, endure and disappear, we see that all of them are fueled by open intelligence.

This gives us the power to be in any situation, including facing death or being with someone who is dying, to just let everything be *as it is*. Again, everything, including death, happens one moment at a time. Whatever is occurring for the dying person in the present moment, the best action the caregivers can take will become obvious in a very dignified, caring, loving and mature way. To have someone totally present—totally available with love and openness, openheartedly and totally welcoming of everything, including death—is a very beautiful gift to share with the dying person.

Open intelligence prepares us for anything. We do not know what is going to happen next; we could hear that in two days the Earth will be destroyed and that we will all die. What are we going to be thinking then? How will we be dealing with that set of circumstances? Open intelligence sustains us regardless of the circumstances. So, we want that kind of preparedness for our entire life and as we enter into death—real stability, no matter what is happening.

Chapter Twenty

THE ULTIMATE RESOURCE

All of the money or wealth ever created or possessed—past, present and future—is held within open intelligence. Open intelligence is all-powerful and is at the root of the provisioning of everything. It gives absolute surety; conversely, money is not something that can give absolute surety. By the direct encounter with this truth in our own experience, we grow to see open intelligence as the surge of total prosperity and as the unimaginable capacity to consistently produce whatever we need or want.

If we are concerned about money or any of the other fundamental issues of life, we rely on open intelligence, and that reliance will clear up the concerns. When we are introduced to open intelligence, we are introduced to the magnificence of nature's intelligence as the ultimate resource.

There are many young people who are totally committed to open intelligence whose parents are giving them lots of advice about security—the same advice that their own parents had given to them: "You've got to get a good job, work hard, save your money, and then you can afford a home and other things that will give you safety, security and comfort." This is well-meaning advice, but they probably do not yet know that we *all* already have a home with lifelong security—open intelligence—and that the food, clothing and shelter that are needed will be provided.

Unless we realize that money does not have an independent nature, there will always be limits on money. For example, if we are very tight with money or at the other extreme of constantly spending more than we have, we would be well served to rest with all the stirrings that thoughts of money bring up. Most people feel that money definitely has an independent nature and that it can make or break them, so money is therefore a very, very powerful data stream.

However, when we see that we have had an inappropriate response to something that actually has no independent nature, we can just relax. It does not mean that we stop working at our job or we stop keeping track of our investments or we do not provide for our daily needs. It just means that, no matter what our money lifestyle is, we are paying full attention; we are no longer limited by the false reality that we have given to money. In being completely at ease with the data of money, we will find that many other data streams are automatically caught up in that pervasive ease.

Most of us have trained ourselves to believe that money has power over us. We unconsciously live from these sorts of automatic assumptions in relation to money, where almost every move we make is related in some way to money issues. We think we are spending too much or we are spending too little, but either way we may feel that we do not have a balance. People can be dominated by concerns about money; for many it is a matter of trying to get more money or skimping and holding on to what they have.

It could be that no matter how much money we have we are still thinking about more money, because no matter how much we get we think that it is never enough. People may have millions of dollars, and it is still not enough for them. This is a good example of the fact that there is no way to get enough money to make money a source of permanent satisfaction and well-being.

OUR GENEROUS NATURE

We are all built of excellence and total open intelligence; no one can give that to us or take it away from us. All we have to do is show up for the relationship with open intelligence exactly as we are—high or low, up or down, this way or that. By acknowledging our basis in open intelligence, every single moment is more and more powerful, and there is never an end to the stream of prosperity and generosity. Every single moment is more enlivened and more filled with the power of open intelligence.

Open intelligence is penetrating, vivid and lucid; it is very personal and very relational. It knows how to evaluate logically the arguments that are used to explain experience, for instance, "I can't be too committed to open intelligence, because I might run out of money." By holding to open intelligence, we find the thorough cut from all data, including the data of thinking that money has some kind of power of its own.

The strategies to save money, to hoard it and to spend it have been going on our entire lives—the great plans to keep the money, get more of it or spend it in the best ways possible. Open intelligence empowers generosity and allows for more resources for more people all of the time, and by relying on our own open intelligence we allow an expanse of generosity to naturally open up.

If we collapse into any data stream, then everything starts to look like that particular data stream. If we collapse into the money-data-stream, then everything looks like that. We are looking at everything from that vantage, but it is like a very narrow tunnel that just keeps going on and on with no end, always with more data related to the initial data.

We find within ourselves that instinctive open intelligence can carry us through in all ways and that it can show us what we need and how what we need can come to us in a beneficial way. We no longer feel that we need to devote our entire life to the accumulation of money in order to have security and comfort. Instead, we come to see where security and comfort really come from. Only from instinctive open intelligence are we able to act in a truly beneficial way. The commitment to this alone is absolutely the best way anyone could spend their life.

When we find our peaceful nature within ourselves, that experience cannot be matched by anything in life. That is the greatest treasure we will ever find in life, and there isn't anything greater. We could have all the money on earth, all the finest foods and the most expensive possessions, but whatever we are looking for in those things cannot even come close to the treasure of our peaceful nature.

We never know what is going to happen, so we want to prepare ourselves with what will endure anything that is happening. That is what we really want to fortify ourselves with—not with more data streams about money and security and other things that will not endure.

By relying on open intelligence we make the best investment we can make. We make an investment with no downside and only an upside. If we invest in something that has no downside, we are an excellent investor! If the world economy should collapse, we know that we have something that will be untouched.

TRUE WEALTH

True wealth is the constant, permanent display of open intelligence—always present, always available. But through the eyes of reification it is impossible to really know what real wealth is. Without the wealth of open intelligence, it is impossible to reveal real wealth, just as it is impossible to reveal perfect love. There is a constant and steady flow of love, the feeling of love, the presence of love, the all-encompassing power of love in everything, and it comes from this simple practice of short moments of open intelligence repeated many times until it is obvious at all times. All ultimate resources are of this nature.

Often we get caught up in feelings of lack and scarcity, thinking that there isn't enough and that we constantly have to work harder in order to have enough to survive. People often have very fixed ideas, for example, "Of course food and shelter come from money. I know they do!" However, this is a perception that has been trained into us, and the only way to subsume these ideas is in our own direct experience. If we continue to believe that money is provisioning everything, then it will not be possible to see what the ultimate resource is.

By relying on open intelligence for short moments, our whole life is completely enriched with incredible abundance of all kinds. How could prosperity and generosity be an exception to that? Look at the enrichment of mental and emotional life, of physical life and of friendships that is brought about by relying on open intelligence. This is a life of a greatly fortunate being. There is no greater fortune than this.

Thinking like this goes completely against everything we have learned about money and how we think about ourselves in regard to money. We have learned that money is a special thing and that we have got to find out how to get it. Then we have got to get some more money, and if we already have enough, then maybe we still want to get more so that we will have *more* than enough! This keeps going on and on until money is one of the first things we think about—adopting money as a special power and force, living in a state of scarcity and stinginess and being afraid. "What about my money? What am I going to do if I don't have enough?"

For many of us there is a conscious or unconscious fear of ending up a homeless beggar, and this fear perhaps drives us to do things we don't really want to do in life—for example, staying in a job or a relationship we don't really want to be in— to make sure we have our basic needs met and that we don't become a homeless beggar.

We have to get real about the structures we have set up for ourselves in the world, because if they are based on the wrong fundamental principal, they will not work. Our intelligence, just *as it is*, is one of generosity and not one of scarcity and stinginess. If we live in a mode of scarcity and stinginess, that is exactly what we will have. If we live in the mode of open intelligence, more and more our heart will open in generosity, to the degree that we will never even have to think about money— how to get it, when to get it, where to get it. Open intelligence is humanity's greatest natural resource, and we are just beginning to mine it. It is an infinite resource; it never stops giving. It tells us exactly what to do in each area of life. All the resources flow naturally from it.

Everything could be seen as scarce—food, money, sex, work, relationships, leisure and whatever else it might be—and if so, there would never be a real sense of prosperity, generosity and ongoing benefit. However, by the power of short moments an expanse of complete benefit opens up, and we see from that first short moment the prosperity and generosity of open intelligence. It is easy to return to it again and again, because we do not forget that initial blast.

In the Age of Human Empowerment and Era of Great Benefit we change the way we look at every single aspect of living. We go from living in perpetual economic uncertainty to economic certainty, where we do not even have to think about where things are coming from or if we will have them. We have gotten so ingrained in money-data; however, making the issue of money into a big deal is unnecessary. What if we chose to rely on open intelligence rather than on the money-data and saw what happened then?

REASSESSING OUR PRIORITIES

Some people are very passionate about wanting to be of benefit and following their dreams of being an artist or a musician or doing something else that does not assure them of a steady income. But they often worry about whether they would ever be able to support themselves if they remain committed to that lifestyle. This is certainly an issue, but it has a very plainspoken answer. There are two ways to pursue life: with short moments and without short moments. A good recommendation would be to educate yourself in short moments and become assured of that. Whether you are working for an income or not, it does not really matter; whether you are earning lots of money or none at all is not the key issue.

Anyone anywhere can set up a career based only on open intelligence, and you do not have to be in a constant state of fear about what might go wrong. Open intelligence engenders fearlessness. "I have a choice about how I want to create my life. Am I going to settle for the conventional ways things have been described and be limited by my fear?" It does not matter which field you are in: you make an agreement right up front to commit to open intelligence.

Just by letting your data be as they are and allowing open intelligence all the while, that is of tremendous benefit to yourself and to the world. You can know that you are always being of incredible benefit, beyond any kind of action that is contrived to produce benefit. Just settling in to your own nature is profoundly beneficial for each of us—and for everyone.

One can live in all kinds of ways, but for sure it is possible to live without a steady income, and there are many ways to accomplish that. The first thing we can do is to reassess our priorities and change the emphasis to short moments of open intelligence, so no matter what we are doing we will have that as our priority. To rely on open intelligence rather than relying on money-data is a very good choice to make. More benefit, more prosperity and more of one's needs are taken care of, but without money-data. How is that going to happen? It is going to happen by the power of relying on open intelligence rather than on the money-data.

After the decision has been made to commit to this sort of life, there may be continuing feelings of fear and scarcity related to money for a while, but by the power of relying on open intelligence and in knowing the simple fundamentals of money, they are not so scary any longer.

A MASTER OF MONEY

The convention of relying on authorities to solve our problems and figure things out for us is coming to an end. Some of us may still be in a little denial about this, but the time of giving over our responsibility to authority will soon be over. We are in an era where we are coming to see that our self-authority and mastery need not be turned over to external authorities and that *we* are responsible.

For example, in the recent financial crash so many people gave their money to the so-called experts who were going to manage the money. "So here, you take my money and handle everything for me, while I buy a million-dollar home even though I only make a few thousand dollars a year." This is just one example of the extremes that were occurring in the financial world, and we can see now that this system was not working. But we are *all* responsible for the breakdown—not just the people who were the so-called experts. We were part of the decision-making process that led to this financial crisis.

More and more we will find a new way of making decisions that does not involve giving up our own self-authority and handing it over to external authorities. By the power of relying on open intelligence, we are able to make a radical and welcome shift in the way we understand money and ourselves. We are trained from early on in life to have all of these data about ourselves and about money, but what a relief it is to not have them any longer. What a relief to find complete self-authority in the realm of money and to know that everything that is needed is already available. This is a hundred percent assurance that is experienced in practical living.

Open intelligence allows for mastery of all data, because there isn't any point from which to view. If we do not have money-data, it does not mean that we do not know anything about money or that we avoid or replace the money-data with some other data. It means that we have complete freedom within the money-data—complete freedom. Another way of saying it would be that we become a master of money instead of being mastered by money. Each person is at basis the master of money—not the other way around—and by the power of open intelligence, more and more can be known about that lifelong.

We all have basic needs for food, clothing and shelter, and we come to understand that open intelligence alone is our primary need. Without it we cannot fulfill our other needs; without it resources will dwindle, but with it we will find resources we never imagined before. Open intelligence may be a resource we never imagined before, so now as we discover it we discover a whole world of new resources.

In the Age of Human Empowerment and Era of Great Benefit the fundamentally unconditioned essence of indivisible pure benefit and the means of mining its resources are demonstrated. The fruition is shown to be the natural place of pure benefit that is fundamentally unconditioned. Its beneficial qualities and activities of body, speech and mind provide a lifestyle that is unimaginable. It isn't conditioned by having the right positive data, and it isn't conditioned by getting the right amount of money.

An individual who is completely taken over by brilliant open intelligence has sovereignty over every single one of their actions, including every thought, emotion, sensation and other experience—and over money as well. This kind of openheartedness can only be found in open intelligence; it cannot be cultivated through behaving in a certain way or through contriving conduct. It can only come from total open intelligence; that is its seat. It is a disposition of giving, giving, giving, giving—openhearted, open-intelligence generosity. The person with this disposition is the wealthiest person on Earth.

Chapter Twenty-One

ORGANIZATIONS AND LEADERSHIP ROOTED IN OPEN INTELLIGENCE

The Age of Human Empowerment and Era of Great Benefit comes about through making open intelligence the core competence for oneself and in all groups, communities, organizations, in society and in the world as a whole. We see groups springing up throughout the world based on the core competence of open intelligence's beneficial energy, and there are many ways to introduce the core competence into institutions and organizations. It can start out in one part of the organization or it can start out as an overall organizational imperative, but however it may begin, with this core competence the organization will not only attract the most committed people, it will also be able to retain them.

Many of the things that are used in organizations now will become obsolete and dispensable as more and more people gather together in open intelligence's beneficial potency. An organization based on open intelligence is designed to get direct feedback so that it can be totally responsive to the needs of the people involved with it. Responsive organizations are being built by people coming together from the grassroots and saying, "We don't want to live the old way anymore, and we are going to organize a new way of responding to life."

In an organization based on relying on open intelligence there is no doubt anywhere in the organization that open intelligence is the core competence. The people in the organization are choosing to have open intelligence as the core competence, no matter what situation they are in. That means that everyone in the organization is trained in open intelligence and has a total commitment to it. Everyone feels that they are unified in their vision, everyone is committed to openness and each action is informed by "what will be of the greatest benefit to all?"

Open intelligence breeds beneficial potencies, and as the laser-like brightness of open intelligence outshines meaningless elaborations, then everything about how to carry out a task or solve a problem becomes very clear. All glass ceilings are gone beyond. By the power of open intelligence there are incredible skillful means available for consistently fulfilling beneficial and creative intent in oneself and in the groups and organizations one is associated with.

An organization with the core competence of open intelligence is a supportive place to be. All of one's service is given and received in the spirit of generosity. In such an organization it is the responsibility of leadership to empower each individual in the organization beyond the individual's expectations of what they think they can do. Being a leader means serving the members of the organization so that each feels totally empowered and supported in their unique strengths, gifts and talents.

As a leader, you build your team so that everyone is in agreement that open intelligence is the core competence, and you make sure everyone on the team receives training in open-intelligence competence. The most competent people can work and serve anywhere they want to, and so they are very picky. If there is an open-intelligence environment available with leadership that fully supports and enables them, then they will want to be there.

Sharing one's direct, actual experience of being an open-ended knowledge and benefit creator with someone else is a beautiful form of leadership in an organization, because in such a setting everyone thrives. Everyone is using their optimal beneficial skills in everything they do throughout the day. The focus isn't all on "me" anymore, because people have released that energy of trying to figure out all their personal data. The energy is used instead for creating beneficial solutions. The environment and expectations have a different definition than organizations that are based on competition and criticism.

AN OPEN-INTELLIGENCE ENVIRONMENT

All of the time that is lost through judging other people, obsessing over disagreements with them, competing with them or mulling over the things we do not like about them—all the data that have taken up so much time in most organizations and businesses—all of this falls away when open intelligence is the core competency of the organization. Even though there might be data hanging around once in a while, it will not be there for long, as the interest in data just gradually disappears.

Remember the old movies where the employees would all gather around the water cooler in the office and gossip about each other, their jobs and the boss? Well, that does not happen in an open-intelligence environment. The consensus is that the people are there for the benefit of all, so all the stuff around the water cooler and text messaging gossip and criticism becomes a lot less interesting!

When everyone relies on fundamental benefit to all instead of getting into all the detours of emotionality and different data streams that make organizations difficult to be in, then the organizational environment organically evolves into a beneficial, effective and solution-oriented workplace.

Where people are committed to the core competence of open intelligence's beneficial energy, teamwork becomes effortless and easy, because there is no interruption by data, and people do not get derailed into a lot of opinionated conversations about what is going on. People are able to work together in a unified and powerful fashion. Through each person's own example of relying on open intelligence, ease and availability are passed on to others. As more and more people recognize the same thing in themselves, they want to join in, and the open-intelligence virus spreads rapidly.

This comes from the richness of everyday experience, from people caring about each other and from their being able to live happily with each other and do great things together. We actually make this come about; every single person who relies on open intelligence has given themselves an enjoyable and beneficial life, and the opportunity to do the same is then offered to everyone who wants to join in.

As we organize ourselves as individuals in open intelligence, we organize organizations in open intelligence and we organize the world in open intelligence. We can now see that result happening around the world in practical, everyday reality. The process is based primarily on word of mouth; people are very excited about what they are involved in and they spread the word to other communities and organizations.

The spirit of seeing how beneficial everyone actually is spreads out everywhere contagiously. This is such an exciting life, because it takes human beings to their real strength. We need desperately to go to this next level; to take the leap from focusing on data to focusing on open intelligence is an exponential leap of an extraordinary kind for human beings.

AN INNOVATIVE WORK ENVIRONMENT

One of the first goals of a leader creating an innovative organization or work environment is to attract people to the team who really want to work there. They see what the leadership is doing and the situation that has been created, and they know they want to work there. They do not need to be convinced that they should come. People who are attracted in this way do not come with the attitude of, "How much can I get out of this; how can I earn the most money and make the best career for myself?" They come in already knowing the guiding principles of the business or organization, and they have taken a stand on serving and being of benefit within the organization rather than grabbing for themselves.

They are there to bring something to the team that is really remarkable. They are there because they want to go beyond where they are now. They know they are capable of a lot more, but they have not found the leadership that will inspire them to realize that capacity and actually evoke it so that it is a reality in their lives.

When a person comes to the team, they are coming because they know the people there have the power and tools to solve problems skillfully. It is not like it is in so many other places—a matter of running around frantically putting out fires here and there—but it is an organizational structure that produces extraordinary results. People know that the power and tools are there to bring about remarkable results, and that is why they want to come and work there.

No matter what is going on with the team—physically, mentally or emotionally—from the vantage of open intelligence it is all seen to be the display of natural perfection. To be of benefit requires letting everything be *as it is*. When the display is left completely unrejected, the power of all-accomplishing activities is released.

When we leave all our data unrejected, that releases immense beneficial power, and this power resides in the simultaneity of abandoning and realization, because we are abandoning an unproductive way of looking at things and realizing a much better way. "Lack of open intelligence" and "instinctive recognition of open intelligence" are inseparable and simultaneous. This is not something that can be figured out mentally; its recognition only comes about from gaining assurance in open intelligence. In all these things that we have tried to abandon, open intelligence is already present. The data are naturally abandoned or resolved in the instinctive recognition of open intelligence, and this is the basis from which the team and the entire organization operate.

Open intelligence opens up the total spaciousness of connection among the members of the team. Imagine an organization that, when the team leaders walked into the room everyone is happy to see them! It is not a matter of, "Oh no, there they are again." The team members do not see leadership as people who are there to merely exert authority. They see them as people who are there to bring out the best in the team, and the team members know they can count on leadership for that.

When the team comes to work, they do not come with the mindset of, "Oh, I can't wait to get out of here." Instead, they come excited to spend the day doing things that really mean something to them, and they even want to spend extra time doing just that. Their work and service in such an environment become a very enriching part of their lives.

THE IDEAL TEAM

The ideal team is one in which everyone knows they are responsible for their own data, so the habit of being controlled by one's data no longer gets in the way. If someone needs support with their data, they know who to go to in the organization to get support for that, and people know that they are well supported. The team really wants to work together, and this leads to complete loyalty within the team. Not only that, the team members feel so enthusiastic about where they are and what they are doing that they want to attract other stellar people to come to work there.

The organization grows in such a way that the people on the team can each become leaders themselves. Not only is a team being trained, but future leaders are being trained at the same time. That allows new projects to be undertaken under the leadership of really clear people who can be counted on and who are now in the position to train other leaders.

The team has the fire in them to meet and exceed any expectations that leadership might have of them. This is a natural disposition for the team members to have—to want to meet and exceed expectations. But it is up to the team leader to inspire that.

People love this sort of environment. It has tremendous energy, and this energy is always enriching. It never feels like a burden. There may be significant challenges that the team members face, but they face them with enthusiasm, because they know that the beneficial power is there to solve the problems. They can also see that this energy is always increasing, because all energy is in fact the energy of the cosmos itself, and the accessibility of this is always increasing and never diminishing.

The power of open intelligence is not based on labels, and it is not based on all the ways things are described in conventional situations. Labels are merely tools of communication—that is all—and open intelligence is discerning, clear, potent insight that does not rely on labels. The power and force of open intelligence does not come from labels; it comes from the clear, potent insight that is the basis of all labels.

A business or organization fails when human and financial resources are dedicated to maintaining labels or a system rather than the outcome for which the system was established. Energy gets devitalized into maintaining the system instead of promoting the intent of the system, which was to benefit or contribute to the whole.

In relying on open intelligence the team does not need labels or rigid systems to arrive at a successful result. It is known exactly how to create a basis to bring about a successful result. Clear, potent insight is always flowing and is part of this tremendous natural energy that is always present. It is spacious and open in all situations and in all circumstances. It is generous, always giving and always grateful.

These principles for guiding the team are totally exceptional, because they are not based on self-promotion, competition and power struggles. Leadership that is perfectly clear knows how to cut right through any of the competitive undercurrents that might be going on within individuals or groups, and it will not allow these distractions to predominate. Competitive undercurrents are devitalizing and cause isolation. Many people find that they can no longer happily work in such an environment, and they will want to leave. What is more, for the people who stay in those types of situations, the environment disempowers them as they struggle to find ways to feel beneficial, safe and secure.

In situations such as that, very often there is a lot of anxiety, tension, fear and struggling, both for individuals in a team and for the team as a whole. However, with the perspective of all-inclusivity, relationships are easygoing and carefree. The work environment isn't all tense and uptight. Each person is empowered with their own sense of mastery, and more and more for the team as a whole there is complete mastery in all situations. The disposition is one of unflinching mastery, and that makes for a powerful, brilliant team, where all the resources of the team and the organization are maximized.

Everyone on the team feels confident that they can exceed expectations, whatever the expectations have been, and the undercurrents of self-promotion, competition and power struggles have been left behind. The discernment to bring this about comes through the activities that are carried out in day-to-day life. It is therefore not some theoretical thing or something that is going to be available some time in the distant future.

Because people are accustomed to the game of self-identification, initially they might be a little reticent or they might hold back from giving themselves fully to the team, but trust will quickly grow, and they will see that the leadership is there for them entirely. Most people will have never had a leader like that, so when they work with leadership based on open intelligence, this is most likely going to be the first time that has happened for them.

SELF-LEADERSHIP

Complete reliance on unflinching open intelligence is the ultimate form of self-leadership, and leadership of oneself is coincident with empowered team leadership. So, if we are looking for self-leadership, the answer is open intelligence, and if we are looking how to work with and lead others, the answer is open intelligence.

Unflinching open intelligence empowers cheerful, caring individuals, organizations and a society that is successful, collaborative, cooperative, socially just, inclusive and compassionate. We want to benefit ourselves, and we want to benefit others, and relying on open intelligence makes this possible. When reliance on open intelligence's beneficial energy is informing the way we think about ourselves and the world, then we see our power to be of benefit.

We no longer see hopelessness and powerlessness. We no longer feel the need to rely on abstract authorities—the ones we call "they," as in, "They are the ones doing this to us," or "They will get it done for us." Instead, we know where the responsibility is; it is *with us*. It is with open intelligence and its beneficial qualities and activities in us. This kind of open-intelligence leadership is an ongoing state of authenticity that is already stable in everyone—a continuously inexhaustible opening of beneficial power.

Open-intelligence leadership naturally includes the responsibility that comes from total self–responsibility for all of one's own data as it is. It is a full-on engagement that comes from knowing oneself so thoroughly and completely and being able to lead oneself so thoroughly and completely through the power of open intelligence. Open-intelligence leadership is the absolute call to open intelligence in oneself. It is ultimate self-governance and self-responsibility.

An exceptional leader elicits open intelligence in their team, no matter how large or small the team is, and is skillful in creating an environment of mutual success. To lead in a powerful way, you need to obtain the consent of everyone on the team to commit to open intelligence; otherwise, that team cannot be empowered. If one person on the team is relying on open intelligence, the team will be more empowered, but it is nothing like when everyone is fully engaged. When the whole team buys into open intelligence, it creates a momentum way beyond that of the individual.

The solution-orientation of open intelligence is always on; it is always looking for the ultimate beneficial solution, and mutual success is instinctively rooted in every aspect of the team. What a delightful way to live: instead of competition and contradiction among people, mutual success is the basis in every experience of the team. It is a mutual success that is really so joyful; the joy cannot be contained and bubbles out naturally.

Unflinching open intelligence empowers a transformation of human culture into an Age of Human Empowerment and Era of Great Benefit; it is as simple as that. This isn't about something happening in the future; this is right now. People have started this era with their commitment to open intelligence. By sharing this worldwide, everyone in the world is participating in the initial stage of this emergence. How exciting is that? How powerful is that? How fortunate is that?

OUR OWN EXAMPLE

In true self-leadership the power of open intelligence is the standard operating procedure. At some point it is not necessary any longer to try to rely on open intelligence; open intelligence's beneficial energy is always on, and our unflinching open-intelligence view influences everyone we meet. We do not even have to say anything; the wordless power, the potency of unending open intelligence comes to the fore and touches people in a profound way.

We do not have to do any blabbing about open intelligence. We show up as an example of our true self, totally enriched with open intelligence's beneficial potency, and that example is enough. Just that has a tremendous effect on people. It starts to become obvious for them; they look around and say, "Wow! Look at those people; they are just like me. I can do that, too." These brilliant examples of open-intelligence benefit have more of an effect on other people than all the talking one could do. It is a power that cuts right through all the history, all the memories and all the projections into the future.

The benefits of open intelligence are so extraordinary and obvious that others choose open intelligence by the power of this example. Especially in an era of scientific and technological advancement, it is really important to be able to show the actual results of open intelligence. People want to know how open intelligence is going to be of benefit to them, and it is all answered in the glowing examples of the people exhibiting the self-leadership of open intelligence.

It is not possible to be a true leader if the leadership is based solely on data. There are things that could come up like, "What will people think of me? If this undertaking doesn't work out as planned, will I continue to be popular and successful?" Whatever it might be, again, open intelligence is the only solution. From your own open intelligence you know what to do and how to act in each situation. Your own decisive, instinctive recognition of open intelligence is inseparable from benefit and service.

If you are giving a talk or a presentation your prime concern will not be, "What are they all going to think of me?" You do not have to try to figure out what to say, what will be acceptable and what your relative hierarchical position is in relation to the other people there. Instead, you are totally present, totally connected, open and alert. You enter into every relationship from the perspective of mutual intelligence and mutual benefit.

There isn't a need to figure out how somebody else is somehow going to be of use to you for your own purposes. That is replaced with a completely open relationship that does not have any definitive factors nailing it down. So, for example, from reified intelligence there will usually be lots of sorting out of thoughts, emotions, sensations and experiences, but from an open-intelligence perspective everything is just completely open and easeful. There isn't anything you need to get, and there is nothing to avoid, replace or indulge. There isn't anything to indulge that is going to make you feel any different than you already do. That is a perspective of complete empowerment.

Imagine everyone in the world empowered by the open-intelligence view—everyone in the world living and cooperating in an incredible way. It is a very real possibility, and a true leader knows how to make this a reality, because they have the power to create it. Each of us shows our own true leadership ability by creating it in each lived situation in each moment of our lives.

Another aspect of skilled leadership is that it has the power to evoke the energy of the entire group—to inspire people and reveal possibilities that they did not even know were present in their current circumstance. This is the power to really show people what they can do and what they are really made of. They are shown their own inherent open intelligence, and they are skillfully put into situations where its presence will just become clearer to them. At some point they will not even be able to remember the data that they had before.

There is unwavering recognition of the basic state and a pervasive evenness throughout all situations. It isn't like conventional life, where there are severe ups and downs and then neutrality or passivity in between. Because of the all-inclusive perspective that is naturally equanimous, there is incredible discernment in every single situation and an ability to remain at ease regardless of what is happening.

In a larger organization where there are many teams, this perspective allows that organization to train all of its teams to form a highly collaborative environment where there is complete seamlessness throughout the organization. There is an intuitive sense of who is doing what and how what they are doing over here fits in with this team over there. There is a real connection between everyone that goes beyond the contrived values of a conventional organization.

This level of leadership represents mastery of all data *as it is*, which is expressed in the ability to re-arrange data to be of maximum benefit. For example, if there are certain assumptions that are prevalent in science, technology or business, the practical, perfected vantage of open intelligence's beneficial potency can understand them in a profoundly innovative way and utilize these new insights to create forms of benefit that were unavailable before. People are given a clear understanding of the way things actually are, and the views that are not serving the benefit of all are seen through and abandoned.

The greatest innovations in knowledge do not come about from within the current conventional learned knowledge. They come about by discovering knowledge that is already present but which has not yet been recognized by anyone. An example would be with the theories of Albert Einstein; he was describing something that was obvious and evident, but no one had ever described it before. So, it was not a matter of discovering knowledge that was not present; the knowledge was already present. The same is true with discovering the law of gravity or the spherical shape of the earth or the solar system—knowledge was already present here-and-now; it just required an innovative vantage from which to recognize it.

Humankind is in transition to a new way of existing. In this Age of Human Empowerment and Era of Great Benefit the things that we have assumed to be true about life are just not going to be seen as true any longer. That is really what it comes down to. We are capable of much more than we have recognized till now.

We really need people who are passionately innovative, and more and more these people will be coming forward. These are people who really feel the force of discovery and inventiveness in every aspect of their lives, and they will bring about the incredible innovations that are to come. In this very critical period of time, these innovations are urgently needed. It is not a time to sit back; it is a time for the expression of abundant open intelligence.

We are no longer relying on conventional ideas about anything, and we do not restrict or limit ourselves in any way. We do not constantly have to reference back to past norms or understandings about the way things work. Here we instinctively recognize the true nature of reality *as it is*, and this is an extremely powerful disposition. Yet at the same time, we must realize that as pioneers of open intelligence, we know only a little. The humility intrinsic to this statement keeps everything within the clear perspective of the benefit of all.

Chapter Twenty-Two

EMPOWERED RELATIONSHIPS ARE THE BASIS OF SOCIAL CHANGE

Balanced View is an innovative model for global standardized education in the actual nature of the human mind. With tremendous precision, skill and insight, Balanced View brings forth the very best of human mind, speech, body, qualities and activities, as well as the unique strengths, gifts and talents of each individual. The Balanced View educational program is the first of its kind, for it provides humans with exacting empowerment, education and mobilization of their most comprehensive intelligence, one that is of benefit to all and which has never before been utilized on a mass scale.

In its initial decade of global use, Balanced View has launched both the Age of Human Empowerment and the Era of Great Benefit. In other words, on the fly it has shifted the paradigms through which we see ourselves and the world. Balanced View is the foundation for empowered relationships and for vast social change in which benefit, prosperity, generosity, life satisfaction and flourishing are the birthright of all human beings.

The Four Mainstays are a combinatory pattern of instruction through which one's identity flourishes and is satisfied. The most comprehensive beneficial intelligence, the primordial intelligence at the basis, is realized and inexhaustibly maintained. In such a combinatory pattern as the Four Mainstays, each element is an essential requirement to the result. If any element is omitted, the result will not reach fruition. For example, with the formula $E=mc^2$, to omit an element of the formula completely changes the result; in fact, the omission makes the formula nonsensical. Such is the case with the Four Mainstays.

The Four Mainstays are the formula for empowered relationships that lead to truly beneficial, permanent and inexhaustible social change. When the beneficial potency of the Four Mainstays pervades local community organizing as well as potent organizing through telecommunications and electronic communications, including the Internet, social change is sweeping and pervasive. Potent organizing means that each skillful means utilized has the direct result of greater benefit for all. Through our own instinctive realization, we are assured of increase in open intelligence's beneficial potency. This is a goal that can actually be measured through the use of ongoing studies.

The Twelve Empowerments Training provides the infrastructure for everyday life. If there is no infrastructure for empowerment such as the one that comes through the education and mobilization from the Twelve Empowerments, then one will keep doing the same disempowered things over and over again and expecting a different result. The solution-orientation brought about by the Twelve Empowerments and the Four Mainstays empowers, enhances and harmonizes all relationships. To have these tools available and not use them is to actively engage in internalized oppression and is to, one could say, consciously choose self-harm.

GOING BEYOND THE INDEPENDENT NATURE OF DATA

The relationship with data is of two types: one type takes as its path the affirmation of the independent nature of data, while the other takes the path of pure benefit. The first path leads to being caught up in indulgence, avoidance and replacement of data to form definitions of life and the world. Focus on the independent nature of data results in a closed intelligence that functions as a collector of definitions and conceptual frameworks.

Open intelligence, however, is grounded in inexhaustible beneficial potency and is free as the data stream itself. Data are the totally pure, spontaneous presence and liveliness of open intelligence. Data, having no independent nature whatsoever, are certainly beneficial; when they are left in their own place with no defining factors, there is only sheer beneficial potency.

When the independent nature of data is gone beyond, the spontaneous beneficial energy of open intelligence is obvious. As the reality of open intelligence settles in, each moment of human life becomes a wonder and a marvel.

Additionally, mind, speech, body, qualities and activities based on open intelligence have a full reach and range of discernment and insight into all thoughts and conceptual frameworks, regardless of their use in any circumstance, and they create the greatest benefit for all.

The search for meaning that underlies all data reification is the assumption of an independent nature in that which has no independent nature, while all along all data are simply the natural, potent glow of open intelligence's vast, all-encompassing benefit. Rather than relating to data as something that is to be changed by some external change agent, instead we turn to spontaneous great benefit, which of itself is already pervasively present in its own place. Thus, when perfect benefit is met upon introduction to open intelligence, it is defined as recognition of reality itself.

The instinctive comprehension and realization of spontaneous benefit for all is the great outshining of all data, which is understood at the crucial juncture of open intelligence and data—the primordially pure, unique expanse of luminosity. It is like the sun and its bright light, which are actually present and shining. Its entity is hot, so it burns off all reified descriptions, leaving only benefit. Open intelligence is a unique heat and is not the kind of heat that causes harm.

Primordially pure light, the great outshining, is the ultimate vehicle of intelligence as well as that of open-ended knowledge and benefit creation. Whoever instinctively realizes the great outshining of data in benefit has this perspective. To exemplify this, one could say that everything is like light pouring into light. Equalness, evenness and non-differentiation are the nature of the great benefit of all data, and this equalness and evenness enables the greatest advances ever to be made in all kinds of knowledge and benefit.

In short moments, great benefit becomes obvious. This means that whenever the great benefit of open intelligence is self-placed and left in its natural condition, there is a fault-free, pure expanse while brilliant intelligence shines forth of its own accord without movement away from that. In that way, the primordially-placed primal benefit of correct knowledge has become manifest. It is necessary to preserve the life force of benefit whose potency is its own entity.

"Self-placed" means that we put ourselves into the power of great benefit in its own natural self-condition. "Primordially placed" means that great benefit is always already placed in its own condition, without actually needing to do anything. In other words, upon authentic introduction to open intelligence and its inseparable powers of great benefit, we instinctively empower everyday life and all circumstances with inexhaustible great benefit. Through the path of self-placement, perfectly stated as "short moments," we are fortunate to instinctively recognize the primordial fruition of the very great and beneficial intelligence and appropriate actions that are already present.

Thus, in Balanced View's system it is asserted that self-arising benefit itself is you and me existing right now in a spontaneously existing way, whereas lesser educational means use cause, condition, conceptual frameworks and accomplishment to achieve intelligence newly. The difference between the two is like earth and sky.

Generally speaking, our skillful means, insight, discernment and power to act are joined to a greater level of beneficial activity. Utilize all skillful means at your disposal to empower, educate and mobilize at the grassroots for potent social change which enlivens benefit, prosperity and generosity for all.

It is of critical importance to start up new organizations and institutions based on the Balanced View model. Change cannot come from within existing organizations, unless there is one hundred percent buy-in and commitment to open intelligence by everyone who works there.

THE FOUR MAINSTAYS LIFESTYLE

We are enacting an empowering imperative through the Four Mainstays lifestyle. "Imperative" means that we don't have a choice—that we must act now. Simultaneously, we must act globally and we must act locally. We must act globally and locally to educate everyone on the power of the mind and on the exact nature of the mind. To avoid reality is denial of its existence, although reality shines with irresistible persistence.

The only way to change the force and the momentum of the way the mind works on a global level is through education. So far, most education has been directed towards disempowering ideas about what human nature is. It is only due to lack of education that people do not know the nature of mind or the definition of their own human nature. Each of us can see how we were all educated to think about ourselves. We were educated to think about ourselves basically as flawed and needing change, whether it related to ideas we learned through philosophy, school, in our family or in the culture at large.

Through education in the nature of mind, our whole life changes completely. We empower the nature of mind through a simple teaching: Balanced View's Four Mainstays, fueled by short moments of open intelligence repeated many times. Through that practice open intelligence becomes obvious all the time. The more open intelligence becomes obvious, the more our speech changes; we don't talk the way we used to talk, and we don't think the way we used to think. We begin to see ourselves as infused with an inexhaustible beneficial potency that we did not know we had. Now life is vastly potent and lively; everything and everyone is the spontaneous presence of our vast intelligence—the nature of mind.

Initially, it feels very good to us personally, but soon we realize that this power within us is the power of the benefit *of all*. The feel-good we feel from resting naturally for a longer and longer duration is the power of the benefit of all, and the benefit of all includes *ourselves*.

Through the introductory trainings, the Twelve Empowerments and Balanced View's Four Mainstays, we are presented with a complete infrastructure for living. Through the authentic introduction to the nature of mind, we discover self-leadership. This potent realization of basic benefit is self-governance of all data streams; thus, we simply come to know ourselves, as well as everything and everyone. We see the great simplicity at the basis of governance of the human species. In the instinctive recognition of open intelligence and its powers of great benefit, there is inexhaustible flourishing of the mind, speech, body, qualities and activities.

We don't have to place a lot of focus on self-concern—and none on self-governance—because beneficial potency is our only energy and nature. All-encompassing benefit is the way we live, the way we speak, what our body does and what our qualities and activities naturally are. Each short moment is one of all-encompassing benefit.

So, I call out to all of you everywhere to stand up and know yourself as you really are. Know yourself as you really are; know your mind as it really is! No matter where you live—if you live under censorship and dictatorship or you live in a more democratic country—whatever it is, go into your mind and settle into its vast expanse of all-inclusive, all-pervasive governance. By going back to basics we are shaping the Era of Great Benefit through the Age of Human Empowerment.

EDUCATION IN THE NATURE OF MIND

Open intelligence is the nature of mind and it is immediately accessible. However, it is of crucial importance to receive an introduction to the full power of the beneficial nature of mind from someone who already embodies its complete potency. Until the inception of Balanced View, this pure transmission of the nature of mind within human society has been just enough to keep our species from going even more berserk than it already has. With the worldwide pervasion of Balanced View, the outshining of reification increases daily, until there is only the perception of beneficial potency.

Education in the nature of mind has its own language—a single language of tremendous significance. It is a language that combines a spontaneous yet defined set of mind-opening similes with gestures, specialized combinations of words and mind-to-mind transmission. The standardization of terminology in the educational method and practice of the nature of mind must be uniform. This is crucial. The numbers 0 through 9 and other symbols are basic and crucial to mathematics. Similarly, yet even more importantly, the Four Mainstays algorithm—based on authentic introduction to the nature of mind—is crucial to life, whether embodied or not, such as in human beings or in artificial intelligence. The Four Mainstays provide a simple, revolutionary operating structure for all aspects of life.

For approximately sixty years humans have given free rein to highly personalized interpretations of the nature of mind, and what we ended up with were very few results of the fruition of the brilliant beneficial potency of open intelligence. There were many confused people and a conundrum of gibberish, wherein there was no common ground for communication about the most important of all knowledge—education in the nature of mind.

In the beneficial potency of open intelligence, we naturally unite; we are spontaneously and globally united in open intelligence. Even though we might have ideas about uniting globally, when we are all wrapped up in reification and we are defining everything and everyone as having an independent nature, that unity is impossible. A united human culture is based on unity within the nature of mind—within each individual knowing exactly what the nature of their mind is. It comes from knowing that the nature of our body and mind and that the nature of our speech, our qualities and activities are all—all—completely infused and pervaded by beneficial potency. This is our natural state; this is reality.

There is the brightly shining sun of pure beneficial potency always primordially present. When that open intelligence which is actually the case is known to be so, knowing it is the actual accomplishment of that beneficial potency. In short, it is reality; all that is required is to know it by setting yourself into its natural condition. Go to any lengths to live the Four Mainstays lifestyle. Do not rely on half measures. Now, as the full force of beneficial potency—intelligence open and free—it is fiercely clear that any application of conceptual effort will mystify or destroy pure knowing.

Rest naturally and potently, without seeking anything.

ASKING FOR EDUCATION IN OPEN INTELLIGENCE

The only solidity, the only comfort, the only relief, the only power is in the nature of mind in open intelligence's beneficial potency. Everyone knows this instinctively, whether they have been educated in it or not. No matter how anyone might seem, even if they may seem totally un-open to any kind of education along these lines, if we just listen to whatever they have to say, skillful means will allow us to connect directly with them. Skillful means and insight allow us to connect directly with everyone without actually saying anything.

A person can sometimes affect an entire group just by being there, without saying anything about the nature of mind. This is how much each human being is asking for education in open intelligence. Everyone is asking for education in open intelligence; no one wants to be left out.

Ultimate fluency sees, speaks and otherwise enacts the potency of inexhaustible benefit and has no interest in the always-increasing workload of reification. Similarly, no one would try to light their way with a match when the sun is shining brightly. Thus, it is of urgent importance to dedicate our mind, speech, body, qualities and activities to open intelligence. Unfortunately, today there are many people who believe they have been introduced to open intelligence, when in fact they have not.

Through reliance on authentic open intelligence, Balanced View has created global organizing at the community level all over the world. On all continents, in all but a few remote countries, we have countless active Balanced View communities in the start-up phase. So, this is how much people want education in open intelligence.

Education is a simple matter. There's no reason to make a big mystery out of it by putting human nature in a category where it has to be looked at and analyzed with diagnostic and statistical tools. First of all, in order to advance in any area—and most specifically in science and technology—each human being doing the work on that science and technology must know the nature of their own mind and have mature and radical breakthrough experience of all aspects of their own nature, whether the aspects are positive, negative or neutral.

Lack of education, which is inseparable from the refusal of all Four Mainstays, can keep us puffed with pride—without even knowing it. Perhaps we feel we know it all already, when this is not the case in any respect. A pervasive form of arrogance today is one which assumes some kind of nondual realization, which actually is an extreme point of view and not any kind of realization at all. The all-encompassing benefit of open intelligence is inclusive of duality and nonduality. There is no point from which to view, no destination to arrive at. Everyone must be given the opportunity for authentic introduction to open intelligence rather than incorrect ideas.

There is in fact a treasure trove of benefit even in lack of education, pride/arrogance, jealousy/envy, desire and aversion; however, this is realized only with authentic introduction to open intelligence's beneficial potency. Along with this there must be a committed relationship with an excellent, accessible trainer who has the toolkit of pure transmission potency, endless key points and pith instructions, widespread community of actual results in their students and demonstration of a wide range of skillful means—including open-ended knowledge and benefit creation.

Most specifically, in afflictive states it is important to have an enormous breakthrough—to see that these afflictive states indeed do *not* have a power or influence of their own. By letting them be *as they are*, they break through into beneficial potency, which is always what they are in the entirety of their appearance. No matter what the name is, open intelligence is present and pervasive. By letting open intelligence be *as it is,* we see that, no matter whether the afflictive state is something during the day or a dream at night, it bursts forth with beneficial potency and shines like sunshine from the sun.

THE ENACTMENT OF EMPOWERMENT

If all data are completely analyzed, all are equal in not being truly established and in having no independent nature. If their pure benefit is established through analysis (as in, for example, the analysis that comes from examining an object in a linear particle accelerator) and of going from coarse to fine, fine to parts, and parts to no parts, then finally there would be the determination of their part-less pure benefit. There would be *only* the purity of great benefit. What a wondrous marvel it is!

This is the simple, moment-to-moment enactment of empowerment in our own life. By this enactment and empowerment of open intelligence, we even see that there are no parts called "moments." We see that all of this is part of human creation. Everything is part of our own mind: time, space, cause and effect—*all* of it.

However, we live within an Earth-society, and Balanced View's Four Mainstays are an education in a simple lifestyle within that society. If we have questions about open intelligence, we can ask someone who is a certified trainer, or we can turn for support to other community members in a worldwide community—with twenty-four hour live online support on the website www.balancedview.org. There are all kinds of media available there, pouring forth like a great river. New magical feats are manifesting daily!

Enact your own open intelligence; empower your own open intelligence; do everything you can through the Four Mainstays. The first Mainstay is the practice of open intelligence in short moments. The second is relying on a trainer—now, that will really do it! By relying on a trainer you have a pal, someone you can talk to about what's actually going on. You can talk to them about their own experience, strength and realization of open intelligence and the empowerment of open intelligence in their own life and yours. That is all a trainer is: it's the buddy system with all-the-way-through empowerment, all the way through life. A trainer is the ultimate friend—not just another yes-person or someone to argue with. This relationship allows for true empowerment which one can then carry into all aspects of life.

The third Mainstay is the training itself, the endless array of all kinds of media to support you in any way conceivable or inconceivable. It just keeps flowing. The worldwide community is the fourth Mainstay of Balanced View, totally empowered in action and in beneficial potency. All of this is inseparable from open intelligence, just like the sky and the color blue are inseparable—all of this totally inseparable.

That is what we do in Balanced View: we meet people who are ready for education in the nature of mind, ready to allow their beneficial potency to be as it is. We educate people in the empowerment of their own mind, the empowerment of their own human nature, to use their speech, their body, their qualities and activities for beneficial action and social change right now in this Age of Human Empowerment and Era of Great Benefit.

BALANCED VIEW RESOURCES

All Balanced View resources necessary for being educated in the nature of mind are available at www.balancedview.org.

The Four Mainstays support network of Balanced View is available worldwide, twenty-four hours a day, seven days a week. The Four Mainstays support everyone interested in training up open intelligence for the benefit of all through: 1) short moments of open intelligence, 2) the trainer, 3) the training, and 4) the worldwide community. The Four Mainstays lifestyle is the support for obvious open intelligence recognition and benefit at all times.

To begin with, please listen to talks and watch videos from the founder, Candice O'Denver, and the other Balanced View trainers. All video and audio talks are free and can be easily downloaded in MP3 and MP4 format. All Balanced View books are available on our website as free downloads, and some can be purchased on amazon.com.

Also found on the website is a schedule of Balanced View trainings offered by certified trainers around the world. Venues range from face-to-face trainings and public open meetings to trainings and meetings offered via the Internet and video-conference.

For participants who wish to contribute to Balanced View, donations are gratefully accepted.

Printed in Great Britain
by Amazon.co.uk, Ltd.,
Marston Gate.